Neoliberal gothic

Manchester University Press

INTERNATIONAL
GOTHiC

Previously published
*Monstrous media/spectral subjects: imaging gothic from the nineteenth century
to the present* Edited by Fred Botting and Catherine Spooner
Globalgothic Edited by Glennis Byron
EcoGothic Edited by Andrew Smith and William Hughes

Neoliberal gothic

International gothic in the
neoliberal age

Edited by Linnie Blake and
Agnieszka Soltysik Monnet

Manchester University Press

Published by Manchester University Press
Altrincham Street, Manchester M1 7JA
www.manchesteruniversitypress.co.uk

British Library Cataloguing-in-Publication Data
A catalogue record for this book is available from the British Library

Library of Congress Cataloguing-in-Publication Data applied for

ISBN 978 1 5261 1344 3 hardback

First published 2017

Typeset by Out of House Publishing
Printed in Great Britain by TJ International Ltd, Padstow

Linnie Blake would like to dedicate this book to her mother, Sheila Robinson – whose lifelong radicalism has never failed to inspire and motivate – and to Ella and Freya Blake who will carry all she has taught us into the future. Agnieszka Soltysik Monnet would like to dedicate it to Christian, for his full-spectrum home economics of nourishing conversation, moral support and loving companionship.

Contents

Contributors

Katarzyna Ancuta is a lecturer at Assumption University in Bangkok, Thailand. Her research interests oscillate around the interdisciplinary contexts of contemporary gothic/horror, currently with a strong Asian focus. Her recent publications include contributions to *A New Companion to the Gothic* (2012), *Global Gothic* (2013) and *The Cambridge Companion to the Modern Gothic* (2014), as well as two co-edited special journal issues on Thai (2014) and Southeast Asian (2015) horror film.

Linnie Blake is Principal Lecturer and Director of the Centre for Gothic Studies at Manchester Metropolitan University. She is the author of *The Wounds of Nations: Horror Cinema, Historical Trauma and National Identity* (Manchester University Press, 2008) and co-editor (with X. Aldana Reyes) of *Digital Horror: Haunted Technologies, Network Panic and the Found Footage Phenomenon* (2015). She has also published on a variety of gothic topics in journals such as *Gothic Studies*, *Horror Studies* and *Cultural Sociology*.

Rebecca Duncan completed her DAAD-funded doctorate at Giessen University (Germany) in 2015. She is the author of the forthcoming *South African Gothic*, and has published articles and book chapters on topics relating to postcolonial and South African textual cultures, the gothic and the speculative, and materialist ecocriticism. She currently teaches in the Division of Languages and Literatures at Stirling University in Scotland.

Tracy Fahey is Head of the Department of Fine Art and Head of the Centre of Postgraduate Studies in Limerick School of Art and Design (LSAD). In 2013 she established the LSAD research centre ACADEMY, where she acts as principal investigator. Her primary research area is the gothic, with special reference to the visual arts. She has chapters on this subject in collections published by Routledge, Palgrave, McParland, Cork University Press, Peter Lang Publishing and Rowman & Littlefield. She is currently working on a monograph, *Contemporary Irish Folk Gothic*, for University of Wales Press. She has also published on gothic bodies and medical gothic, contemporary gothic art, transgressive body-based art and a/r/tography. In 2010 she founded the art collaborative, Gothicise, who create site-specific projects that interrogate the relationship between site and narrative. Her short fiction has been published in thirteen anthologies to date by US and UK presses, and her collection *The Unheimlich Manoeuvre* was published in July 2016. In 2016, two of her short stories were long-listed for honourable mentions in *The Year's Best Horror* (ed. Ellen Datlow).

Stéphanie Genz is Senior Lecturer in Media Studies at Nottingham Trent University. She specialises in contemporary gender and cultural theory. Her book publications include *Postfeminist Gothic: Critical Interventions in Contemporary Culture, Postfeminism: Cultural Texts and Theories* and *Postfemininities in Popular Culture*. Stéphanie's current work centres on sexist liberalism/liberal sexism in post-recessionary culture that belies assumptions of gender equality and sexual freedom.

Steffen Hantke has edited *Horror*, a special topic issue of *Paradoxa* (2002); *Horror: Creating and Marketing Fear* (2004); *Caligari's Heirs: The German Cinema of Fear after 1945* (2007); *American Horror Film: The Genre at the Turn of the Millennium* (2010); and, with Agnieszka Soltysik Monnet, *War Gothic in Literature and Culture* (2016). He is also author of *Conspiracy and Paranoia in Contemporary American Literature* (1994) and *Monsters in the Machine: Science Fiction Film and the Militarization of America after World War II* (2016).

Karen Macfarlane is Associate Professor in the Department of English at Mount Saint Vincent University in Halifax, Nova Scotia. Her most recent publications have been on Lady Gaga, the queer icon and the monster ('Monstrous House of Gaga'); textuality, empire and the monster ('Here be monsters', in *Text Matters* (2016)); and the reanimated mummy in *fin-de-siècle* British adventure fiction ('Mummy knows best ...', *Horror Studies*). She has an article forthcoming in *Gothic Studies* on the creepy little girl. Her current research focuses on monsters in popular culture at the turn of the nineteenth and twentieth centuries.

Barry Murnane is Associate Professor and Fellow in German at St John's College, Oxford. Before moving to Oxford he worked at the universities of Freiburg and Halle-Wittenberg in Germany. He has written widely on the gothic from the eighteenth century to the present day, including a monograph on Kafka, several edited volumes on German gothic, and essays on topics ranging from Horace Walpole to neoliberalism. His most recent work has focused on the gothic and medical humanities.

Agnieszka Soltysik Monnet is Professor of American Literature and Culture at the University of Lausanne in Switzerland. She is the author of *The Poetics and Politics of the American Gothic: Gender and Slavery in Nineteenth-Century American Literature* (2010), and the editor of several collections of essays, including *The Gothic in Contemporary Literature and Popular Culture* (with Justin Edwards, 2012). She is also the co-editor of a special issue of *Gothic Studies* (with Marie Lienard-Yeterian, Manchester University Press) on 'The gothic in an age of terror(ism).' Her essays and reviews have appeared in journals such as *Victorian Literature and Culture, European Journal of American Studies, Comparative American Studies, Gothic Studies* and *Novel.*

Aspasia Stephanou is an independent scholar and publisher. She is currently writing her second monograph, *Inhuman Materiality in Gothic Media.*

Series editors' preface

Each volume in this series contains new essays on the many forms assumed by – as well as the most important themes and topics in – the ever-expanding range of international 'gothic' fictions from the eighteenth to the twenty-first century. Launched by leading members of the International Gothic Association (IGA) and some editors and advisory board members of its journal, *Gothic Studies*, this series thus offers cutting-edge analyses of the great many variations in the gothic mode over time and all over the world, whether these have occurred in literature, film, theatre, art, several forms of cybernetic media, or other manifestations ranging from 'goth' group identities to *avant garde* displays of aesthetic and even political critique.

The 'gothic story' began in earnest in 1760s England, both in fiction and in drama, with Horace Walpole's efforts to combine the 'ancient' or supernatural and the 'modern' or realistic romance. This blend of anomalous tendencies has proved itself remarkably flexible in playing out the cultural conflicts of the late Enlightenment and of more recent periods. Antiquated settings with haunting ghosts or monsters and deep, dark secrets that are the mysteries behind them, albeit in many different incarnations, continue to intimate both what audiences most fear in their personal subconscious and the most pervasive tensions underlying western culture. But this always unsettling interplay of conflicting tendencies has expanded beyond its original potential as well, especially in the hands of its greatest innovators, to appear in an astounding variety of expressive, aesthetic and public manifestations over time. The results have transported this inherently boundary-breaking mode across geographical and cultural borders into 'gothics' that now appear throughout the world: in the settler communities of Canada, New Zealand, and Australia; in such postcolonial areas as India and Africa; in the Americas and the Caribbean; and in East Asia and several of the islands within the entire Pacific Rim.

These volumes consequently reveal and explain the 'globalisation' of the gothic as it has proliferated across two-and-a-half centuries. The General Editors of this series and the editors of every volume, of course, bring special expertise to this expanding development, as well as to the underlying dynamics, of the gothic. Each resulting collection, plus the occasional monograph, therefore draws together important new studies about particular examples of the international gothic – past, present or emerging – and these contributions can come from both established scholars in the field and the newest 'rising stars' of gothic studies. These scholars, moreover, are and must be just as international in their locations and orientations as this series is. Interested experts from throughout the globe, in fact, are invited to propose collections and topics for this series to the Manchester University Press. These will be evaluated, as appropriate, by the General Editors, members of the Editorial Advisory Board and/or other scholars with the requisite expertise, so that every published volume is professionally put together and properly refereed within the highest academic standards. Only in this way can the International Gothic series be what its creators intend: a premiere worldwide venue for examining and understanding the shape-shifting 'strangeness' of a gothic mode that is now as multi-cultural and multi-faceted as it has ever been in its long, continuing and profoundly haunted history.

Acknowledgements

This book grew out of the International Gothic Association research community and its biennial conferences, as well as a shared fascination with political work on the contemporary gothic. As we see the human and natural destruction caused by the current neoliberal agenda and its unsustainable pursuit of ever-increasing profit piling up around us, we felt that a volume of essays acknowledging the way that the gothic has been creatively and critically engaging with this situation was not only timely but long overdue. We would like to thank all the contributors for their assiduous and original work, Manchester University Press for accepting and supporting the volume, Audrey Loetscher for her work on the index, and John Ledger for his generous permission to use his artwork, *I Believe in Capitalism,* on the cover.

Linnie Blake and Agnieszka Soltysik Monnet

Introduction: neoliberal gothic

Over the course of the past twenty-five years, as neoliberal economics has transformed the geopolitical landscape, monsters have overrun
popular culture. Film and literature, graphic novels, fashion and music,
computer and online gaming have all appropriated the gothic's ghosts
and witches; vampires and werewolves; ancient castles, curses, quest-
ing heroes and secrets from the dark past. And in the last five years, the
transnational zombie horde has become ubiquitous.[1]

This collection of essays engages with the geopolitical context of
the gothic's migration from the periphery to the fast-beating heart of
popular culture – specifically the rise to economic and cultural predominance of global neoliberalism. It is no coincidence, we contend,
that the characters and plots of the historic gothic have come to dominate popular culture over the course of the past thirty years. For as neoliberalism has come to dominate the ways we live, work, think, interact
and introspect, harnessing the epistemological incertitude of the postmodern project in service of its aims,[2] the gothic's ability to give voice
to the occluded truths of our age has resulted in a global proliferation of
gothic, and gothic-inflected, cultural artefacts. This collection engages
with the ideological dimensions of such texts: specifically, the ways in
which they articulate the social and existential consequences of thirty
years of globalised laissez-faire capitalism. We contend, in other words,
that the gothic texts of the neoliberal age can be seen to undertake the
same kind of cultural work that was carried out by the gothic mode in
earlier periods of socio-economic turbulence. And, as in earlier periods,
we can see a variety of ideological allegiances at play in gothic texts of

the neoliberal age – ranging from the revolutionary to the radical to the downright reactionary.

For all its wild improbability, the gothic has always engaged with the context of its own production, whether that be the regicidal upheavals of the age of revolutions, the squalid emergence of the industrial metropolis or, in the United States, the creation of the world's first post-colonial democracy. The first wave of gothic novels has frequently been read, for example, as a philosophical and psychological response to the Enlightenment's rationality, its will to overturn the social hierarchies of old and to bring forth a new discourse of human rights.[3] Thus, blending chivalric and contemporary romance, novels such as Horace Walpole's foundational *The Castle of Otranto* (1764) would establish the mode's lexicon of medieval castles and monasteries, lascivious clergy, disinherited aristocrats, Faustian pacts and secrets from the dark past that would enable successive generations to question the contemporary world, its power-relations, values and objects of terror.

The Victorian gothic refashioned the eighteenth century's preoccupations to produce a range of monsters, mutants and lunatics more fitted to an increasingly urban and industrialised world, a whole new gothic lexicon emerging as the British Empire stretched across the globe and new scientific theories, such as Darwinian evolution, reshaped the ways in which people thought about what it was to be human. Broadly realist writers, such as Charles Dickens and Robert Louis Stevenson, established the city as a new kind of gothic landscape whilst romantics, like the Brontës, capitalised on the wild spaces beyond the city to pioneer a new kind of domestic gothic in which the home itself became a site of horror. By the end of the century, the Victorian cult of death had transmuted into a pervasive sense of decay, as libertines such as Oscar Wilde's Dorian Gray and ancient evils such as Bram Stoker's Dracula[4] embodied the fears of a generation, for whom the foreign horde threatened to overrun the imperial capital whilst the Englishman himself became a corrupt shadow of his former heroic self.

In the United States, meanwhile, a range of writers had drawn on the symbolic machinery of the eighteenth-century English Gothic to illuminate their own concerns. Washington Irving had looked back to the nation's bloody foundation, exploring in his tales the traumatic legacy of revolt against colonial rule, his characters Ichabod Crane and Rip Van Winkle becoming, in turn, canonical literary figures.[5] Nathaniel Hawthorne, himself the descendant of a judge at the Salem Witch Trials, would return repeatedly to the nation's prehistory to conjure up a

world of cursed families and haunted New England villages surrounded by dark woods that later writers such as Stephen King would
make their own. Edgar Allan Poe's poems and tales would challenge
the nineteenth century's optimistic and democratic *Zeitgeist* with wild
and hallucinatory visions of etiolated families, deranged con-men, aristocratic killers, and strange supernatural happenings. Thus American
gothic came into being, steeped in the troubles of its colonial past and
discomfited profoundly by the demands of a rapidly unfolding and
unstable market economy (a series of economic recessions prevented
Poe from starting a literary journal and kept him on the edge of poverty
for most of his adult life). This pattern of gothic writing interrogating
the contemporary *Zeitgeist* would spread across the world, moreover,
as successive nations adopted the mode's lexicon to explore their own
most troubling times.[6] It is to this tradition of social engagement and
analysis that the gothic of the neoliberal age discussed in this collection contributes.

This is not to argue that there is necessarily a radical intent to
gothic texts – whether those texts be drawn from the historic past
or the mass cultural present. The gothic is no stranger to regressive attitudes to gender, ethnicity and class, after all.[7] And gothic
texts can reveal the hidden tensions of the societies that produced
them without proffering any attempt at formulating a solution.[8] The
same can be said of gothic texts of the neoliberal age. An important
distinction needs to be drawn, in other words, between those contemporary texts that adopt the characters, plots, settings and thematic machinery of the gothic to lend a frisson of historic romance
or transgressive sexuality to tales that range from the politically dis-
engaged to the downright reactionary,[9] and those texts that deploy
gothic conventions specifically to expose and critique the material actualities of the present.[10] This collection focuses on the latter
category. We explore literary, televisual, filmic and dramatic works
from countries as geographically distant and culturally diverse as
Britain and Mexico, the United States and Ireland, Germany, Korea,
and Japan. Like neoliberalism itself, we argue, such works have both
a nationally specific context and a global awareness. They articulate distinct national histories, identity paradigms and divergent
modes of socio-cultural organisation. But they are unified by a will
to interrogate the ways in which neoliberal economics has impacted
the modern world, has pervaded our very consciousness and, in so
doing, has refashioned the very subjectivities we inhabit.

What, then, is neoliberalism as we conceive of it?

Based on the economic theories of Friedrich von Hayek, the 1980s neoliberalism pioneered by Ronald Reagan in the USA and Margaret Thatcher in the UK rested on a radical individualism that eschewed those principles of state welfare, social progress and equality of opportunity on which the postwar consensus in the UK and the Great Society in the US had rested.[11] Economic planning was decried in favour of an ostensible deregulation of the markets, whilst cuts to public spending, the suppression of trade unions, lower taxes and a transfer of public services to the private sector were enacted wholesale. The results were manifold. The neoliberal subject was recast as agent of his or her individual destiny, repeatedly refashioning him- or herself in whatever image the market demanded whilst being held fully responsible for any failure to prosper. As politicians pledged their allegiance not to the welfare of the electorate but to the financial freedoms of the market, a widening gulf of inequality became all too apparent. In developed nations, this manifested itself in the form of bankruptcies, unemployment lines, homelessness and public health crises.[12] Globally, organisations such as the International Monetary Fund and the World Bank exported this ideology in the form of loans extended to developing countries in exchange for a wholesale dismantling of state welfare programmes and the suppression of collectivist organisations such as trade unions.[13] At the heart of all this was an insistent avowal that markets could regulate themselves, that they could generate phenomenal wealth and that this wealth would, somehow, trickle down to each and every stratum of society.[14]

As the Latin American debt crisis of 1982 and later the global financial crisis of 2008 illustrated, however, neoliberalism failed to deliver either economic stability or widespread prosperity – this because its core tenets were at best an illusion and at worst a deliberate deception. Far from being the most democratic model of economic organisation, as was claimed in 1989 with the fall of the Berlin Wall, neoliberalism's hostility to collectivism has strongly militated against participatory democracy, depriving the working class of any say in government, curtailing union power and placing the business of politics in the hands of outsourced organisations such as think tanks and non-governmental organisations. In the neoliberal world, as Richard Seymour has argued, policies are no longer 'democratically deliberated and decided upon', as it is now for 'a technocratic layer of experts' to supply 'the policy ideas, the ideological thematics, the dense intellectual justifications' of government (Seymour, 2014: 27). Echoing this, of course, is the fact that the ideological privatisation of the public sector has resulted in an exponential growth in corporate profitability along with a concomitant polarisation of society's 'haves' and 'have nots' into those reliant on residual state services and those able to resource their own healthcare, housing and education – the provision of which was once deemed a cornerstone of a developed society.

Clearly, the role of the State has shifted under neoliberalism from the provision of social welfare to the facilitation of global trade, this including the handover of billions of dollars of public funds in bank bailouts whenever the system that was 'too big to fail' teetered on the abyss (Seymour, 2014: 13). Such bailouts were coupled with a programme of so-called 'austerity' measures that effectively forced the public to pay for the mistakes of the banking sector. A kind of 'voluntary deflation', austerity seeks to 'restore competitiveness' by 'cutting the state's budget, debts and deficits', this manifesting as a reduction in 'both wages and public spending', measures that targeted the poorest and most vulnerable members of society (Blyth, 2013: 2). And in economic terms, as several of the chapters in this collection explore, such measures have resulted in a spiralling of national debt coupled with never-ending cuts to public expenditure. So, as the plight of Ireland and Greece attests, austerity measures have proved a recipe for social disaster that has nonetheless reinscribed neoliberal economic models at the very heart of the State.[15] If one's goal is growth, in other words, neoliberal austerity programmes are entirely ineffective. If one's aim is to advance the neoliberal agenda, however, austerity is a startling success. Accordingly, many of the chapters in this collection explore this disjunction between the professed aims of neoliberal economics and the personal and social cost to the most disadvantaged members of society.

As David Harvey has argued, the neoliberal agenda is markedly imperialistic, for 'any hegemon, if it is to maintain its position in relation to endless (and endlessly expanding) capital accumulation, must endlessly seek to extend, expand, and intensify its power' (Harvey, 2003: 35). In the 1990s, the 'soft power' of the Clinton administration had sought to deliver both freedom and prosperity through the integration of a post-cold war global market. This process ended with the 'War on Terror', the invasion of Iraq marking a shift to a less consensual and considerably more coercive model of imperialist expansion. Thus the Bush Doctrine set about 'stretching the boundaries of pre-emptive action to embrace preventive war, rejecting deterrence, demoting allies, putting the United States on a permanent war footing and firmly believing in the efficacy, necessity and morality of absolute military preponderance' (Gurtov, 2006: 48). Sold to the public as a justifiable response, not only to the events of 9/11 but to the ongoing terrorist threat, the 'War on Terror' became the militarised face of neoliberalism, entrenching a sense of continuous crisis in the public mind whilst undertaking an ostensibly justifiable curtailment of civil liberties at home and overseas that, itself, served the corporate agenda.

The chapters in this collection address themselves to all these themes – the disempowerment of the public sector; the social consequences of underinvestment in health, education and welfare; the imperative to economic growth and capital accumulation; the economic might of the corporation and the economic precarity of its workers; the rise of militarism; the denigration of rights discourses; and the emergence of neoliberal subject as mutable avatar of capital flow. The economic crash of 2008 is a consistent theme across the collection as each chapter explores how the gothic mode enables writers, dramatists, directors and fine art practitioners to grapple with the ethical, existential and social ramifications of global neoliberalism and proffer solutions that range from the revolutionary to a form of liberal appeasement that champions public welfare whilst refusing to challenge capitalism as a model.

Part I. Neoliberal gothic monsters

Since its inception, the gothic monster has provided a ready means of mobilising alterity discourses, the abject otherness of the vampire, the werewolf and the zombie enabling a critique of social norms and values, available models of identity and the monstrosity that lies within us all. Whilst the gothic monster proliferates across this collection, the three chapters that begin our study focus on the ways in which it has come to embody contemporary subjectivity formations and economic relations in a culture driven by a Social Darwinist *Zeitgeist* in which only the fittest survive and the victims are held responsible for their 'failure' to compete.

What are notable in all three chapters here are the ways in which neoliberalism's insistence that there is 'no alternative' to it are embodied in the gothic texts under consideration, sometimes overtly and sometimes in their inability to posit a viable mode of being outside the neoliberal matrix of bio-power. Aspasia Stephanou's chapter, 'Game of fangs: the vampire and neoliberal subjectivity', thus traces the vampire's evolution from the nineteenth-century past of industrial capitalism to the neoliberal present's accelerated violence and corrupt precarity. Stephanou argues that the selfish individualism and hedonic consumerism of neoliberal subjectivity have come to be embodied in the contemporary vampire, itself characterised by a desire for unlimited expansion and the extension of life beyond its biological limits. For, as the predatory capitalists of Jody Scott's *I, Vampire* (1984) and Guillermo del Toro and Chuck Hogan's *The Strain Trilogy* (2009, 2010, 2011) attest, such practices are ultimately destructive of all life, collapsing the future into a state of exploited exhaustion. As the world-weary vampires of Jim Jarmusch's *Only Lovers Left Alive* (2013) attest, western subjectivity has become so etiolated that it has come to sustain itself by feeding off other, more vibrant cultures. The contemporary vampire, for Stephanou, thus comes to embody all we may become at the hands of a rapacious neoliberalism that threatens first to consume and thus to destroy everything that is truly of value in the world.

Such concerns are echoed in Stéphanie Genz's chapter, 'Austerity bites: refiguring *Dracula* in a neoliberal age', which explores the political, social and cultural contradictions that have emerged in the wake of the 2008 global economic crisis – a period that, as we have seen, has been characterised by substantial cuts to public expenditure, bank bailouts and mass unemployment. For just as anti-capitalist protestors have targeted the self-serving avarice of the greedy banker class, Genz argues, so have gothic texts come to embody and explore the contradictory field of forces set in motion by neoliberalism itself. For Genz, the vampire, as eminently commodifiable figure, both reflects and responds to capitalist imperatives, mobilising Fredric Jameson's sense that capitalism is both the best and the worst thing to happen to humanity, both 'catastrophe and progress all together' (Jameson, 1993: 86). Ranging across contemporary texts and theoretical positions, Genz focuses on the NBC television mini-series *Dracula* (2013–), which perfectly encapsulates our own post-recessionary subjectivity: weary of capitalism and trapped between the politics of austerity and the ongoing ideological imperative to partake in the neoliberal dream. With Dracula himself transformed into a benevolent American capitalist who throws down a challenge to the forces of monopolistic greed, the series therefore undertakes a thinly veiled critique of the economic interests that drove the US-led 'War on Terror'. But, Genz argues, whilst the series may deploy the machinery of the gothic to evoke the neoliberal inter-play of freedom and coercion, emancipation and subjugation to which we are all subject, it proffers no way out of the political uncertainty and economic instability of the present beyond the promotion of a 'kinder' form of capitalism that is capitalism nonetheless.

Barry Murnane's 'Staging spectrality: capitalising (on) ghosts in German postdramatic theatre' also addresses state capitalism but turns our attention away from the vampire and towards the ghost, focus-ing on the ways in which such spectral figures have come to dominate new German theatre, specifically as a means of representing the eco-nomic order that emerged globally following the fall of the Berlin Wall. Beginning with Heiner Müller's *Germania 3: Gespenster am Toten Mann* (*Germania 3: Ghosts on the Dead Man* (1995)), Murnane traces the ways in which the spread of capitalism in the former German Democratic Republic has become encapsulated by the aesthetic of spectrality. This, he argues, has come to dominate postdramatic theatre – which itself eschews the development of character and unified plot. Exploring the way Dea Loher's *Manhattan Medea* (1999) traces the patterns of trans-national migration and capital flow that emerged following the Balkan wars, he illustrates how the figure of the ghost both critiques the spec-tralising tendencies of contemporary global capital and yet remains subject to reappropriation by it. For as gothic spectrality has become culturally prominent in Germany, he argues, the figure of the ghost has been effectively normalised in contemporary cultural and political theory. The result is an integration of the ghost into the State-sponsored economic models of the German cultural landscape that quashes the radical potentiality of the gothic mode. Thus, as Genz too has argued, the gothic ably evokes the neoliberal present but is unable to offer an alternative, having been skilfully reappropriated by the very forces it critiques.

Part II. Biotechnologies, neoliberalism and the gothic

Global pharmacology has come, over the course of the past thirty years, both to embody and to advance the neoliberal capitalist agenda, a very limited number of companies dominating the research, development and distribution of drugs across the world.[16] And this gives them the corporate power to co-opt any institution, including elected govern-ments, that may stand in the way of their profits. As is indicated by the case of Tamiflu® in the developed world and anti-retrovirals in Africa, neoliberal pharmacology is no longer devoted to developing and producing useful new drugs that may in some way benefit humanity. Instead, pharmaceutical corporations are driven to sell drugs regardless of their efficacy, to suppress the unfavourable results of clinical trials, to invent new diseases purely for profit, or to magnify the threat of minor outbreaks and to offer unethical incentives to healthcare professionals across the world to prescribe their products.[17] Meanwhile, in the sphere of biotechnology, the transnational trade in human organs has become a highly gothic encapsulation of global economic relations, the citizens of poor nations becoming little more than an aggregate of commodified body parts that may be resold, at a profit, to the ailing citizens of richer nations. Such developments have given rise to a slew of gothic novels, films and television series that interrogate the agenda of the biotech sector.[18] We focus on three examples here: cinematic depictions of the international organ trade in Asia, big pharmacology and the television zombie in the United Kingdom, and literary representations of the dehumanised South African poor. In a world in which each of us is repeatedly interpellated by neoliberal capitalism and penetrated by the drugs and medical procedures it sells, each of these studies points to the ways in which gothic texts may reaffirm our common humanity, expose often hidden economic relations and explore ways of being that challenge the neoliberal consensus.

Katarzyna Ancuta's chapter, 'The return of the dismembered: representing organ trafficking in Asian cinemas', explores the gothic dimensions of the transnational organ trade as a spatial manifestation of neoliberal capital flow. Ancuta illustrates how existing economic hierarchies in Asia have become materially actualised in the trade of human organs – with countries like Japan, South Korea, Hong Kong and Taiwan buying body parts from the comparatively impoverished nations of Pakistan, Bangladesh, the Philippines, Myanmar, Cambodia, Thailand and China. In the latter two countries, moreover, the vast disjunction between those who benefit from global neoliberalism and those who are exploited by it becomes most sharply realised, these being the 'places of procedure' in which organs are transferred, like capital, from the poor to the rich. Thus, Ancuta argues, the highly gothic motif of organ transplantation becomes an affective (and therefore effective) metaphor for neoliberalism's impact on East, South and Southeast Asia. Her analysis of texts ranges across the continent and includes consideration of the Korean films *Sympathy for Mr Vengeance/ Boksuneun naui geot* (dir. Chan-wook Park, 2002) and *The Man from*

Nowhere/Ajeossi (dir. Jeong-beom Lee, 2010), the Hong Kong film *Koma/Jiu ming* (dir. Chi-Leung Law, 2005), the Taiwanese *Declaration of Geneva* (dir. Wu Derrick, 2013), the Philippino film *Graceland* (dir. Ron Morales, 2012), and the Japanese films *Children of the Dark/Yami no kodomo-tachi* (dir. Junji Sakamoto, 2008) and *Casshern* (dir. Kazuaki Kiriya, 2004). Each functions, in a nationally specific way, as a gothic exploration of neoliberalism's exploitation of the global poor, whilst all affirm that our very humanity is being compromised by such capitalised acts of bio-violence.

Linnie Blake's chapter, 'Catastrophic events and queer northern villages: zombie pharmacology *In the Flesh*', engages with similar themes, focusing on Dominic Mitchell's BAFTA-award-winning drama series *In the Flesh* (BBC, 2013–14). This is set in a bleak northern English landscape in the period immediately following The Rising – when the recently dead emerged from their graves and wrought all manner of cannibalistic havoc on the living. Restored to personhood by a daily dose of the drug Neurotriptaline, the bodies of the Risen become, a complex liminality on which are written the political imperatives of our own neoliberal age. Allegorising the impact on the poor, the sick and the disabled of five years of ideologically driven austerity measures under the Coalition Government, and condemning wholesale the immigration hysteria that has gripped the United Kingdom up to the present moment, the series wholeheartedly condemns the inhumanity of our leaders whilst exploring the politics of fear that sets person against person and tears communities apart. As such, Blake argues, it allows for a significant interrogation of contemporary subjectivity in an age in which we all exist (to varying degrees) as hybrids of organism, machine and drug, endlessly penetrated by global pharmacology, the corporate machinations of which intersect with discourses of national security across the world.

Rebecca Duncan's chapter, 'Gothic vulnerability: affect and ethics in fiction from neoliberal South Africa', is thematically contiguous with the two chapters that precede it. Duncan explores the ways in which traditional gothic devices have been mobilised in the literary culture of post-apartheid South Africa as a means of negotiating the ways in which global neoliberal capitalism builds on colonialism's hierarchies of race and gender to consolidate the vulnerability of particular groups. Focusing on the ferociously political yet self-consciously commercial work of the South African author Lauren Beukes, Duncan examines the ways in which the multivalent dehumanisations of neoliberalism are encapsulated in repeated scenes of the sentient body being reduced to little more than matter. Like Ancuta, she illustrates how neoliberal acts of violence against the subject may be interrogated by contemporary gothic texts that, in so doing, may enable us to think through strategies of resistance to the economic actuality of neoliberal economics and the ideologies of selfhood and society they entail.

Part III. The gothic home and neoliberalism

The third part of this collection moves from the global to the local, focusing on the family home as the primary site of everyday life under neoliberalism. Addressing the ramifications of the economic crash of 2008, these two chapters return us to one of the gothic's most beloved tropes – the haunted house. In so doing, both explore the ways in which neoliberal capitalism has penetrated our most private spaces, refashioning us and the ways we live accordingly.

Karen E. Macfarlane's chapter, 'Market value: *American Horror Story*'s housing crisis', explores the ways in which the events of 2008 challenged the dream of the family home as traditional encapsulation of the American myths of hard work, self-reliance and (world-leading) social mobility. Exploring the first season of the television series, she charts the ways in which the post-2006 owners have become trapped in the house by the current economic situation, becoming akin to its long-term resident ghosts. Held hostage by their unsellable investment and reminded at every turn that their lives are subject to penetration by the spectral alterity of forces beyond their control, the series' protagonists, for Macfarlane, have come to embody the crisis in models of national identity engendered by global capital flow in general and by the economic collapse of 2008 in particular. Here the Ramos family, driven from the house by racist ghosts, enacts the collapse of the US sub-prime mortgage market, which loaned money specifically to black and Hispanic borrowers at inflated interest rates regardless of income. Though this makes them the only family to own the house without dying in it, it also underscores the ways in which neoliberalism has not only failed to eradicate longstanding ethnic hierarchies in the United States but has exploited them for its own ends. For Macfarlane, the haunted house of the neoliberal age becomes a potent symbol, not only of neoliberalism's failure to deliver on its promises of wealth generation but, as we have seen in Ancuta's Asia and Duncan's South Africa, of the way it has retrenched historic inequalities among class and ethnic groups. Those foolish enough to buy into the neoliberal dream are doomed. Those excluded from it have had a lucky escape but remain dispossessed, inferior and not quite American enough.

Tracey Fahey's chapter, 'Haunted by the ghost: from global economics to domestic anxiety in contemporary art practice', also explores the impact of the 2008 crash on the domestic space, this time with reference to Ireland. Fahey investigates how the boom years of the Celtic Tiger led to the overproduction of housing stock that would never be inhabited or bought, the European Debt Crisis giving rise to 650 so-called 'ghost estates' – housing developments left either partially occupied or unfinished by developers bankrupted by the crash. These eloquent monuments to a vanished prosperity (itself driven by excess and greed) are read through Derridean hauntology as places adrift in time, houses that have lost their value as commodities, haunted by the spectre of what might have been. Thus reanimated and reimagined by the Irish artists and film-makers Aideen Barry, Elaine Reynolds, Eamonn Crudden and Anthony Haughey, the ghost estates are shown to embody the price paid locally for failures in global economic policy, the domestic sphere having become an anxious and unstable space, and its inhabitants mere ghosts of a future that never came to pass.

Part IV. Crossing borders

As the seductive yet deadly figure of the undead-yet-living vampire attests, the gothic has long walked the line between modes of being, models of identity and competing conceptualisations of what is both desirable and good. This preoccupation with states of liminality is encapsulated in this collection's final two chapters. Here the borders of the nation state become a permeable membrane through which the toxic waste of first world technology seeps out alongside the murderous economic imperatives of the neoliberal agenda.

Steffen Hantke's chapter, 'Gothic meltdown: German nuclear cinema in neoliberal times', focuses on three stylistically divergent 'nuclear incident' films produced for television and cinematic distribution and aimed at different target audiences: *Die Wolke/The Cloud* (dir. Gregor Schnitzler, 2006), *Der erste Tag/The First Day* (dir. Andreas Prochaska, 2008) and *Unter Kontrolle/Under Control* (dir. Volker Sattel, 2011). For Hantke, the nuclear power plant is an exemplary gothic site of neoliberal ideology. Here monopolised and transnational corporate power intersects with the modern security state. And when the plant malfunctions, spilling radioactive poison into the environment, discourses of individual and collective citizenship, bodily autonomy, and social and economic enfranchisement and disenfranchisement are all called into question. Adapting the conventions of American disaster and post-catastrophic survival cinema to the German context, all three films are shown to deploy the gothic mode's representational strategies to explore the networks of power that hold the neoliberal world in place. For whether we inhabit national, transnational or even postnational spaces, the undead hand of neoliberal economics continues to exert a hold on all our lives.

The final chapter in the collection is Agnieszka Soltysik Monnet's 'Border gothic: Gregory Nava's *Bordertown* and the dark side of NAFTA'. This examines the Mexican–American border as a gothic space created by a combination of postcolonial power relations and the new economic and political conditions created by the North American Free Trade Agreement (NAFTA). It focuses on Gregory Nava's gothic thriller *Bordertown* (2006), which tells the story of a young Indian *maquiladora* worker who is raped and left for dead but manages to survive and tell her story to a journalist. The film, Soltysik Monnet argues, not only draws heavily on gothic imagery and representational practices (particularly in its depiction of unsafe working practices) but engages with the very issues that inform theoretical work on the neoliberal politics of the frontier, biodisposability and death.[19] Thus, she illustrates, border towns such as Ciudad Juárez become contemporary underworlds, created by neoliberal practices that prey especially on young female workers, often from indigenous tribes. Grounding the film within its distinctive cultural context (specifically the fact that hundreds of young women have been murdered around Juárez in the last twenty years and almost none of these crimes have been solved) Soltysik Monnet explores the film's indictment of the governments of both the United States and Mexico. Both have colluded with the corporations that own the factories in which these women work to draw a pall of secrecy over the murders. Thus, the combined forces of neoliberalism, sexism and the lingering postcolonial disenfranchisement of native populations are seen to have created a climate of constant fear for women working in the border factories of the film, their murders being effectively sanctioned by the state. The gothic visual rhetoric of the film is therefore not merely an aesthetic choice but is also a rhetorical strategy that resonates productively with contemporary cultural theory about the human cost of neoliberal policies.

Conclusions

Although they range across continents and focus on a variety of media, the chapters in this collection all demonstrate the ways in which global neoliberalism has impacted on the lives, dreams and subjectivities of people across the globe. They demonstrate, therefore, the ways in which international gothic texts provide an effective and affective means for viewers and readers to explore the often unspoken nature of their economic condition. Ultimately, what emerges most forcibly from the collection is a sense of economic, existential and humanitarian crisis – the neoliberal experiment having led us to war, to environmental catastrophe and to levels of inequality unprecedented in modern times. Alongside this is an awareness that the gothic is ideally positioned, as a mode, to evoke and interrogate such turmoil, focusing as it does on the monstrous, the liminal and the domestic in ways that undermine dominant ideologies, question old truths and envision different ways of being. It is entirely appropriate, we contend, that ours is a culture inhabited by monsters. For thirty years of neoliberal experiment have done extraordinary violence to our societies and ourselves, leaving us unable, it seems, to find a way out of the darkness.

Notes

1 The zombie's cultural predominance as the new millennium's monster of choice is witnessed by the extraordinary proliferation of novels, television programmes, films and games that showcase its insatiable hunger to consume both human beings and the societies they inhabit. Notable novelistic examples include *World War Z* (2006) by Max Brooks, Jonathan Maberry's *Patient Zero* (2009), Jon Ajvide Lindqvist's *Handling the Undead* (2009), *Dust* (2010) by Joan Frances Turner, and M. R. Carey's *The Girl with All the Gifts* (2014). In terms of television programming, *The Walking Dead* (AMC, 2010–) has become the most popular programme on US television, its Season 4 premiere attracting an audience of over 20 million people (see Biebel, 2013). As the zombie has grown in popularity, moreover, it has moved across media and genres: films have become television programmes (*Zombieland*, 2013), graphic novels have been adapted for TV (*The Walking Dead*, 2010–; *Rachel Rising*, 2012), and both games (the *Resident Evil* franchise, 2002–16) and novels (*Warm Bodies* (Marion, 2010); dir. Jonathan Levine, 2013) have been made into films. Zombie films themselves have ranged from low-budget comedy (*Midget Zombie Takeover*, 2013) to politically engaged explorations of the contemporary

workplace (*Dead Man Working*, 2013) to comments on the 'War on Terror' (*The Revenant*, 2009). They have given a new twist, moreover, to more established genres such as the ghetto movie (*Gangs of the Dead*, 2006), the road movie (*Deadheads*, 2011) and the Western (*Gallowwalkers*, 2013).

2 See Harvey (1989), Jameson (1991) and Callinicos (1990).

3 See Punter (1980).

4 Oscar Wilde, *The Picture of Dorian Gray* (1890); Bram Stoker, *Dracula* (1897).

5 Both 'The Legend of Sleepy Hollow' and 'Rip Van Winkle' were published in *The Sketchbook of Geoffrey Crayon* (1820).

6 For detailed consideration of the global dimensions of the gothic see Byron (2013), and Byron and Townshend (2013).

7 From its earliest manifestations, the gothic has displayed highly misogynistic tendencies, both in the form of sexual violence against women (as in Matthew Lewis's *The Monk* (1796)) and of a more nebulous sense of threat (as in Ann Radcliffe's *The Mysteries of Udolpho* (1794)). William Beckford's *Vathek* (1786) and Charlotte Dacre's *Zofloya; or, The Moor* (1806) delved into the terror of ethnic alterity, a theme developed in H. Rider Haggard's *She* (1886) and Charlotte Brontë's *Jane Eyre* (1847), and later still in H. G. Wells' *The Island of Dr Moreau* (1896) and R. L. Stevenson's *The Strange Case of Dr Jekyll and Mr Hyde* (1886). Meanwhile, the mode's historic class politics have been avowedly bourgeois, resulting in extreme depictions of both the aristocracy and the working class: Count Dracula himself typifying the former, whilst the latter (although catered to in the Victorian period in penny dreadfuls such as *Varney the Vampire* (1847)) emerge frequently as objects of horror, both in Europe and in the gothic tradition of the American South.

8 The highly gothic 'miseries and mysteries' genre inaugurated by Eugène Sue in his *Mysteries of Paris* (1843) and critiqued by Karl Marx in *The Holy Family* (1845) is a case in point. Whilst it revelled in the dark and perverse underside of Paris, Sue's novel reduced its proletarian characters to sympathetic caricatures and failed to envision a political solution to the social problems depicted. In the United States, the genre would descend into melodramatic sensationalism that effectively demonised the working classes for the titillation of a bourgeois readership.

9 Examples of gothic-clad conservativism are numerous. We would point, in particular, to the gender politics of television programmes such as *The Vampire Diaries* (2009–) and the heteronormativity of novels such as *Warm Bodies* (Marion, 2010). Both adopt the *mise-en-scène*, plot and character types of the gothic, but eschew its capacity for social engagement and political critique.

10 Examples of gothic radicalism are equally numerous. We would point, in particular, to Max Brooks' novel *World War Z* (2006) – an accomplished exploration of international relations and global economics – and to television series such as *In the Flesh* (2013–14) and films such as George A. Romero's 'Dead' sextet, both of which deploy the zombie as an exploration of the rights and responsibilities of humanity and the inherently oppressive nature of the neoliberal State.

11 In the UK, this was characterised by a belief in active government dedicated to reducing social inequality – a mixed economy in which core industries were owned by the State – industrial relations policies that entailed conciliation with the trade union movement – and a commitment to state welfare, health and education. In the USA, the 'Great Society' initiative promoted by Lyndon B. Johnson would echo

the aims, if not the method, of the British, seeking to tackle poverty and inequality through State investment in education, medical care, the inner city and transport. See Dutton (1991), and Milkis and Mileur (2005).

12 David Harvey writes informedly on this in *The Condition of Postmodernity* (1989).

13 'They reversed the nationalizations and privatized public assets, opened up natural resources (fisheries, timber, etc.) to private and unregulated exploitation (in many cases riding roughshod over the claims of indigenous inhabitants), privatized social security and facilitated foreign investment and freer trade. The right of foreign companies to repatriate profits from their Chilean operations was guaranteed' (Harvey, 2005: 8).

14 As a recent Oxfam report has indicated, however, the 'trickledown' theory is entirely fallacious, a widening gulf of inequality having opened up between social classes and nations that threatens to consign future generations to ever-worsening poverty (Oxfam, 2014).

15 In the wake of the global financial crisis of 2008, the European Debt Crisis occurred when several EU countries (Greece, Portugal, Ireland, Spain and Cyprus) found themselves unable to repay their government debt or bail out indebted banks without the help of outside parties such as the European Central Bank or the International Monetary Fund. The result was a swingeing programme of austerity forced on sovereign governments by the EU, impacting most markedly on the poorest members of society.

16 These include American companies Pfizer, Merck, Johnson and Johnson, Bristol-Myers Squibb, and Wyeth; British companies GlaxoSmithKline and AstraZeneca; Swiss companies Novartis and Roche; and the French company Aventis.

17 For a full discussion of the topic see Goldacre (2012).

18 These include Margaret Atwood's *Oryx and Crake* (2003) and *The Year of the Flood* (2009), the Canadian TV series *ReGenesis* (The Movie Network, 2004–8) and the US vampire movie *Daybreakers* (2009).

19 Specifically Gloria Anzaldúa's *Borderlands/La frontera* (1987), Henry Giroux's notion of the 'biopolitics of disposability' and Achille Mbembe's 'Necropolitics' (2003).

References

Anzaldúa, Gloria. 1987. *Borderlands/La frontera: The New Mestiza*. San Francisco: Aunt Lute Books.

Atwood, Margaret. 2003. *Oryx and Crake*. London: Bloomsbury Press.

Atwood, Margaret. 2009. *The Year of the Flood*. London: Bloomsbury Press.

Bibel, Sara. 2013. 'The *Walking Dead* Season 4 Premiere Is Highest Rated Episode Ever with 16.1 Million Viewers & 10.4 Million Adults 18–49'. *Zap2it*, 14 October. http://tvbythenumbers.zap2it.com/2013/10/14/the-walking-dead-season-4-premiere-is-highest-rated-episode-ever-with-16-1-million-viewers-10-4-million-adults-18-49/208857/.

Blyth, Mark. 2013. *Austerity: The History of a Dangerous Idea*. Oxford: Oxford University Press.

Brooks, Max. 2006. *World War Z: An Oral History of the Zombie Wars*. New York: Crown.

Byron, Glennis, ed. 2013. *Global Gothic*. Manchester: Manchester University Press.

Byron, Glennis and Dale Townshend, eds. 2013. *The Gothic World*. Basingstoke: Routledge.

Callinicos, Alex. 1990. *Against Postmodernism: A Marxist Critique*. London: Polity.

Carey, M. R. 2014. *The Girl with All the Gifts*. London: Orbit.

Dutton, David. 1991. *British Politics since 1945: The Rise and Fall of Consensus*. Oxford: Blackwell.

Goldacre, Ben. 2012. *Bad Pharma: How Drug Companies Mislead Doctors and Harm Patients*. London: Fourth Estate.

Gurtov, Melvin. 2006. *Superpower on Crusade: The Bush Doctrine in US Foreign Policy*. Boulder, CO: Lynne Reinner.

Harvey, David. 1989. *The Condition of Postmodernity*. Oxford: Blackwell.

Harvey, David. 2003.*The New Imperialism*. Oxford: Oxford University Press.

Harvey, David. 2005. *A Brief History of Neoliberalism*. Oxford: Oxford University Press.

Jameson, Fredric. 1991. *Postmodernism, or, The Cultural Logic of Late Capitalism*. London: Verso.

Jameson, Fredric. 1993. 'Postmodernism; or, The cultural logic of late capitalism'. In T. Docherty, ed., *Postmodernism: A Reader*. London and New York: Harvester Wheatsheaf, 62–92.

Lindqvist, Jon Ajvide. 2009. *Handling the Undead*. London: Quercus.

Maberry, Jonathan. 2009. *Patient Zero: A Joe Ledger Novel*. New York: St Martin's Griffin.

Marion, Isaac. 2010. *Warm Bodies*. New York: Simon & Schuster.

Mbembe, Achille. 2003. 'Necropolitics'. In Stephen Morton and Stephen Bygrave, eds, *Foucault in an Age of Terror: Essays on Biopolitics and the Defence of Society*. London: Palgrave Macmillan, 11–40.

Milkis, Sidney M. and Jerome M. Mileur, eds. 2005. *The Great Society and the High Tide of Liberalism*. Amherst: University of Massachusetts Press.

Oxfam. 2014. 'Working for the Few: Political Capture and Economic Inequality'. 20 January. www.oxfam.org/sites/www.oxfam.org/files.

Punter, David. 1980. *The Literature of Terror*. London: Longman.

Scott, Jody. 1986. *I, Vampire*. London: The Women's Press.

Serres, Michel. 1982. *The Parasite*. Baltimore, MA: Johns Hopkins University Press.

Seymour, Richard. 2014. *Against Austerity*. London: Pluto.

Turner, Joan Frances. 2010. *Dust*. New York: Ace Books.

Filmography

Bordertown. 2006. Dir. Gregory Nava. El Norte Productions.

Daybreakers. 2009. Dir. Peter Spierig and Michael Spierig. Lionsgate.

Dead Man Working. 2013. Dir. L. E. Salas. Left Stage Productions.

Deadheads. 2011. Dir. Brett Pierce and Drew T. Pierce. FroBro Films.

Gallowwalkers. 2013. Dir. Andrew Goth. Boundless Pictures.

Gangs of the Dead. 2006. Dir. Duane Stinnett. Outside Productions.

In the Flesh. 2013–14. BBC.

Midget Zombie Takeover. 2013. Dir. Glenn Berggoetz. Driving with Our Eyes Shut/ Cold Spring Productions.

Rachel Rising. 2012. Alcon Television Group.
ReGenesis. 2004–8. The Movie Network.
The Revenant. 2009. Dir. D. Kerry Prior. Putrefactory Productions.
The Vampire Diaries. 2009–. Warner Brothers Television.
The Walking Dead. 2010–. AMC.
Warm Bodies. 2013. Dir. Jonathan Levine. Mandeville Films.
Zombieland. 2013. Dir. Ruben Fleischer. Amazon.

Part I

Neoliberal gothic monsters

1

Aspasia Stephanou

Game of fangs: the vampire and neoliberal subjectivity

> I am prodigiously adaptable. A survivor in every sense.
> (Scott, 1986:6)

> One feeds on another and gives nothing in return.
> (Serres, 1982: 182)

In contemporary culture the omnipresence of vampirism coincides with a specific kind of subjectivity produced under neoliberal capital. Taking a cue from Noémi Szécsi's *The Finno-Ugrian Vampire* (2012), vampirism becomes a way of life: 'You must suck out their blood before they suck out yours' (Szécsi, 2012: 4). In this chapter I will examine the figure of the vampire as symptomatic of contemporary neoliberal subjectivity and the way it relates to the current understanding of capitalist relations. The popularity of the vampire in contemporary literature and film suggests a world in which violence, predatory and greedy attitudes, and uncontrollable desires characterise and define human relations. Neoliberal vampires are entrepreneurs of themselves, fashioning themselves and profiting from their own labours. Vampires are the selfish individuals whose predatory and rapacious behaviour destroys solidarity and being in common.

From novels such as Jody Scott's *I, Vampire* (1984), John Marks' *Fangland* (2007) and Matt Haig's *The Radleys* (2010) to Guillermo del Toro and Chuck Hogan's *The Strain Trilogy* (2009–12), vampirism has come to represent the neoliberal subject's compulsion to devour and consume in a dangerous world based on exploitation, competition, consumerism, profit and growth. More particularly, Jody Scott's novel and Jim Jarmusch's latest film, *Only Lovers Left Alive* (2013), are vivid examples of neoliberal subjectivities that bring into focus neoliberalism's Janus face. Scott's novel represents the hyperactivity of the worker and mobilisation of psychic energies experienced in the 1980s and 1990s, whereas Jarmusch's film sheds light on the darker side of neoliberalism's exhaustion of energies and depression, evident after the outbreak of the financial crisis in 2008. It is significant to note that neoliberalism is not merely a form of governing economies but also a way of governing individuals, and cultivates those existential conditions that produce a particular kind of subjectivity. The neoliberal subject is not only a manager but also a slave of him-/herself, investing in his/her own self at the same time that s/he is being exploited by the system that produces him/her. The idea of neoliberal vampire subjectivity is not a whimsical formulation but reflects the character of neoliberalism and its unholy births.

The attraction to vampires reveals society's fascination with the psychopath and criminal whose power and freedom to exploit and manipulate social norms enable them to follow unhindered their selfish goals. For example, Adam Kotsko in *Why We Love Sociopaths: A Guide to Late Capitalist Television* (2012) argues that the fascination with sociopaths is not rebellious but 'serves only to reinforce our collective Stockholm Syndrome' (Kotsko, 2012: 77). If the world around us is characteristically anti-social and lawless, populated by sociopaths, then it is inevitable that we become enthralled by them, finding their pseudo-rebellious behaviour appealing, seeking to emulate their successful lives but also becoming them in order to avoid being destroyed by them. Our fascination, then, with vampires points towards the omnipresent and generalised pattern of parasitic relations, and the threat posed by those predatory humans caught in the spell of voodoo economics and compelled to feed on each other, maximising their human capital at the expense of others. The proliferation of cultural representations of vampire corporations and capitalism thus shows, not the distant chaotic future, but the current state of politics and economy. Within this context self-interested people invest in their own survival and increase of wealth, while others trudge across the abandoned spaces of bankrupt cities reduced to the status of the living dead. Images on television after the Greek government-debt crisis in 2009 attest to the effects of neoliberal policies on the population: thousands of unemployed Greeks are left homeless, hundreds of thousands use soup kitchens daily, the rate of HIV infection is on the rise because of budget cuts to health, there is widespread depression and the suicide rate has increased dramatically (Ferris-Rotman, 2011; Smith, 2012; Lynn, 2011). Dimitris Christoulas, for example, who shot himself in front of the Greek Parliament, had written a suicide note explaining that 'The government has annihilated all traces for my survival' (Lowen, 2012). With austerity measures, then, the disenfranchised are bled dry so that the banks are resuscitated. Bailing out banks at the expense of ordinary people is something experienced in the European debt crisis, with Cyprus being the most recent example, and makes Matt Taibbi's comparison of Goldman Sachs (and every other big bank) to a 'great vampire squid' very timely (2010).

Beginning with *Dracula* and Franco Moretti's reading of Dracula as an ascetic, I want to move from industrial capitalism based on a Protestant ethic to contemporary neoliberal capitalism that is based on acceleration, violence, insecurity and corruption.[1] While in Bram Stoker's *Dracula* the count accumulates only as much blood-money as he needs without wasting a drop, now vampire capitalists violently appropriate every resource, expanding their power beyond limits. At the same time, according to Moretti, vampire capital, like today's predatory capitalism, is 'the capital which, after lying "buried" for twenty long years of recession, rises again to set out on the irreversible road of concentration and monopoly' (Moretti, 1982: 74). With deregulation and the elimination of modernity's principles and bourgeois law, capitalism now 'has turned into a criminal system and keeps working towards the expansion of the realm of pure violence, where its advancement can proceed unhindered. *Splatterkapitalismus*: the end of bourgeois hegemony and of the enlightened universality of the law' (Berardi, 2009a: 52). Similarly, Christian Marazzi describes the attempts of twentieth-century financialisation as 'parasitic' and 'desperate' (2011: 26). This is why criminal behaviour that characterises the vampire, as well as other fictional monsters, has become normalised. As Franco 'Bifo' Berardi points out:

> Crime is no longer a marginal function of the capitalist system, but the decisive winning factor for deregulated competition ... Torture, homicide, child exploitation, the drive to prostitution, and the production of instruments of mass destruction have become irreplaceable techniques of economic competition. Crime is best suited to the principle of competition. (2009a: 52–3)

Nowhere is this more obvious than in Guillermo del Toro and Chuck Hogan's *The Strain Trilogy*. The voracious capitalist Eldritch

Palmer and the Nazi vampire Thomas Eichorst set into motion their plans for the mass destruction of humanity and the reorganisation of wealth and power. By utilising Nazi techniques of biopolitical control and managing those inferior lives through blood camps, they seek to secure the survival of the few and powerful while sacrificing those they deem expendable. Within this realm, power is grounded on terror, and violence turns humanity into waste, bled dry and emptied out. Berardi notices that neoliberalism favours the monopoly over the free market in the guise of a 'predatory lumpenbourgeoisie' that took advantage of the crisis of traditional capitalism in the 1970s, appropriating large shares of social capital (Berardi, 2009a: 62).[2] This is also mirrored in *The Strain Trilogy* with Palmer's parasitic profits through his appropriation of natural resources and the control of the financial markets so that his power will extend beyond humanity's natural limits. As a capitalist, he invested in a vampire future where he would be the only powerful and wealthy immortal.

Indeed exploitation, production of scarcity, violent imposition and rules based on force are now the forms of neoliberal capitalism (Berardi, 2009b: 83). In this respect, as Berardi argues in *The Soul at Work*, competition becomes the universal belief of the last decades while solidarity is eclipsed. Human relations are based on competition and aggressive impulses, transforming humans into ruthless and lustful antagonists driven by the corrupted smell of blood/money. As Berardi writes, the loss of eros results in 'the investment of desire in one's work, understood as the only place providing narcissistic reinforcement to individuals used to perceiving the other ... [as] a competitor and therefore an enemy' (2009b: 80). When hyper-capitalism liberates itself from Humanism and the Enlightenment's values, what is left is 'pure, endless and inhuman violence' (Berardi, 2009b: 132) where individuals are locked in competition and guided by their obsessions with acquisition, possession and accumulation. The family of vampires presented in *The Radleys* is no exception to this. The normalised vampires' everyday pursuits, work routine, the conveniences of a supermarket life, and the constant management of their aggressive appetites numbed with commodified blood and other everyday products exemplify contemporary life subjugated to the rhythms of mechanical struggle, unhappiness and anger. As will be discussed later, Jody Scott's entrepreneur vampire, Sterling O'Blivion, takes enjoyment from working in the Max Arkoff dance studio, instructing her teachers to increase sales while being aware of the antagonisms and limiting relations between them. In John

Marks' *Fangland* the threat of vampirism is not only linked to a notorious Eastern European criminal, but is also associated with the vampiric and predatory nature of the media and journalists that let the vampire in. The television news-magazine people are playfully likened to bloodsuckers (Marks, 2007: 27–8), while vampirism is spread through the viral language of the contaminated tapes that arrive at the television network, called Fangland.

The parasite is here a useful figure to understand the relations within neoliberal culture. In *The Parasite* (1982) French philosopher Michel Serres develops a model of parasitism based on relations of 'taking without giving' in the fields of information theory, economics, politics and anthropology. The anachronistic presence of the vampire seems uncannily fitting to define the cultural ether of today characterised by the reproduction of the same and repetitive exploitation. Contemporary culture, unable to produce the new, appears nostalgic for older periods and seeks the restoration of old values. As Serres points out:

> Our world is full of copiers and repeaters all highly rewarded with money and glory. It is better to interpret than to compose … The modern illness is the engulfing of the new in the *duplicata*, the engulfing of intelligence in the pleasure [*jouissance*] of the homogeneous. Real production is undoubtedly rare, for it attracts parasites that immediately make it something common and banal. (Serres, 1982: 4)

The vampire does not create anything new but depends on its human host for food. It feeds on the human and gives nothing in return; it is merely an exploiter. Serres takes on the figure of the vampire itself, which he associates with death, and juxtaposes it with life and work. The vampire capitalist leeches the workers, forces them to give their flesh and blood: 'Certain pale, cadaverous shades move about, wandering in a world like some netherworld, almost dead already, and even greedier, thirstier, for fresh blood, the blood of those who work. Innumerable vampires and bloodsuckers attached in packets to the rather rare bodies of the workers' (Serres, 1982: 87). Therefore, if we extend the metaphor of the parasite to the whole of society, it can be said that today's neoliberal subject is at the same time the parasite and the host, eater of others and eaten by others. There is a whole nexus of relations based on this schema of consumption and exploitation. Maurizio Lazzarato, for example, defines neoliberalism as a system of exploitation based on the capitalist relation between creditors and debtors, masters and slaves, those who have and those who have not. The parasite, then, as the one who feeds on others, but is also exploited by others, is an appropriate figure to describe contemporary subjectivity and human relations.

But the parasite does not merely poison the organism of the host but strengthens the system by reinforcing resistance and increasing the host's adaptability, giving it the means to fight the parasite. Serres notices that parasitism can facilitate the creation of new species, but also destroy through epidemics those species that are unable to adapt to the new conditions. It is possible to argue that today those individuals who are able to adapt to the current state of affairs by playing the neoliberal game and sharpening their fangs against anyone who threatens their selfish interests are the survivors. Contrary to these parasites, the individuals who are unable to play according to the new rules of the game are quickly marginalised and ostracised. An illustration of this is the increasing gap between the poor and the rich, and the resulting anxiety of being unable to participate in consumer culture and achieve success in terms of career, job or income. Henry Giroux refers to the ways populations and groups become 'redundant, disposable, or criminalized' (Giroux, 2011: 32). Poor minority youth in America, for example, can merely choose among the military, prison or their exile in dead zones of invisibility (Giroux, 2011: 32). Given the fact that neoliberal life is predicated on the freedom of consumer choice, the inability to participate due to inadequate financial income results in ostracism, aggression and violence (Bauman, 2005). In this game of fangs only the fittest survive, and an ideology of Social Darwinism is perpetuated that seeks to exclude by spreading fear and polluting relations. In a culture conditioned by the sadomasochism of competition, dominant ideology crushes any form of egalitarian living, rendering humanity anodyne and undead.

In such an impoverished world, one's subjectivity is significantly defined by work, just as the business of being a vampire and feeding itself defines the vampire's life. Work

> eats its worker, devouring his flesh and his time; it is slowly substituted for his body. This invasion causes fear. Who am I? This, there, written in black on white, fragile, and this is my body, has taken the place of my body, frail. This is written in my blood; I am bleeding from it, and it will stop only with the last drop. The work parasites the worker; no, soon he no longer exists. He dies of it. And he can do nothing about it. He lives from it … The work parasites me, and I parasite it. (Serres, 1982: 131–2)

In neoliberalism, where work increasingly defines one's being, the individual is imprisoned in repetition and competition, where work takes over one's life and it is no longer possible to segregate leisure and work. Working oneself to death, and the compulsion to repeat it without escape, reduce human relations to cash exchange and alienation. As Carl Cederström and Peter Fleming argue in *Dead Man Working* (2012), the rituals of capitalism are essentially an anti-life, condemning one to the grave of work: 'From the daily tedium of the office, to the humiliating team building exercise, to the alienating rituals of the service economy, to the petty mind games of a passive-aggressive boss: the experience is not one of dying ... but neither of living. It is a living death' (2012: 4). When we become the job itself then life is put to work. If, in Fordist capitalism, work was separate from leisure time, and the brains of the workers were severed from their bodies, now the whole of one's existence is occupied by work. Work is something we are, rather than something we do. Irregular hours and part-time contracts dictate different patterns of work and demand that one is always available for work, while one's desire and knowledge become useful and productive (Mitropoulos, 2005). Checking emails at any time of the day, networking during leisure time or producing intellectual work during one's holidays, or even thinking while dreaming, have become a way of living. Now managers, aware that one is more creative at home, encourage work outside the office. Moreover, one's private life is now invited at work, where photographs and personal items, or visits from one's children, become ways to encourage productivity at the workplace. As Peter Fleming and Andrew Sturdy (2011) emphasise in their study of management practices in controlled environments such as the call centre, today employees are encouraged to *'just be themselves'*, express their lifestyle choices, personality, sexuality and difference so that their 'authentic' or 'non-work' personalities are captured as emotional labour. In a perverse way, images of blood farms presented in vampire films (*Blade Trinity, Daybreakers*) and fiction (*The Strain Trilogy*) depicting humans drained of their blood in organised labour camps and factories testify to the current situation and the living death experienced under neoliberalism.

Life in 24/7 capitalism is exhausted while sleep becomes the enemy of productivity and profit. Within the global neoliberal framework, to be sleepless is something to be desired so that production and consumption carry on as the human body adapts to new conditions that are more suited to the creatures of the night. Without any distinction between sleep and restoration, humanity lives in a 'permanent state of fearfulness from which escape is not possible' (Crary, 2013: 33).

The reconceptualisation of time and work, of the private and public spaces, creates the conditions for monotonous reproduction, apathetic consumerism and automatism where one is depleted of any meaningful political response. Vampire texts offer many examples of life in a permanent state of undeath, waking and surveillance. It is not only vampire life itself that is characterised by vigilance and supervision to guarantee its survival, but also human life. In apocalyptic landscapes where vampires pose a constant threat, humanity remains in a permanent and exhaustive state of alert vulnerability.[3] A more vivid example is captured in the representation of blood farms where humanity is kept in a state of non-death in controlled environments managed by vampire scientists.[4] On the one hand, in del Toro and Hogan's *The Strain Trilogy*, 24/7 blood farming is characterised by efficiency and functionality, while, on the other hand humanity survives in a condition of neutralisation, watching rerun programmes and dispossessed of time (*The Night Eternal*). This is clearer in the adaptation of *The Strain Trilogy* into a television series entitled *The Strain*, where the loss of the boundary between day and night infects life with insecurity so that no one feels safe at any time.

The neoliberal subject and the vampire share voracious appetites that congeal around the idea of conspicuous consumption characterised by compulsion and excess. Monstrosity and the vampire can be understood as the underside of enjoyable consumption, and as the criminal figures that threaten to destabilise the illusion and fantasy of neoliberalism's economic stability. Neoliberal ideology might stress that everyone is a winner, but in a competitive environment there are winners and losers, consumers and criminals. Significantly, a vampire-criminal system produces the vampires-criminals it needs. Jodi Dean, following Paul A. Passavant, indicates how the double imaginary figures of neoliberal governmentality – the consumer and the criminal – embody and, at the same time, occlude neoliberalism's fantasies and nightmares. For Dean, 'Under neoliberalism, the disciplined worker and consumer-citizen of the social welfare state fragment into myriad, shifting, imaginary identities that converge around the strange attractors of the insatiable shopper (shopaholic) and incorrigible criminal' (Dean, 2009: 63). The propaganda of neoliberalism that promises consumer enjoyment can easily turn into the threat of loss where the excessive and unregulated consumer appears to be as volatile and dynamic as the neoliberal market itself (Dean, 2009: 68–9). Because no risk in neoliberalism is acceptable, any risk is imagined as monstrous and unbearable (Dean,

2009: 71). As economic conditions become more desperate, and thus the fantasy of free trade is shown to be false, the criminals become more dangerous and monstrous, and the more they have to pay because there is no one else to take the blame (Dean, 2009: 72). The criminal is an apt figure to embody contemporary subjectivity because s/he, like the normalised vampire of fiction, is a normal individual who might, at any given time, act in a horrifying manner. Dean very succinctly recognises that the response to crime is pre-emptive: 'get them before they can get you' (2009: 71). The threat of the vampire, then, represents fears of being deprived of life and opportunity, of losing in the neoliberal game.

It is exactly this mentality of dog-eat-dog and dangerous predation that is so widespread today: an attitude, however, that diverts attention away from neoliberalism's volatility. For example, in *The Radleys* the desire to consume blood is distinguished between good and bad consumption. Their compulsion-addiction to blood is considered good when the vampire family follows the pattern of a successful economic citizen and responsibly acquires the blood-product. The uncle who indulges in the old vampire ways of hunting for his prey is unable to participate in the economy and his vampiric feeding is deemed a bad choice. At the same time, the daughter's unpredictable feeding on a boy, and his resulting death, demonstrate how the vampiric consumer can at any time become the unregulated consumer. What these uncontrolled vampires embody is the brutal face of neoliberalism's criminality and danger. They express the displaced anxieties about the monstrosity of the neoliberal system itself. In other words, neoliberal representations of volatile and dangerous vampires are indicative of a transformation in current relations and the ways understandings of self and Other have undergone radical change under neoliberal capitalism. The Other is perceived as a possible threat to one's enjoyment.[5] As one's life is exposed to the risks of the entrepreneurial business and one's economic security is destroyed, the Other is imagined as more monstrous and dangerous. When the criminal, deviant or monster is punished, the Other's suffering becomes a source of satisfaction for the majority because someone has finally paid for the collapse of the economy.

Jody Scott's *I, Vampire* expands this idea of vampirism as a compulsion that the subject is unable to resist. This 1984 novel also touches upon an early conceptualisation of neoliberal postfeminism. In the novel, Sterling O'Blivion is a 700-year-old vampire who works as an instructor and manager at the Max Arkoff dance studio in Chicago. Her selfhood and job attitudes, as well as the idea of vampirism as something completely normal, make this a particularly interesting novel that captures neoliberal life, competitive lifestyles and precarious living conditions. Scott's earlier novel, *Passing for Human* (1977), which shares similar characters with *I, Vampire* and is considered to be its loose sequel, describes an alien's anthropological research trip to Earth and her attempt to save Earth from an alien invasion. What is interesting is Scott's satire of humanity and her description of 'Earthies' cannibalising each other. Sterling O'Blivion's personal point of view is similar. She appears to be proud of the people she employs and the way she transforms them into greedy, competitive, ruthless little vampires. At the same time, the Max Arkoff Studio, as she clearly points out, 'does business in the time-honoured way. We go for the jugular' (Scott, 1986: 22). Scott's novel demonstrates in a unique way not only how the vampire has been normalised in postmodern fiction, but also how indistinct the border between humanity and vampirism is. Paradoxically, in her attempt to invert the conception of the vampire as alien Other, by representing humans as dangerous and predatory, Scott creates a female vampire who resembles the very character of humanity she critiques. As O'Blivion points out, 'vampires are as human as anyone; in fact, more so. A vampire scratches her flea bites, worries about the job market and hopes some nice person will send her a valentine. But nobody wants to believe there is none so monstrous it isn't her own mirror image' (15).

Sterling O'Blivion appears to conform to the image of the feminist as masculine, predatory (penetrating) and destructive, portrayed by backlash ideology. As she explains, her

> compulsion is all that sets her above the ruck of women: that scent of conquest, the noble chase, a game of wits, figuring out how I can penetrate and feast without getting my neck broken. And then the thrill of victory forever new, the ritualized ecstasy as I master the unconscious victim and at long last that slow, marvellous caress on the tongue as the Ruby slips down my throat. (Scott, 1986: 5)

O'Blivion sounds here like a thirsty entrepreneur driven by a compulsion to accumulate the precious liquid, describing the hunt as a chase and a game of wits, a competitive game of master and slave that ends with the domination of one over the other. Vampirism is constructed around the idea of compulsion as conquest, a play of hierarchies and what separates losers from winners. Vampirism is about risk and reward, the adrenaline of winning and the enjoyment of the other's suffering.

As an entrepreneur, O'Blivion has learned how to adapt and survive within the precarious and unexpected conditions of postmodern life. She is the ideal candidate for a successful life within neoliberal culture's accelerated rhythms, ruthless antagonism and undying desire for more profit. As she explains, unlike humans who 'get eaten alive by this cannibal culture' she survives (23). She is 'attached to ... [her] job by an umbilical cord' working at the studio 'ten or twelve hours a day, teaching, selling courses, managing, squeezing pennies' (24) in a 'libidinous frenzy' as she encourages everyone to 'fill our time with these activities so we won't ever need to think' (26). As everything moves fast she infects her employees with a sole message: 'Sell, sell, sell'. O'Blivion suffers from overstimulation injected with the 1980s confidence and positivity of neoliberal ideology for entrepreneurial spirit, profit and success. Her subjectivity is animated by her dependence on work and the fast pace of the dance studio.

The vampire not only feeds on the adrenaline and sweat of her employees but also cultivates a similar attitude in the studio, conditioning them to become predators and voracious consumers. She exhorts the instructors:

'Homo homini lupus!', quoting Dante, Cervantes, and Marcel Proust; giving pep talks, making charts, forcing them to compete with each other in a desperate frenzy; insisting that they spent every minute of their spare time collecting bills and receipts for the IRS; or using their pocket calculator to figure capital gains breaks, health benefits, or retirement plans; or, if religious, quibbling with God; or if not religious, polishing their teeth, curling their lashes, applying lacquer to their toenails, and preparing for wonderful, glossy dates with handsome closet cases who lift weights. (26)

As work dominates one's leisure time and existence, and as one works beyond work hours in order to fashion and improve oneself multiplying one's assets, life is put to work and the subject is programmed to perform a regulated set of actions that are meant to provide financial compensation. Overexcited and obsessed with identity, Sterling O'Blivion's employees are conditioned to an uninterrupted flow of enjoyment and work on the self, unable to switch off from the circuit of continuous stimulation, pathological excess of expressivity and information overload. Scott's prose imitates this frenzy of energies as 'Everyone is in a mad rush, changing costume to a drumbeat in the back room, straining and complaining under the narcotic of ritual dancing, a skittery swampfire of thousand-year lost causes' (26). The image of the dance instructors 'gyrating like the demons in a painting by Hieronymous

Bosch' (27) or skittering like cockroaches and bursting with energy are apt examples of neoliberal capital's manic–depressive dynamic, risky fluctuations and unexpected losses. For Berardi, the psychic and emotional state of the cognitive worker is indicative of the economic situation (2007: 79). For example, the financial euphoria of the 1990s, the 'culture of Prozac', was part and parcel of the economy. According to Berardi, during the 1990s, western economy's operators and managers made decisions under the influence of drugs and in a state of chemical euphoria that stimulated productivity and competition (Berardi, 2007: 79). However, as these energies were slowly exhausted, euphoria was followed by depression. As Berardi points out, the current state of exhaustion and depression is not the result of the economic crisis, but its cause (2007: 79). The cognitive worker, after working profitably for years, falls eventually into depression because his/her emotional, intellectual and physical system can no longer respond to the hyperactivity of the market or that of psycho-pharmaceuticals (2007: 79). So in Scott's novel, the fervid emotion, wild applause and violent convulsions of the dance teachers and students soon turn into stillness and emptiness, 'Nothing but confetti, half-empty cups, and silence' (Scott, 1986: 28).

For O'Blivion, contemporary existence is painful because it demands cruelty towards one's colleagues and relationships, as well as sacrificing one's morality and ethics. The vampire's understanding that the 'dance biz is so agonizing' but satisfying her 'craving for punishment' (27) – as she tortures her pupils with instructions that punish and reward so that they buy more courses – is part of the mentality of our times. Resembling 'mighty hunters cornering a woolly mammoth at cliff's edge' is how the vampire describes the greedy attitudes of the teachers towards their clients at the dance studio. Cultivating a selfish consumerism but also staying ahead of one's game is a vampire's strategy. As O'Blivion explains, 'We have clever parties to build up competition between our branch studios. It costs a fortune to run a studio. You can't sit around trading baseball cards; you've got to *compete*; you've got to *hustle* in order to get ahead and stay ahead, and drown the funny things that are going through your mind' (27).

Unlike Jody Scott's vampire child Sterling O'Blivion, who is energetic and living for her work, the vampires in Jim Jarmusch's film *Only Lovers Left Alive* (2013) are emptied out and withered. The film is not injected with adrenaline and vampiric frenzy, and, paradoxically, the vampires appear bored and worn out in their repetitive and ageless existence. Unlike neoliberal capital of the 1980s and 1990s, which was characterised by euphoria, endless energy, growth and positivity, the capital of the 2000s is different. Its speedy rhythms and relentless desire for more profit and expansion have a pathological effect on contemporary subjectivity, whose mental energies are used up and exploited beyond recuperation. In the film both Adam and Eve embody such decrepit subjectivities, their lives dangerous anachronisms that are peculiarly contemporaneous with the haunting deathliness of western culture. The vampire is fundamentally associated here with whiteness and is portrayed as a ghastly apparition, exhausted and lifeless.

The film is concerned with the ancient lives of a vampire couple, played by Tilda Swinton and Tom Hiddleston, rendered in dark and claustrophobic settings that capture the vampires' sterility and entrapment in a meaningless American world. The eternal lovers live in different worlds. Adam is a reclusive and depressed rock star with a cult following who is currently living in America. Once acquainted with Byron, and now a misanthrope, Adam is isolated in the ghost town of Detroit itself, rendered undead by the cold hand of financial capital. His house is a shrine to the past and is littered with old recording equipment and memorabilia from lost epochs. It is an outdated microcosm of the outside world, surrounded by the haunting sounds of old instruments and archaic apparatuses. The sounds of screeching records and uncanny technologies are not reassuring or comforting but oppressive, shrouding with a heaviness that is suffocating. Similarly, his Romantic individualism reminds one of John Polidori's Byronic vampire, who is a moral parasite and totally absorbed in himself. Adam's need for blood is supplied by a medical doctor in exchange for money, while the Renfield figure of Ian supplies him with guitars and a wooden bullet with which he considers terminating his long, boring and bloodless life. Adam's life is dominated by psychic automatisms and repetitive habits, as well as by unhappiness, depression and the thought of suicide. Cederström and Fleming describe contemporary subjectivity in a similar way, pointing out that the dead man working, finding himself 'paralyzed, crippled, and only half alive', seeks 'to reinvent death by crafting his own private terminus' through recourse to drugs or suicide (Cederström and Fleming, 2012: 8).

On the other hand, Eve resides in northern Morocco, in the alive and exotic Tangier where her mentor, the Elizabethan poet and playwright Christopher Marlowe, provides her with fresh blood. Unlike Adam's desperation due to his monotonous lifestyle, Eve is a happier vampire who enjoys the slow rhythms of life in exotic reverie. However, as she passes through the winding streets of timeless Tangier her haunting whiteness taints the dark bodies of the oriental people. Dressed in white clothes and gloves, with a marble pallid complexion, she, like Adam, embodies nothing but death. What seems to keep her more alive than Adam is the blood and the culture of Tangier on which she parasitically feeds.

When Adam and Eve drive through the streets and deserted houses in Detroit, there is a sense of loss and mourning about western civilisation. Detroit, once celebrated as Motown or Motor City, was the automotive centre of the world. By 2013, Detroit's economic decline left the city bankrupt. The film, in its movement through the sterile wombs of gigantic grandiose theatres, unveils the eerie remains of the city and reminds one of those emblematic images of Detroit's buildings circulating in popular culture as the fruits of the so-called 'ruin porn' photography.⁶ It is not only the evacuated Detroit, the stillness of the western landscape, but also the existential void, the archaic aestheticism, and Adam's nostalgia for the past that reveal the miserable hollowness at the core of American culture. At the same time, Detroit's location is indicative of neoliberal capital's insatiable appetite. The city's past creativity and productivity are exhausted and depleted by the mouth of neoliberal capital, which has now moved to other exploitable nations and workforces that will eventually be left in ruins as production moves elsewhere.

The western neoliberal subject, embodied by Adam and Eve, has reached a standstill. The vampires float through the streets like ether, shadows and ghostly containers hungry for blood and life. Both Adam and Eve are pale and extremely white, embodying death, sterility and bareness. There is nothing more to consume in the western world. Blood, life and creativity are lacking. The solution to this is offered elsewhere, in the eastern exoticism of Tangier. The ancient Tangier acts as an antidote to the sterility of Detroit's corpse. Adam is shown to be mesmerised by Lebanese singer Yasmine Hamdan, and the Orient's creativity, music and life bring him back to reality and inject his boring existence with new life. He hopes that Hamdan's song will not become famous because it will then be transformed into capital. Tangier does not only satisfy their aesthetic desires; there, their previously dormant predatory instincts and violence are revivified as they parasitically feed on a young oriental couple.

Jarmusch's film links vampirism and western culture to whiteness and death. Richard Dyer, in *White* (1997), associates the colour white and white people with death and bringing death. He locates 'the horror of vampirism … in colour: ghastly white, disgustingly cadaverous, without the blood of life that would give colour' (210). The vampires are dead and white, and when they consume their victims they leave them white and pale until they become dead too. Thus, in the act of vampirism, white western culture feeds off the Other and threatens to destroy and assimilate all difference. With its references to the Romantics, sensibility, and taste, the film also offers a critique on the hegemonic status of western culture, turning towards the East as the site, not only of Romantic creativity, but of oriental creativity, power and difference. The film looks elsewhere for different conceptions of selfhood, and away from the competition and predation of western ideologies. The neoliberal parasitic subject and the vampire are quintessentially western phenomena, obsolete and exhausted. The path towards the liberation of the social space from economic domination and parasitic relations is only possible through a withdrawal into passivity and silence, away from the realm of work, productivity and competition. The East becomes a possible outside space for new configurations of selfhood that do not submit to institutional regulations or surveillance, and more stable social forms involving reciprocity and co-operation. More importantly, while for the neoliberal mind the East is the focus of the 'War on Terror', Tangier in the film, as an emblem of the East, terrorises the war economy of neoliberalism by passively resisting its grip. In this way, the vampires are able to move from living death towards the more authentic life of Tangier.

Notes

1 Corruption should be understood here as the result of the neoliberal policies of deregulation and privatisation of the State's industries and services. See Ohemeng and Owusu (2014), 180.

2 Traditional capitalism here refers to Fordist and industrial capitalism, which decomposes in the 1970s, given that traditional methods are no longer able to guarantee the survival of capitalism. It is implemented by a post-Fordist mode of accumulation that depends no longer on the labour power of the factory worker but on immaterial labour (emotional and intellectual labour). See Hardt and Negri (2000), 28.

3 See Cronin (2010).

4 See Rod Hardy's film *Thirst* (1979), David S. Goyer's *Blade Trinity* (2004), the Spierig Brothers' *Daybreakers* (2009), and Guillermo del Toro and Chuck Hogan's *The Night Eternal* (2012).

5 In Lacanian psychoanalysis *jouissance*, or enjoyment, refers to an excess of enjoyment: a pleasurable pain, horrible fascination, or a surplus stimulation characterised

by uneasiness. For Slavoj Žižek, our hatred for our neighbour, the immigrant or the 'monstrous' Other derives from the belief that they have access to an imagined primordial and absolute bodily enjoyment. For example, racist attitudes are associated with envy about the Other's enjoyment, exemplified by the dislike of one's neighbour's weird customs or unfamiliar language (Žižek, 1993: 200–5).

6 The term 'ruin porn' was arguably used for the first time on 1 August 2009, in a blog post, 'Something, something, something, Detroit', written by Thomas Morton in *Vice Magazine*, in which Detroit photographer and blogger James Griffioen is quoted using the term (Morton, 2009).

References

Bauman, Zygmunt. 2005. *Work, Consumerism and the New Poor*. Buckingham: Open University Press.

Berardi, Franco 'Bifo'. 2007. 'Schizo economy'. *Substance* 36(2): 76–85.

Berardi, Franco 'Bifo'. 2009a. *Precarious Rhapsody: Semiocapitalism and the Pathologies of the Post-Alpha Generation*. London: Minor Compositions.

Berardi, Franco 'Bifo'. 2009b. *The Soul at Work: From Alienation to Autonomy*. New York: Semiotext(e).

Cederström, Carl and Peter Fleming. 2012. *Dead Man Working*. Winchester and Washington: Zero Books.

Crary, Jonathan. 2013. *24/7: Late Capitalism and the Ends of Sleep*. London and New York: Verso.

Cronin, Justin, 2010. *The Passage: A Novel*. New York: Ballantine Books.

Dean, Jodi. 2009. *Democracy and Other Neoliberal Fantasies: Communicative Capitalism and Left Politics*. Durham, NC: Duke University Press.

Dyer, Richard. 1997. *White*. London: Routledge.

Ferris-Rotman, Amie. 2011. 'Insight: In Greek crisis, HIV gains ground'. *Reuters*, 11 November. www.reuters.com/article/2011/11/11/us-greece-hiv-f-id USTRE7AA37P20111111.

Fleming, Peter and Andrew Sturdy. 2011. '"Being yourself" in the electronic sweatshop: New forms of normative control'. *Human Relations* 64(2): 177–200.

Giroux, Henry A. 2011. *Zombie Politics and Culture in the Age of Casino Capitalism*. New York: Peter Lang Publishing.

Hardt, Michael and Antonio Negri. 2000. *Empire*. Cambridge, MA and London: Harvard University Press.

Kotsko, Adam. 2012. *Why We Love Sociopaths: A Guide to Late Capitalist Television*. Winchester and Washington: Zero Books.

Lowen, Mark. 2012. 'Greek unrest after pensioner suicide beside parliament', *BBC News*, 5 April. www.bbc.com/news/world-europe-17620421.

Lynn, Matthew. 2011. *Bust: Greece, the Euro and the Sovereign Debt Crisis*. New Jersey: John Wiley and Sons.

Marazzi, Christian. 2011. *Violence of Financial Capitalism*. New York: Semiotext(e).

Marks, John. 2007. *Fangland*. London: Vintage Books.

Mitropoulos, Angela. 2005. 'Precari-Us?'. *Republicart*, March. http://eipcp.net/transversal/0704/mitropoulos/en.

Moretti, Franco. 1982. 'The dialectic of fear'. *New Left Review* 136: 67–85.

Morton, Thomas. 2009. 'Something, something, something, Detroit'. *Vice Magazine*, 1 August. www.vice.com/read/something-something-something-detroit-994-v16n8.

Ohemeng, Frank L. K. and Francis Y. Owusu. 2014. 'Beyond neoliberal public sector reform: A case for a developmental public service in sub-Saharan Africa'. In Charles Conteh and Ahmed Shafiql Huque, eds, *Public Sector Reforms in Developing Countries: Paradoxes and Practices*. London and New York: Routledge, 175–92.

Scott, Jody. 1986. *I, Vampire*. London: The Women's Press.

Serres, Michel. 1982. *The Parasite*. Baltimore, MA: Johns Hopkins University Press.

Smith, Helena. 2012. 'Greek homeless shelters take in casualties of debt crisis'. *Guardian*, 10 February. www.theguardian.com/world/2012/feb/10/greek-homeless-shelters-debt-crisis.

Szécsi, Noémi. 2012. *The Finno-Ugrian Vampire*. Trans. Peter Sherwood. London: Stork Press.

Taibbi, Matt. 2010. 'The great American bubble machine'. *Rolling Stone*, 5 April. www.rollingstone.com/politics/news/the-great-american-bubble-machine-20100405.

Žižek, Slavoj. 1993. *Tarrying with the Negative: Kant, Hegel and the Critique of Ideology*. Durham, NC: Duke University Press.

2

Stéphanie Genz

Austerity bites: refiguring *Dracula* in a neoliberal age

> Neoliberalism ... is relentlessly engaged in the production of an unchecked notion of individualism ... In its current historical conjuncture, the authoritarian state is controlled by a handful of billionaires ... their families ... and a select class of zombie-like financial and corporate elite who now control the commanding economic, political and cultural institutions.
>
> (Giroux, 2014)

As I finish watching the first season of NBC's television mini-series *Dracula* (2013–), I am reminded of Henry Giroux's compelling description of our contemporary 'second Gilded Age' typified by 'the moral sanctioning of greed, the corruption of politics by big money, and the ruthlessness of class power' (Giroux, 2014: 2). Giroux provides a scathing attack on free-market fundamentalism and individualism adopted by neoliberalism's pro-corporate agenda, which supports deregulated 'casino capitalism' and the demise of the social State. Indeed, ever since crisis hit global capitalism in 2008, we have been all too familiar with stories about reckless financiers and corrupt banking practices that have caused suffering for millions of families, workers, children and jobless public servants. Cultural commentators en masse have berated bankers' seemingly unchecked greed and narcissism, which no longer just point to 'a character flaw among a marginal few' (Giroux, 2013: 261) but now come to be seen as postmillenary moral evils symptomatic of a market-driven society (Hall, 2011; Gilbert, 2013). As Stuart Hall suggests in his analysis of the political, social, and cultural contradictions that have emerged in the wake of the global economic crisis, neoliberalism appears to be 'in crisis' but 'it keeps driving on' (Hall, 2011: 728). While Michael

Douglas famously held up robber baron power in the 1980s corporate drama *Wall Street* (dir. Oliver Stone, 1987) – encapsulated by the now classic axiom 'greed is good' – the bare materialistic and exploitative nature of capitalism and the social and personal costs of neoliberalism have been increasingly unmasked in the context of substantial cut-backs, bailouts, mass unemployment and austerity measures that have characterised the post-2008, recessionary world. The ideals of a free-market economy – based on the right to make profits and amass personal wealth – have been the target of a range of anti-capitalist protests that highlight the self-serving and avaricious practices of the 'masters of capital', exemplified by the widely reviled image of the 'greedy banker'.

In this chapter, I want to discuss how the contradictory field of forces set in motion by the unfolding economic crisis are articulated in the 2013 televised version of *Dracula* that provides a new outlet for the commodification of the vampire and the corporatisation of the gothic. The vampire is of course an eminently commodifiable figure – much scholarly, often Marxist-orientated, work has focused on the vampire as a character that responds to and reflects capitalism (Gelder, 1994). The gothic as well has become a much sought-after, lucrative badge – particularly in its more consumerised, celebrity-focused and mainstream variant, epitomised, for example, by *The Twilight Saga* (2005–8). As I argue, *Dracula* (2013) highlights not only the increasing humanisation of the vampire (Zanger, 1997), but also a specifically postrecession, capitalism-weary environment caught between the need for simultaneous restoration of growth and austerity. In this recent incarnation, the foreign, racial Other of Stoker's original narrative poses as an American entrepreneur intent on bringing modern science – in the form of wireless electrical transmission – to Victorian society in order to take revenge on an all-powerful business elite, known as the 'Order of the Dragon', whose wealth lies in oil reserves. Here, the links to the US-led 'War on Terror', its thinly disguised economic agenda and the conquest of Middle Eastern oil are plainly apparent. In this context, the figure of the vampire as an insatiable capitalist sucking on the life-blood of others evolves and responds to the transient nature and changing perceptions of this profit-geared ideology, proffering the possibility of a 'good' capitalism that might be free from financial monopoly and greed. If, as Nina Auerbach famously asserted, 'every age embraces the vampire it needs' (1995: 145), *Dracula* (2013) might have much to tell us about our uncertain, politically and economically unstable times.

Capital vampires and neoliberalism (in crisis)

Grounded in the idea of the 'free, possessive individual' and the ubiquitous and all-encompassing character of 'wealth', neoliberal ideas
represent a widely circulating current that affects cultural practices
of commodification, production and consumption (Hall, 2011).
Propagated prominently by the Thatcher and Reagan regimes of the
late 1970s and 1980s, neoliberal ideas, policies and strategies have
incrementally gained ground globally – 'setting the pace', as Hall
puts it, by 're-defining the political, social and economic models and
governing strategies' (2011: 708).[1] Market discipline and rationale
irrevocably entered all aspects of social life under 'Third Way' politics in the 1990s,which promoted particular types of entrepreneurial,
competitive and commercial behaviour in citizens – Tony Blair and
Gerhard Schroeder famously advocating that 'the state should not
row, but steer; not so much control, as challenge' (quoted in Genz,
2006: 335). In a bid to maximise their 'human capital' and release
their market potential, neoliberalism's entrepreneurial subjects were
encouraged to adopt individualist values of self-reliance and responsibility in their effort to marketise their identities (or self-brands) in the
most productive and lucrative manner. While the opportunity of prosperity and entrepreneurship might have been viewed with optimism
in the pre-recession decades, post-2008 neoliberalism's market-driven
logic appears less as an individual entitlement than a compassion-
less corporate contract that absolves debt-ridden governments from
civic obligation and public welfare. Nowadays, the neoliberal mantra
of choice and self-determination is still present but becomes inflected
with the experiences of precarity and risk and the insistence on self-
responsibilisation.[2] We seem to have entered what Giroux (2011)
calls a Darwinist 'survival-of-the-fittest' world, in which freedom and
equality have become unaffordable luxuries for the vast majority of
the population: 'Corruption, commodification, and repressive state
apparatuses have become the central features of a predatory society in
which it is presumed irrationally "that markets should dominate and
determine all choices and outcomes to the occlusion of any other con-
siderations"' (Giroux, 2013: 258).

In some ways, it could be argued that the bare-faced 'economic
Darwinism' we are currently witnessing and experiencing is rooted in
the very principles of 'classic' liberal economic and political theory of the
eighteenth century that saw the rise of the first commercial-consumer

society. As Foucault highlighted in his Biopolitics Lectures delivered in the mid-1970s, liberalism 'entails at its heart a productive/destructive relationship [with] freedom' – 'freedom in the regime of liberalism is not a given … [It] is something which is constantly produced. Liberalism is not acceptance of freedom; it proposes to manufacture it constantly, to arouse it and produce it, with, of course, [the system] of constraints and the problems of cost raised by this production' (2010: 64, 65). Stuart Hall raises a similar point by referring to the 'Janus-faces of Liberalism' and its practice of 'splitting', whereby it entails 'progress, but simultaneously the need to contain any "threat from below"', 'emancipation and subjugation' (2011: 715, 710). These antinomies re-emerge within neoliberalism, which, like its antecedent, harnesses political ideas of individual freedom and empowerment to the economic ideas of the free market (Hall, 2011). Yet crucially, under neoliberalism the laissez-faire attitude of classical liberalism – associated with thinkers such as Adam Smith and rooted in the unshakeable belief in the 'sacred rights of private property' and of free men to 'truck, barter and exchange one thing for another' (Smith, 2007 [1776]: 136, 15) – is replaced by an institutional framework and governmental logic designed to 'liberate' those same individual entrepreneurial freedoms (Harvey, 2005). As Gilbert notes, neoliberalism advocates a programme of 'deliberate intervention by government' to constitute self-regulating and self-actualising citizens by adopting a conception of the individual as both 'the ideal locus of sovereignty and the site of governmental intervention' (2013: 9, 11).[3]

In a postindustrial, post-recessionary capitalist context, liberalism's progressive and regressive characteristics are transformed and inflected further towards a market logic that sanctions an ethos of greed and expands a 'politics of disposability' to those who are regarded as 'failed consumers, workers, and critics' (Giroux, 2011: 592). In effect, in order to deal with the crisis in private speculation, the austerity agenda implemented by neoliberal governments mobilises specific ideas of self-sufficiency and self-responsibilisation that interpellate the individual as consumer while simultaneously undermining the very capacity of citizens to consume (Gilbert, 2013: 18). Neoliberal subjects are thus legitimised as self-governing consumer-citizens through discourses of choice and free will, with freedom itself being manufactured by their ability to compete in what Foucault calls the 'game of enterprises' (2010: 173). In this sense, the crash of neoliberal economics has led to a more 'intensified neoliberalism' that reduces collective egalitarian principles to the individual pursuit of opportunity and promotes consumer mentality as the only mode of agentic subjectivity (Gilbert, 2013: 19, 21). In the face of its own failure, neoliberalism is upheld and sustained – at times, through the invocation and marketisation of a nostalgic, wartime ideal of perseverance, of 'carrying on regardless' – with the result that, as Hall notes, 'exercising "consumer choice" is the next best thing to freedom itself' (2011: 722).[4] Here, freedom can no longer be defined as a civil right but instead is delimited by a market rationale and produced by individualistic consumer-agents who are responsible for their own success and failure. In a post-2008 world constrained by social and economic cut-backs and joblessness, this distorted notion of freedom further reinforces and validates acquisitive and competitive modes of citizenship that discard those who struggle to fulfil their consumer/civic duties, and accumulate (economic and human) capital, as redundant and ultimately dispensable.

Of course, capitalism has long been defined by its ability to consume in excess – in Marx's words, 'liv[ing] the more, the more labour it sucks' (quoted in Auerbach, 1995: 32). Marx in particular made use of the figure of the vampire as a ravenous and exploitative capitalist to describe capital as 'dead labor' that is 'vampire-like' and 'lives only by sucking living labor' (Auerbach, 1995: 32). Ken Gelder reminds us that 'Marx drew on the metaphor of the vampire time and time again to describe its processes', and repeatedly depicts 'capital as a vampire nourishing itself upon labour' (1994: 20). The vampiric relationship between capital and labour not only involves production but also creates consumer aspirations and wants without which capitalism could not prosper and thrive. As Robert Latham suggests, 'Marxists … have been forced to admit that the desire animating capitalism is more complex than mindless gluttony, that … [it] involves libidinal investment, an erotic complicity' (2002: 130). Here, the individual labourer is seen to be 'irreversibly penetrated by and infected with consumerist desire, an unquenchable, acquisitive lust', and thus becomes a 'willing accomplice' of the 'capitalism-vampire' that offers seductive promises (e.g. perpetual youth) and 'an ever-expanding realm of commodities' (130).[5] In the current climate of austerity, such lusty and complicit consumer behaviour and willingness to submit to the vampire-capitalist have understandably been dampened and replaced by a more resigned and uncommitted compliance, or in Gilbert's words a 'disaffected consent' that is conditional and grudging rather than enthusiastic.[6] This atmosphere of disaffectedness and disenchantment also allows for a reinvigoration and rebranding of the capitalist vampire, which now has to be seen to eschew selfish individualism – indicative of a debt-crazed, boom-and-bust economy and greedy bonus culture – in favour of what, in 2012, British Prime Minister David Cameron referred to as 'socially responsible and genuinely popular capitalism' that 'reconnect[s] the principles of risk, hard work, and success with reward' and where 'open markets and free enterprise can actually promote morality' (Cameron, 2012).

In this respect, Dracula specifically has been discussed and reimagined by a number of scholars as a figure who is entangled with and comprises capitalism. Classic Marxist interpretations depict the vampire count as 'an excessive form of capitalism' that 'must be exorcised' in order for '(British) capitalism to rehabilitate itself, to cohere as an "organic" process with a "human face" which used money responsibly and sensibly' (Moretti, 1988; Gelder, 1994: 19). Here, Dracula is represented as a selfish and despotic monopolist, remorselessly and greedily accumulating capital – not unlike the reckless 'banksters' of late who are publically condemned for adopting a regressive economic rationality that sacrifices 'the public good, public values, and social responsibility to a tawdry consumerist dream' (Curtis, 2013: 76; Giroux, 2013: 257). Often seen as setting the prototype of the modern vampire, Dracula participates in this consumer vision both intra- and extra-textually – spawning a multitude of rereadings and reimaginings – and thus comes to be seen as a 'highly productive piece of writing: or rather, it has become productive through its consumption' (Gelder, 1994: 65). As Gelder writes, '[t]o read this novel is to consume the object itself, Dracula, and, at the same time, to produce new knowledges, interpretations, different Draculas' (Gelder, 1994: 65).

In the next section, I focus on the 2013 addition to the Dracula franchise in order to re-examine the figure of the vampire capitalist in the context of the recent social and economic crisis – emblematic of the ambiguities of (neo)liberalism itself and its interweaving of contradictory strands (e.g. social conservatism and free-market economics) (Hall, 2011: 713). Here, the vampire still functions as a capitalist creature but it adapts and responds to the vicissitudes of capitalism in its current neoliberal guise, proving William Patrick Day's claim that vampires are exceedingly commodifiable figures that 'are highly reactive to the market, providing a sensitive barometer of the social reality in which they exist' (Day, 2002: viii). Dracula (2013) keeps pace with the cultural moment by addressing contemporary fears of insecurity and precarity – symptomatic of an overarching climate of terror and 'national authoritarianism' that thrives on a perception of constant lurking threats (Giroux, 2013: 264) – and the promise of a 'new start', a more affluent future in which democracy is no longer under threat.[7] The new, post-crash *Dracula* highlights (neo)liberalism's twin imperatives of emancipation and subjugation, with Dracula himself no longer reduced to the position of greedy capitalist sucking capital/labour/life but instead fighting to produce freedom and (geo-magnetic) power in order to destroy the tyranny of corporate monopoly. Under neoliberalism's tutelage, the vampire becomes a philanthropic, scientifically inclined and forward-thinking industrialist, the figurehead for a 'good', responsible capitalism freed from financial volatility, risk and speculation. In this latest ideological and cultural remodelling, the neoliberal vampire-entrepreneur walks a tightrope between complicity and critique, being firmly situated and operating within the matrix of capitalist power without replicating uncritically its relations of domination.[8] While this might not amount to a bottom-up counter-politics along the same lines of anti-capitalist protests that have been erupting in a number of recession-ridden countries in defence of economic justice and radical reform – for example in the UK most recently in the shape of the 'Million Mask March'[9] – Dracula's transformation from a 'creature of night and shadow' (season 1, episode 6) to a producer of 'light' and freedom allows us to think about how popular culture reflects and comments on the transitory and mutable nature of capitalism and how the vampire reaffirms itself as a cultural metaphor that simulates, infiltrates and (potentially) opposes Capital.

Vampire entrepreneurialism

Set in the same late Victorian era as Stoker's original novel, *Dracula* (2013) introduces the count not as an archetypal Other from a distant past defined by serfs and lords, by necromancy and superstition – in Auerbach's words, 'an alien invader from occult order of being' (1995: 23) – but as a thoroughly westernised entrepreneur as 'American as God, guns and Bourbon' (1.1). Posing as wealthy industrialist Alexander Grayson, complete with fake accent and brash disregard for English manners and class hierarchy, Dracula's threat lies less in his embodied danger of sexual contamination and hunger for domination than in his revolutionary designs to dismantle corporate capitalism and environmentalist interests in solving the world's energy problems and providing cheap electricity. While Stoker's aristocratic prototype represented an excessive and foreign form of monopoly capital and 'old money', this twenty-first-century New World 'colonial interloper' has embraced the ethos of the American Dream and the neoliberal ideal of freedom that includes the opportunity for prosperity and success, and an upward social mobility achieved through hard (self-)work (season 1, episode 1). As Dracula/Grayson tells the struggling journalist Jonathan Harker, 'a man should never be ashamed of ambition, only the lack of it' – with similar advice being given to his love interest, medical student Mina Murray, 'when it comes to dreams, one may falter but the only way to fail is to abandon them' (season 1, episode 2). Determined to lead Victorian society 'out of the darkness' and inaugurate an enlightened 'new era' no longer plagued by 'fear, hatred and brutality' (season 1, episode 1), this new enterprising Dracula regularly gets his hands dirty, doing metalwork and constructing a generator that will deliver wireless electricity and release humanity from its dependence on oil reserves that are controlled by the nefarious 'Order of the Dragon', an ancient cabal whose objectives appear to be both religious (e.g. the extermination of vampires) and economic (corporate control of oil resources).[10] This linkage of religious anxieties and crony capitalism is certainly legible within the context of the US-led 'War on Terror' against what George W. Bush famously called the 'axis of evil' in his 2002 State of the Union Address, particularly the coalition operation 'Iraqi Freedom' (2003–10), which saw Iraq's domestic oil industry largely privatised and dominated by foreign firms and mega-corporations.[11]

In this sense, the Order's age-old crusade against vampires – fuelled by a deep-seated and fundamental fear of the Other that has been employed historically in the service of, among others, colonial, nationalist, patriarchal and religious discourses (Pickering, 2001) – transmutes into a modern form of economic imperialism based on predatory corporatism and its mantra of doing just about anything to increase profits.[12] If Dracula can be positioned on the productive side of (neo) liberalism's relationship with freedom (Foucault, 2010), then the Order represents without doubt its destructive, subjugating tendencies – in Stuart Hall's words (neo)liberalism involves 'liberty now for some, an unending apprenticeship to freedom for others' (Hall, 2011: 710). *Dracula* (2013) reproduces (neo)liberal forms of governmentality and individualism that conceptualise the self as a rational, entrepreneurial actor determined by the capacity for autonomy and self-care, while seemingly severing links with capitalism's disreputable, immoral and irresponsible mutations that have rendered it 'unpopular', without of course ever disputing that the neoliberal subject's primary responsibility is to the market. Unlike Dracula's 'benevolent' capitalism, the Order of the Dragon epitomises a market-driven and class-based culture of greed, cruelty and ruthlessness that needs to be defeated and dismantled from the inside out by the vampire-entrepreneur:

> Their corruption and their hubris is unbridled ... Murder, torture, rape, wholesale slaughter. That is the stock in trade for the Order of the Dragon and it has been for over 500 years ... In the past they asserted their will more directly by the cross ... Now they do their dirty work via private clubs and boardrooms. They employ business, politics and oil and that last thing will be their undoing. They believe it will fuel the next century and if they control it, they control the future. But from the moment we demonstrate the viability of geomagnetic technology, no more money, no more power, no more Order of the Dragon. (1.1)

Dracula's Americanised and individualised industrialism is thus opposed to the corporate elitism and hereditary privilege of the upper-class order that actively seeks to propagate social and economic inequality through commercial monopoly.[13] Here, vampire capitalism becomes a means to decontaminate and oppose Capital in its predatory, elitist and corporate outgrowth – sucking its polluted life-blood and 'wiping out [its] source of power, [its] vast wealth' in order for ostensibly more democratic, socially responsible forms to emerge (1.1).

In some ways, one could argue that this 2013 reinterpretation of *Dracula* follows a by-now conventional narrative trajectory and well-trodden path of many twentieth- and twenty-first-century vampires that have become increasingly more sympathetic, humanised and secular. As Gelder suggests, '[t]he vampire is seen ... as more of a symptom than a cause. That is the vampire is to be redeemed – the problem lies, instead, with the upstanding heroes' (Gelder, 1994: 66). Similarly, Day proposes that the vampire has undergone a 'liberation' in the last third of the twentieth century, when it has been transformed from monster into an outsider figure with utopian aspirations – what Milly Williamson describes as 'a misfit with a good image' (Day, 2002: 33; Williamson, 2005: 186). Vampire narratives such as *The Vampire Tapestry* (1980) and popular vampire shows and films such as *Buffy the Vampire Slayer* (1997–2003) and *The Lost Boys* (1987) utilise the figure to interrogate societal norms and hierarchies and depict alternative gender, sexual, racial and family formations. In these texts, vampires lose many of their metaphysical and folkloric dimensions – whereby any evil acts can be attributed to individual personality rather than a cosmic battle between God and Satan – and become communal instead of solitary, a condition that permits them 'to love, to regret, to doubt, to question themselves, to experience interior conflicts and cross-impulses' (Zanger, 1997: 13–14). As Zanger summarises, 'the new vampire has become socialized and humanized, as well as secularized' – 'this new, demystified vampire might well be our next door neighbour as Dracula ... could never pretend to be' (1997: 22, 19).

Critics have been divided over how to read this more ordinary and earthly vampire, who can experience human emotions and mimic human relationships and has the capacity for self-examination and self-loathing. Zanger, for example, laments the vampire's move from 'magical to mundane' that demotes the figure from a 'metaphysical "other"', towards the metonymic vampire as social deviant ... eroding in the process of transformation many of the qualities that generated its original appeal' (1997: 17). Devoid of its mythic status, the vampire is deposed to mere outsider and loses 'that monolithic force possessed by Dracula, his unalterable volition' (22). In recent years, this process of humanisation and socialisation appears to have reached its apotheosis in the thoroughly domesticated and sanitised consumer-vampires of the *Twilight* franchise that have willingly relinquished the figure's key function and threat – its blood-sucking ability – in favour of a 'vegetarian' diet, sexual abstinence, married monogamy and conspicuous consumption. Other writers have focused less on the contamination of vampiric essence and instead redefined the vampire as a site of identification that allows us to comment on the human world. For instance, in the late 1980s, Margaret Carter suggested that 'late twentieth-century America finds itself in a mood to see the vampire's traditional outsider status very appealing' (1988: 23). For Auerbach as well, the lure of the vampire lies not in its embodiment of cosmic evil but in its 'intimacy and friendship' (1995: 14). The new vampire is seen to reflect a change in cultural values towards the outside/otherness and thus, as Williamson argues, it offers a 'way of inhabiting difference' and embracing the 'painful awareness of outsiderdom' (2005: 1–2).

In his 2013 incarnation, Dracula is painfully aware of his outsider status, both in terms of his vampire existence between darkness/light, life/death and his unique historical position on the cusp between the old and new world, between past and modernity. As he tells Jonathan Harker, who in this revisioning is transformed into a penniless but ambitious journalist desperate to climb the ranks of aristocracy: 'I understand this struggle [between the old and the new]. I myself am descended from a very old family but my mind is always fixed on the future. I surround myself with things that speak to both, the ancient and the new' (1.1).[14] In particular, Dracula puts his faith in scientific progress and medical discoveries in order to 'give nature a helping hand' and 'facilitate a great change', which involves not only collective liberation from economic extortion and literal enlightenment in the form of 'free, safe, wireless power' but also an individual attempt to lift the curse of vampirism and reclaim his humanity (1.1). Echoing Stoker's original tale, *Dracula* (2013) reinforces progress and rationality but, unlike its predecessor, which ended with 'the reinstatement of Victorian middle-class social and moral structure' (Hollinger, 1997: 206), these modern values are now embodied in the figure of the vampire who represents not just an 'eternal present', but a potentially more democratic, egalitarian but nonetheless capitalist future (Abbott, 2009: 5). Invoking Darwinian evolutionary theories, Dracula wants to 'redefine [his] species' and 'walk in the sun like any other man' (1.1 and 1.3). Disclosing his vampire identity to his loyal employee Renfield – himself a social outcast as a black lawyer in a racist capitalist world – Dracula is emphatic that he will be 'reborn a man once more': 'I live in the darkness but I yearn for the light, even though it burns, I want life' (1.7 and 1.10). This refusal of otherness is a common trait among many sympathetic vampire characters who want to regain their lost humanity in order to become viable subjects and accepted and respected citizens who have the right to marry (*True Blood*) and even have children (*Twilight*). As Williamson explains, at the core of the vampire is the 'desire to signify', 'to matter in the light of day and not just in the shadows' (2005: 2). In *Dracula* (2013), this desire for humanity is given further potency by the fact that vampirism has been thrust unwillingly upon the central character – who, it is revealed, was a medieval master huntsman who defied the Order of the Dragon (1.8) – as a punishment. In this reading, Dracula was not sired but created by the self-same hierarchical, capitalist structure whose downfall he wants to orchestrate, and thus, in some ways, he can be seen, if not as innocent, at least as a persecuted and tragic hero who is caught in circumstances outside his control.

Adopting neoliberalism's entrepreneurial ethos of self-responsibility, self-care and determination, Dracula resolves to become the master of his own fate and engage in what Anthony Giddens calls the reflexive 'project of the self', where the crafting of identity is not understood as static but comes to be seen as a biographical narrative that demands constantly to be worked on, updated and improved.[15] For Dracula, the construction of personal biography and self-identity necessitates a number of 'lifestyle choices' that inevitably conflict with his vampire persona, which is experienced as an involuntary and imposed production. This conscious self-work is a key requirement of neoliberal citizenship and involves the creation of an updated/upgraded self, capable of optimising his quality of life and functionality in the marketplace. As Sarah Banet-Weiser has suggested, here we need to make a distinction between the economic strategies of commodification – which transform social and cultural life into something that can be bought and sold (2012: 4–5) – and the cultural practices of self-branding that demand individual labour and create personal identity that is experienced as 'authentic': 'Principles of contemporary branding … authorize branding the self as authentic, because self-branding is seen not as an imposition of a concept or product by corporate culture but rather as the individual taking on the project [himself] as a way to access [his] "true" self' (2012: 61). For the post-recessionary Dracula, individual entrepreneurship becomes not only the conduit for self-realisation and self-(re)branding but also a means towards a supposedly more socially responsible capitalism.[16] In order to defeat the Order of the Dragon, Dracula finds an unlikely ally in his former nemesis Professor Van Helsing, whose medical and scientific genius helps the vampire to develop a method of wireless electrical transmission, as well as seek a cure for his vampiric blood-lust and intolerance to sunlight. Resolute that he will 'defy this blasted curse they placed on my head', he decides not to kill or feed but to 'live as a man or not at all' (1.7). Moreover, in an attempt to dissemble his vampire identity, Dracula severs his own kinship relations by killing his vampire-offspring – representative of the 'old vampire' who is animalistic, sexually aggressive and irrational – for his lack of (neoliberal) self-control and discretion (1.4). Tellingly, he also resolves to abide by established moral/romantic codes by not seducing Mina – archetypal 'New Woman' and aspiring physician – because 'to simply take [her] … would be an abomination' (1.2).

Notwithstanding these narrative innovations, *Dracula* (2013) also feeds into familiar vampire tropes and provides enough points of similarity that allow us to read this latest addition within the ever expanding corpus of Dracula texts. While his relationship with Mina might be characterised by uncommon reticence and self-restraint, his reputation as sexual predator remains assured by his frequent couplings with other female characters, in particular the highly sexualised vampire hunter Lady Jayne, who for the most part of the first season remains unaware that her American industrialist lover is also the demonic creature she is meant to hunt and kill. The raunchy and explicit sex scenes not only bolster audiences' voyeuristic viewing pleasures but also reassert the vampire as an exceedingly erotic, insatiable creature whose bite will transform his (female) victims into predatory but alluring vampires themselves. As David Punter and Glennis Byron note, nineteenth-century vampires such as Dracula in particular 'function[ed] to police the boundaries between "normal" and "deviant" sexuality' (2003: 269), ultimately reaffirming heteronormative monogamy through the exorcism and expulsion of the vampire's transgressive sexuality. In addition, the series' spectacle of sex – which includes gay/lesbian encounters among a number of characters, including Mina's friend Lucy – can be related more generally to a wider cultural shift that allows for a broadening of sexual narratives and more permissive attitudes to sex, resulting in what Brian McNair calls the expansion of the 'pornosphere' in which accelerating flows of sexual information have led to a 'less regulated, more commercialised, and more pluralistic sexual culture' (2002: 11).[17]

Ultimately however, any suggestions of sexual licentiousness are undercut by the series' final confirmation of hetero-conventions that see Dracula and Mina fulfilling their romantic potential and thus causing a rift with her former fiancé, Jonathan Harker, who enters into an alliance with both the Order of the Dragon and Van Helsing, intent on killing the count. In this sense, we are left in much the same position as with earlier *Dracula* offerings, most notably Coppola's 1992 film version, which transformed the myth into an epic romance with matching tagline ('Love Never Dies').[18] While the first season's finale might be more in keeping with romance than horror, *Dracula* (2013) does not follow the inherently patriarchal-conservative model of other vampire narratives such as *Twilight* that uphold traditional conceptions of family, sexuality, gender and belief. Significantly, Mina is not a virginal vampire bride like Meyer's chaste damsel Bella Swan, having previously given her virginity to her human lover Jonathan and later rejected him because he wanted her to 'dedicate herself to more natural womanly pursuits' (1.2). In this sense, Dracula's conquest of Mina is less vampiric seduction than a (neoliberal) act of choice and free will that allows both partners to pursue the individual lifestyles they have constructed for themselves. If *The Twilight Saga* presented patriarchal capitalism as benign – trans-coding heterosexual monogamy as a 'happily ever after'– then *Dracula* (2013) highlights the constraints, violence and horrors that lie at the heart of the social and economic hierarchies that it enforces. The solution provided here is clearly in favour of individual entrepreneurship and identity-making – representative of an updated, allegedly fairer, responsible and altogether more 'popular' capitalism where subjects are called upon to conceive of themselves as self-actual-ising actors and exercise their individual agency as a capitalist 'choice' within the marketplace – and thus thoroughly neoliberal. At the same time, Dracula's struggles against vampire capitalism are of course inher-ently contradictory and self-defeatist – as Renfield tells him, 'without Dracula, you can never defeat the Order of the Dragon' (1.8).[19] The neoliberal vampire thus faces the well-known contemporary conun-drum that, as Fredric Jameson succinctly put it, 'capitalism is at one and the same time the best thing that has ever happened to the human race, and the worst ... [T]he cultural evolution of late capitalism [is] catas-trophe and progress all together' (Jameson, 1993: 86). Under neoliber-alism, the vampire endures and evolves to reflect this interplay between freedom and coercion, emancipation and subjugation, which is at the heart of the liberal regime.

Notes

1 Of course, as Hall emphasises, neoliberalism is not 'a single system' and has many variants: it is 'not one thing. It combines with other models, modifying them. It bor-rows, evolves and diversifies. It is constantly "in process". We are talking here, then, about a long-term tendency and not about a teleological destination' (2011: 708).

2 As British Prime Minister David Cameron's 2009 speech at the Conservative Party conference makes explicit: 'We've got to stop treating children like adults and adults like children. It is about everyone taking responsibility. The more that we as a society do, the less we will need government to do' (Cameron, 2009). Cameron's solution is the much-touted concept of the 'Big Society', in which everyone 'steps up' to fill the gap in public spending that has resulted in the closure or privatisation of local amenities (libraries, sports facilities, youth clubs etc.). Drawing on another of Cameron's *bons mots*, 'Aspiration Nation' – which positions the individual's will to compete in neoliberal society as a moral imperative – Leftist commenta-tors have been highly critical of this conservative appropriation of the rhetoric of social democracy: ' "Big Society" is ... a sham idea and a shabby, cavalier, duplici-tous interference in freedom of thought. The over-arching theme is a shift of power and wealth back to the already rich and powerful. A demonization of the working class ... is well advanced ... In the "Big Society", it seems, equality has gone out of fashion' (Hall, 2011: 721).

3 According to Gilbert, '[t]his is the key difference between classical liberalism and neo-liberalism: the former presumes that, left to their own devices, humans will naturally tend to behave in the desired fashion. By contrast the latter assumes that they must be compelled to do so by a benign but frequently directive state' (Gilbert, 2013: 9).

4 Foucault's insights about liberalism as 'a consumer of freedom' are also instructive here: 'The new governmental reason needs freedom therefore, the new art of government consumes freedom. It consumes freedom, which means that it must produce it ... Liberalism formulates simply the following: I am going to produce what you need to be free. I am going to see to it that you are free to be free' (2010: 63).

5 This also highlights the branding power of gothic in general and the commodification of the vampire that transforms it from a dangerous and inherently subversive demonic force into a popular and saleable corporate concept that can easily be moulded by the 'new dominant logic of marketing' to appeal to almost any audience (Goulding and Saren, 2007: 227). In particular, in recent years, the vampire has been introduced to youth markets with two of the most successful vampire franchises being located within the 'teen genre' – *Buffy the Vampire Slayer* (1997–2003) and *The Twilight Saga* (2008–12) – both texts using the figure of the vampire to articulate many of the issues and fears faced in adolescence.

6 As Gilbert writes, 'We know that we don't like neoliberalism, didn't vote for it, and object in principle to its exigencies: but we recognise also that unless we comply with it, primarily in our workplaces and in our labour-market behaviour, then we will be punished (primarily by being denied the main consolation for participation in neoliberal culture: access to a wide range of consumer goods)' (Gilbert, 2013: 13).

7 Littler refers to this as the 'cruel optimism' of neoliberalism: 'the affective state produced under neoliberal culture ... is cruel because it encourages an optimistic attachment to the idea of a brighter future whilst such attachments are, simultaneously, "actively impeded" by the harsh precarities and instabilities of neoliberalism' (Littler, 2013: 62).

8 This lesson (i.e. that power is not something unitary that exists outside us) is of course inherently Foucauldian: as Foucault reminds us, there are no 'spaces of primal liberty' in society, as power is diffused throughout the social field and it 'is "always already there"', so that 'one is never "outside" it' and 'there are no margins for those who break with the system to gambol in' (Foucault, 1980: 141, 142).

9 On 5 November 2014, as part of the annual global Million Mask March organised by the Anonymous network, protesters marched towards Parliament Square in London, wearing facial coverings. The masks themselves have become a symbol of civil disobedience following the 2006 film *V for Vendetta*, which depicts a totalitarian vision of Britain, where protesters donned Guy Fawkes masks and gathered on 5 November to rally against their oppressors. See for example http://www.independent.co.uk/news/uk/home-news/million-masks-march-2014-thousands-gather-for-anticapitalist-protest-in-london-9842407.html.

10 The use of religion as a justification for eliminating the vampiric Other can also be read in a post-9/11 context that marshalled neocolonialist, neoliberal discourses of national selfhood in the West's 'War on Terror' and led to ritualised spectacles of violence, such as the systematic emasculation and sexual violation of predominantly Muslim detainees at prisons such as Abu Ghraib.

11 See for example http://edition.cnn.com/2013/03/19/opinion/iraq-war-oil-juhasz/.

12 Giroux also highlights the interconnection between religious and economic rationales within neoliberalism: 'In this discourse [of economic Darwinism], the economic order is either sanctioned by God or exists simply as an extension of nature. In other words, the tyranny and suffering that [are] produced through the neo-liberal theatre of cruelty [are] unquestionable, as unmovable as an urban skyscraper' (Giroux, 2011: 165).

13 For more on the growing inequality between rich and poor, see for example www.theguardian.com/society/2014/sep/15/how-super-rich-got-richer-10-shocking-facts-inequality.

14 Some critics use this reading of the boundary-breaking vampire to interpret the figure as transgressive and even queer. As Kathryn Kane argues, 'The vampire is a queer figure because it is disruptive; the vampire breaks down categories, transgresses boundaries, and upsets the very premises upon which systems of normality are structured' (2010: 103).

15 As Giddens explains, with the decline of traditions – what he designates 'the post-traditional order of modernity' – identities in general have become more diverse and malleable and, today more than ever, individuals can construct a narrative of the self. This is the reflexive 'project of the self' that takes place 'in the context of multiple choice' and allows individuals to negotiate a range of diverse lifestyle options in forming a self-identity (Giddens, 1991: 5). Here, self-identity is not a set of traits or characteristics but a person's own reflexive understanding of their biography. In this sense, the more society is modernised, the more subjects acquire the ability to reflect upon their social conditions and change them.

16 This echoes David Cameron's 2012 speech on 'moral capitalism' that insists that 'we should use this crisis of capitalism to improve markets, not undermine them' (Cameron, 2012).

17 As Feona Attwood summarises, today's sexualised culture is characterised by a 'preoccupation with sexual values, practices and identities; the public shift to more permissive sexual attitudes; the proliferation of sexual texts; the emergence of new forms of sexual experience; the apparent breakdown of rules, categories and regulations designed to keep the obscene at bay; our fondness for scandals, controversies and panics around sex' (Attwood, 2006: 78–9).

18 Vampire scholars in general have been critical of Coppola's big-budget blockbuster. According to Fred Botting: 'Dracula is less tyrannical and demonic and more victim and sufferer, less libertine and more sentimental romantic hero … In moving from horror to sentimentalism, Coppola's film … advocates a more humane approach to vampirism, one based on love, tolerance and understanding … With Coppola's Dracula, then, Gothic dies, divested of its excesses, of its transgressions, horrors and diabolical laughter, of its brilliant gloom and rich darkness, of its artificial and suggestive forms. Dying, of course, might just be the prelude to other spectral returns' (Botting, 1996: 178–80).

19 The outcome of this battle is likely to be played out in the second season of the series, which, after being cancelled by NBC in 2014 because of poor ratings, will be produced by Netflix, a provider of on-demand internet media.

References

Abbott, Stacey. 2009. *Celluloid Vampires: Life after Death in the Modern World*. Austin: University of Texas Press.

Attwood, Feona. 2006. 'Sexed up: Theorizing the sexualization of culture'. *Sexualities* 9(1): 77–94.

Auerbach, Nina. 1995. *Our Vampires, Ourselves*. Chicago: University of Chicago Press.

Banet-Weiser, Sarah. 2012. *Authentic TM: The Politics of Ambivalence in a Brand Culture*. New York: New York University Press.

Botting, Fred. 1996. *Gothic*. London and New York: Routledge.

Cameron, David. 2009. 'Putting Britain back on her feet'. www.politics.co.uk/features/opinion-former-index/legal-and-constitutional/cameron-speech-in-full-$1332736.htm.

Cameron, David. 2012. 'Moral capitalism'. www.newstatesman.com/uk-politics/2012/01/economy-capitalism-market.

Carter, Margaret. 1988. *Dracula: The Vampire and the Critics*. Ann Arbor: UMI Press.

Curtis, Neal. 2013. 'Thought bubble: Neoliberalism and the politics of knowledge'. *New Formations: A Journal of Culture, Theory and Politics* 80–1: 73–88.

Day, William Patrick. 2002. *Vampire Legends in Contemporary American Culture: What Becomes a Legend Most*. Lexington: University of Kentucky Press.

Foucault, Michel. 1980. *Power/Knowledge: Selected Interviews and Other Writings 1972–1977*. Brighton: The Harvester Press.

Foucault, Michel. 2010. *The Birth of Biopolitics: Lectures at the Collège de France*. Basingstoke: Palgrave.

Gelder, Ken. 1994. *Reading the Vampire*. London and New York: Routledge.

Genz, Stéphanie. 2006. 'Third Way/ve: The politics of postfeminism'. *Feminist Theory* 7(3): 333–53.

Giddens, Anthony. 1991. *Modernity and Self-Identity: Self and Society in the Late Modern Age*. Cambridge: Polity.

Gilbert, Jeremy. 2013. 'What kind of thing is "neoliberalism"?'. *New Formations: A Journal of Culture, Theory and Politics* 80–1: 7–22.

Giroux, Henry. 2011. 'The disappearing intellectual in the age of economic Darwinism'. *Policy Futures in Education* 9(2): 163–71.

Giroux, Henry. 2013. 'The disimagination machine and the pathologies of power'. *Symploke* 21(1–2): 257–69.

Giroux, Henry. 2014. 'Neoliberalism and the machine of disposability'. www.truth-out.org/opinion/item/22958-neoliberalism-and-the-machinery-of-disposability.

Goulding, C. and M. Saren. 2007. '"Gothic" entrepreneurs: A study of the subcultural commodification process'. In B. Cova, R. V. Kozinets and A. Shankar, eds, *Consumer Tribes*. Burlington, MA: Elsevier, 227–42.

Hall, Stuart. 2011. 'The neo-liberal revolution'. *Cultural Studies* 25(6): 705–28.

Harvey, David. 2005. *A Brief History of Neoliberalism*. Oxford: Oxford University Press.

Hollinger, Veronica. 1997. 'Fantasies of absence: The postmodern vampire'. In J. Gordon and V. Hollinger, eds, *Blood Read: The Vampire as Metaphor in Contemporary Culture*. Philadelphia: University of Pennsylvania Press, 199–212.

Jameson, Fredric. 1993. 'Postmodernism; or, The cultural logic of late capitalism'. In T. Docherty, ed., *Postmodernism: A Reader*. London and New York: Harvester Wheatsheaf, 62–92.

Kane, Kathryn. 2010. 'A very queer refusal: The chilling effect of the Cullens' heteronormative embrace'. In M. A. Click, J. Stevens Aubrey and E. Behm-Morawitz, eds, *Bitten by Twilight: Youth Culture, Media and the Vampire Franchise*. New York: Peter Lang, 103–18.

Latham, Robert. 2002. *Consuming Youth: Vampires, Cyborgs, and the Culture of Consumption*. Chicago: University of Chicago Press.

Littler, Jo. 2013. 'Meritocracy as plutocracy: The marketising of "equality" under neoliberalism'. *New Formations: A Journal of Culture, Theory and Politics* 80–1: 52–72.

McNair, Brian. 2002. *Striptease Culture: Sex, Media and the Democratisation of Desire*. Abingdon: Routledge.

Moretti, Franco. 1988. *Signs Taken for Wonders: Essays in the Sociology of Literary Form*. London: Verso.

Pickering, Michael. 2001. *Stereotyping: The Politics of Representation*. Basingstoke: Palgrave Macmillan.

Punter, David and Glennis Byron. 2004. *The Gothic*. Oxford: Blackwell.

Smith, Adam. 2007 [1776]. *An Inquiry into the Nature and Causes of the Wealth of Nations*. Ed. S. M. Soares. Amsterdam: Metalibri.

Williamson, Milly. 2005. *The Lure of the Vampire: Gender, Fiction and Fandom from Bram Stoker to Buffy*. London: Wallflower Press.

Zanger, Jules. 1997. 'Metaphor into metonymy: The vampire next door'. In J. Gordon and V. Hollinger, eds, *Blood Read: The Vampire as Metaphor in Contemporary Culture*. Philadelphia: University of Pennsylvania Press, 17–26.

3

Barry Murnane

Staging spectrality: capitalising (on) ghosts in German postdramatic theatre

European theatre has long been preoccupied with the spectralising and dehumanising effects of postmodern and neoliberal economics, commerce, and labour relations. This thematic focus can potentially be explained by the structural importance of performances and performativity they both share. In his landmark study of 1999 entitled *Postdramatisches Theater*, Hans-Thies Lehmann responded to a trend in contemporary theatre practice since the 1960s towards deconstructing the central parameters of classical dramatic theatre.[1] Widespread forms analysed by Lehmann include multimedial installations; performances that operate with a theatrical text that is no longer dramatic in any established sense, ranging from monologic or choric blocks of text to intertextual collages; and most notably situational performances, happenings, and scenic arrangements focusing on the ceremonial, bodily dimension of the theatrical performance itself.[2] Likewise, Richard Sennett has identified a performative dimension in neoliberalism's flexible working models; he sees a 'corrosion of character' as economic subjects are forced to make different 'roles' their own, thereby rendering 'individuality' and identity every more spectral (Sennett, 1998). Likewise, so-called 'phantom firms', the temporary performances of economic entities characterised by frequent and rapid changes of identity and location, are further key mechanisms in a neoliberal world order that uncannily resemble the staged performances of postdramatic theatre.

Drawing on the work of Robert Wilson, Tadeusz Kantor, Heiner Müller and Elfriede Jelinek, among others, Lehmann's study illustrates how in the final third of the twentieth century a form of theatre had developed that in varying degrees had abandoned the assumptions and structural cornerstones of traditional dramatic representation presented on a proscenium stage. In place of a coherent plot that develops the illusion of representing 'real' life on stage through the actions of rounded, psychologically credible figures and role-play, postdramatic theatre foregrounds the artificiality and contrived nature of the dramatic theatre. In its multimedial, ceremonial-performative and text-based variants, such formal experimentation creates a phantasmagorical theatre of disembodied voices that fluctuates among reality, dream and fantasy to produce the kind of 'hauntological' model of space and time that Jacques Derrida has identified at the heart of the spectre (Derrida, 1994: 10). Drawing on Heiner Müller's description of his work as a 'Totenbeschwörung' (séance) and a 'Dialog mit den Toten' (dialogue with the dead),[3] Lehmann identifies such spectralising intertextual practices as one key manifestation of postdramatic theatre's return to the ceremonial and ritualistic origins of theatre, turning the stage into a haunted space (Müller, 1990: 64; Lehmann,1999: 116–17 and 135–6). In one of its variants, postdramatic theatre is a 'ghost-theatre', in which the language becomes depersonalised, the figures on stage are controlled by the citational architecture that gives rise to them in the first instance, and ultimately they appear to be ghostly revenants (Lehmann, 2002: 284–5). The importance of postdramatic theatre's spectral figurations derives initially from, but ultimately exceeds, the theoretical reflexion on theatrical practices and their formal results that give rise to the form in the first instance. Postdramatic spectres and undead figurations are more than simply self-reflexive metaphors for complex formal experiments and citational practices; their real importance derives from their links to extra-theatrical discourses such as neoliberal economics, labour relations and migration.

I wish to argue in the following chapter that in their self-conscious construction of, and thematic reflection on, the spectacular and 'culinary' or narcotic illusions of the theatre (to use a Brechtian phrase), postdramatic models of theatre are able both to mimic *and* to break critically with the spectralising and performative tendencies of late capitalism and neoliberalism as these began to manifest themselves most clearly from the early 1990s (Brecht, 2005: 102). Neoliberalism and its financial models are responsible not only for an increasing de-realisation of the financial sphere – social life itself becomes equally spectralised in this regime, as the phantom firms and vampire-like 'corrosion of character', identified by Sennett above, underline. Thus, postdramatic theatre attempts to stage the abstract, numinous financial structures of neoliberalism, capitalising on its ghosts in order to ground its own phantasmagorical formal experimentation. In the case of the works under discussion, this experimentation enacts a spatialised representation of neoliberalism's phantasmagorical effects in order to conduct an economic critique, although this latter point is not necessarily transferable to other more self-reflexive examples of the postdramatic mode. Importantly, this experimentation is engaged not simply in re-presenting the spectral patterns of finance, but rather also in opening these spectres up for critical reappraisal. Some of the most convincing examples of postdramatic theatre simultaneously deconstruct both dramatic models of representation and the performative and spectralising culture of neoliberalism discussed here. Beginning with a discussion of the structural similarities and links between neoliberal financial models and postdramatic theatre, the following chapter will analyse an early German response to the rise of neoliberal ideology and economics following the fall of the Berlin Wall in 1989. Heiner Müller's *Germania 3.Gespenster am Toten Mann* (*Germania 3: Ghosts on the Dead Man*) (Müller, 2002 [1995]) documents the expansion eastwards of western ideology from the perspective of a playwright from the former German Democratic Republic (GDR) and develops an image of western consumerism and finance as a motor for new forms of haunting. I will finish by analysing Dea Loher's later *Manhattan Medea* (1999) as an example of gothic postdramatic theatre that employs spectral figures in order to reproduce and critique the spectral financial models at the heart of an established global, neoliberal world order.

The spectral dramaturgy of neoliberalism

In the progress of western models of neoliberal finance and economics towards global dominance, critics and economists have identified 1989 as something of a milestone. The opening up of so-called emerging markets across Europe offered the basis for an economic growth and corporate expansion that seemed almost unlimited (Birringer, 2003: 27–9, 31–2). Fuelled by new communication technologies and an unprecedented acceleration in the transfer of data, the euphoria of apparently limitless growth in ever 'newer' markets seemed to render the liberalisation of the financial markets beyond all criticism (Stadler, 2011: 229–30). In addition, deregulated financial systems offered investors a new means of generating capital, providing businesses with expansion capital and precipitating growth. Under such conditions the cornerstones of neoliberal ideology such as market fundamentalism, the belief in the positive powers of competition, free trade and the deregulation of financial affairs seemed sacrosanct as neoliberal economic models provided a swift response to the needs of the socio-economic collapse of the eastern bloc while itself thriving on what appeared to be an endlessly growing demand and supply.

At the core of neoliberalism's visions of everlasting growth in a deregulated, competition-driven market is a progressively 'fictional' financial sphere (Stäheli, 2013: 6–75). Descriptions of stock market speculation and financial trade as speculative fictions have accompanied economic discourses since at least the mid-nineteenth century: the idea that 'present futures (i.e. speculative predictions) influenced the future of the market' (Stäheli, 2013: 66) by becoming important elements of actual trading practices led to broad scepticism about a moment of immateriality and derealisation: 'the economy transformed from a space of material exchange into an absolutely immaterial place' (Stäheli, 2013: 68). In contemporary trading in deregulated synthetic or structured financial products, such as asset-backed securities, futures trading, hedging and sub-prime papers – some of the key tools in generating the new sources of capital underpinning economic growth, and a cornerstone of neoliberal financial models – this immateriality of the market has become increasingly spectral (Polt-Heinzl and Vogl, 2011: 319).[4] Now products are traded, which are always already abstract mathematical projections rather than biophysical objects, which have become little more than a virtual digital numbers game.[5] According to prominent accounts, these financial models are responsible for an increasing derealisation of the financial sphere and social life alike bordering on the gothic in their own right. Sociology and financial analysis base their descriptions of these phenomena in the vocabulary of the gothic. In this regard Colin Crouch has looked critically at some of the vehicles for this trade: so-called 'phantom firms'. These are entities that are characterised by frequent and rapid changes in identity and relocation through mergers, takeovers, name changes, sub-contracting, outsourcing and problematic taxation jurisdiction, and are key mechanisms in maximising shareholder value. In the constant process of self-invention and reinvention demanded by such flexible business models, stable corporate identities seem to become increasingly immaterial, little more than vehicles for generating profit (Crouch, 2004: 37–8). It is not only the companies that take on an invisible, ghostly status; traders also become increasingly mobile, intangible (Lilge, 2012: 109–11). In neoliberalism the classical opposition between work and capital seems somehow decentred, as outsourcing, and what Richard Sennett has described as the 'corrosion of character' through a heightened demand for flexibility of the workforce, have led to increasingly precarious social and industrial relations (Sennett, 1998: 11). In some cases, employment conditions can even become spectral: Sennett describes how the abstract accounting systems and programmes at the heart of the New Economy and the financial boom of the early 2000s have led to a level of automatism in business and finance that renders actual employees ever more defunct, unleashing what he has termed 'the specter of uselessness' (Sennett, 2006: 92–9). Finally, in an age in which governments are themselves increasingly outsourcing key services, even those social systems of checks and balances that are still active begin to develop an intangible, phantom status of their own (Crouch, 2004: 41). When the economy has become abstract in this way, Marx's vampiric and spectral capitalism – where the accumulated labour of the dead sucks, 'vampire-like', the life out of the worker and where commodity fetishism sees objects and financial processes attain a 'phantom-like objectivity' ('gespenstische Gegenständlichkeit') and apparent automatic logic of their own (Marx, 1976: 340, 128) – seems only to have become even more spectral.

These neoliberal practices not only raise questions as to the spectrality of everyday socio-economic and financial matters – that is to say their status in terms of intangibility, immateriality and genuineness – they are furthermore indicative of homologies, points of intersection or functional similarities, between postdramatic theatre and economic or financial activity. Insofar as the neoliberal order demands working relations that are constantly flexible and in which short-term contracts dependent on 'productivity' are the norm, it furthermore produces an almost theatrical lifestyle in which employees are required constantly to redefine themselves, their skills and ultimately their tasks as a form of role-playing (Bröckling, 2007: 247–9). The organisation of employment as 'projects' seems in many ways to be the apotheosis of what Guy Debord once described as the modern 'society of the spectacle',[6] albeit in a different context: role-play, show, intrigue and performativity have given rise to a new quality of immateriality of social life (Debord, 1983). It is almost as if the free-floating signs and phantom agents of neoliberalism's financial markets have become the actors in a phantasmagorical theatre of their own, a spectral dramaturgy played out on an increasingly deregulated, spectral stage. If everyday life becomes theatrical, then how does the theatre – or more specifically postdramatic theatre – react to this? In postdramatic theatre's critical relationship to the creation of an illusion of reality on stage, in its self-reflexive insistence on the theatrical situation and the constructed nature of the performance as opposed to both the unconscious performativity of everyday life and financial activity, a neuralgic point in this homology becomes important. Postdramatic theatre develops from, and indeed explicitly addresses, the illusory character of conventional drama-based theatre; in its self-conscious construction of, and thematic reflection on, the spectacular and narcotic illusions of the theatre, postdramatic theatre's models are able to both mimic *and* critically break with the spectralising and performative tendencies of late capitalism and neoliberalism; in its reproduction of these patterns in its own phantasmagorical spaces and performances these tendencies are made available for reflection and critique. This can be registered in various ways.[7] Some of the most convincing attempts simultaneously to deconstruct both dramatic models of representation and the performative culture of neoliberalism have come from René Pollesch. In his *Heidi-Hoh* Trilogy (1999–2001) and *Prater* Trilogy (2001–2), for example, Pollesch plays out the insecurities of performing roles in which the 'personal' and 'private' have become subject to economic negotiations and regulations.[8] Another response has been to integrate actual documentary material –management and training methods, typical actions, linguistic jargon etc. – into the textual body or the performative scenarios, as for example in Urs Widmer's *Top Dogs* (1996), Moritz Rinke's *Republik Vineta* (*Republic of Vineta*, 2000) or Kathrin Röggla's *draußen tobt die dunkelziffer* (*Outside Rage the Undetected Cases*, 2005). Others, such as the collective Rimini Protokoll, have engaged actual financial 'experts' – bankers, investors, academics – to perform in plays, thereby rupturing any neat sense of division between the worlds of the theatre and finance (such as *Karl Marx: Das Kapital, Erster Band* (*Karl Marx: 'Capital', Volume I*), 2006).[9] Other groups have staged the performances outside the theatre in offices, banks, public spaces etc., such as the performance of Roland Schimmelpfennig's *Push Up 1–3* by Lokstoff in the Bülow office tower in Stuttgart (2005/6).

In the more extreme forms of postdramatic theatre, in which depersonalised forms of speech replace clearly identifiable characters or psychologically credible personal identities – through either textual montages or other intertextual, citational practices tending towards choric and haunted forms of speech – a form of theatrical representation has developed in which the abstract and immaterial-spectral nature of the capital markets, hedge funds and other financial mechanisms can be addressed directly themselves. This is most notably the case in Elfriede Jelinek's 'financial comedy' about a scandalous investment scam surrounding the Meinl Bank in Austria, *Die Kontrakte des Kaufmanns* (*The Merchant's Contracts*, 2009), which engages with the phantasmagorical intangibility and performative nature of financial transactions through textual montages. Jelinek's focus is on the autopoeitic trading of abstract financial 'products', which she repeatedly presents as empty, arbitrary phrases and linguistic orders, piling intertext upon intertext, word-play upon word-play, jargon upon jargon to create an intense circulation of words and signs that mimics the abstract and immaterial nature of derivative financial markets.[10] In her case postdramatic theatre responds to the increasing spectralisation of financial and socio-economic discourses with its own spectral formations.

Heiner Müller and the ghosts of 1989

In the various accounts of the rise to dominance of postdramatic practices in German-language theatre, Heiner Müller has long been a central example. One of the best-known intellectuals in the GDR and arguably the most important German playwright since Brecht, Müller's collaborations with directors such as Benno Besson and Robert Wilson established his reputation at the forefront of experimental theatre in the West as well. *Germania 3: Gespenster am Toten Mann* (1995) is the only play Müller wrote after the fall of the Berlin Wall (Müller, 2002: 253–96).[11] A montage of nine scenes stretching from the First World War until the early 1990s, *Germania 3* moves more or less chronologically from Stalin, through the battlefield at Stalingrad, Hitler's bunker, the last days of the Second World War, 1950s GDR, to the early years of German unification, although this chronology is programmatically disturbed from the beginning by the anachronistic appearances of Ernst Thälmann (who was executed by the Nazis in 1944) and Walter Ulbricht patrolling the Berlin Wall (W5: 255) (Haas, 2004: 125). Like his other works, *Germania 3* is intensely intertextual – confronting quotes and intertexts from different historical periods and locations to deconstruct the psychological depth of the figures on stage, or revealing the words spoken as citations or variations of other texts and hence depersonalized – turning the stage into a haunted space (Lehmann, 2002: 284–5). Earlier texts such as *Die Hamletmaschine* (*The Hamlet-Machine*, 1977) and *MEDEAMATERIAL* (1982) also consist of mono-logic speech blocks and are devoid of rounded dramatic characters that speak them (Lehmann, 2000: 12–13); indeed, *Hamletmaschine* begins by highlighting the fact that the speaker is actually dead, the performance taking on the form of a séance after Hamlet has died: 'Ich war Hamlet. Ich stand an der Küste und redete mit der Brandung BLABLA' (I was Hamlet. I stood at the shore and talked with the surf BLABLABLA) (Müller, 2001a: 545). As this ghostly voice suggests, this destruction of dramatic form is related to Müller's credentials as a gothic writer. His plays and performances generate a surreal mix of strange voices, cita-tions and ghostly apparitions of which gothic figures, like violent can-nibals, murderers, vampires, doubles and ghosts are the outward sign (see Murnane, 2011). Although clearly dominated by the focus of a 'dialogue with the dead' (Müller, 1990: 64) as a means of engaging with Germany's violent and traumatic history in the modern era, depicting spectral traces of violence emerging from the historical fault lines of the past, Müller's final play also documents the arrival of the free-market economy in the former socialist bloc countries. It is this dimension that I wish to analyse more closely now as an early observation of neoliberal ideology in German theatre, at once reproducing its phantasmagorical dimensions in Müller's anti-dramatical modes of presentation, thereby opening them up to critical reappraisal by the audience.

Germania 3 importantly suggests a new generation of ghosts in the post-1989 spread of neoliberal economics in the former GDR. This is encapsulated in the fifth scene, 'Der Gastarbeiter' ('The guest-worker'). Set in a haunted castle at the end of the war (W5: 271), the widows of three executed German officers ask a Croatian SS-soldier to kill them in order to avoid the oncoming Russians. While all four go into the house a stage direction states: 'Wenn es wieder hell wird, sitzen am Küchentisch die drei toten Männer der Witwen' (When the stage is lit again, the three widows' dead husbands are sitting at the table) (W5: 273). These ghosts are later joined by those of the widows (W5: 274) before a final break in the scene shows 'Zwei junge Männer' in 'Mode 1990' (two young men in 1990s fashion) who have inherited the 'Geisterschloss bei Parchim' (haunted castle near Parchim). In this one scene alone, Müller creates a haunting tableau of German history in all its violent incarnations, a postdramatic Grand Guignol of brutal and haunting proportions.

'The guest-worker' shows a subtle change of focus in Müller's post-dramatic spectres. In the middle of the scene, the chronology is disrupted by a passage in which the Croatian soldier has created a new identity for himself and relocated to post-1945 West Germany as one of the many 'guest-workers' recruited from Southern and Eastern Europe to help drive the Federal Republic's industry. In the postwar era, as a guest-worker in suit, shirt and tie driving his German car, the former SS-officer is an uncanny remnant of Germany's violent fascist past at the heart of the capitalist economic revival of the 1950s and 1960s, a familiar socialist criticism of western capitalism as a continuation of fascism by different means. The Croatian's story then proceeds to include another instance of migration. He returns to his homeland from his encounter amongst the capitalist spectres of German fascism to kill his wife and children before returning to the West in an effort to destroy all remnants of his peasant identity. As such the play begins to explore an uncanny blind spot in the post-1989 expansion of western ideology in Central and Eastern Europe as developed by Slavoj Žižek in *Tarrying with the Negative* (Žižek, 1993): the kind of chauvinism and violence that would later explode into ethnic violence in the Balkans in the 1990s.

Žižek sees the transnational processes of economic deregulation, restructuring of cultural politics, liberalisation of the media and commercialization following the collapse of the Iron Curtain with scepticism, highlighting an uncanny and troubling nature at the core of this expansion of western social order into the first so-called 'emerging' markets of Central and Eastern Europe in the 1990s (Žižek, 1993: 208). Unlike in Western Europe, where liberalised markets had grown over several decades, the rapid transition to the free market in Central and Eastern Europe left many confused, threatened and disenfranchised; political participation and liberty proved equally limited both under a new regime of economic interests and with competing local and supraregional redefinitions of cultural identity. The stream of political and economic migrants to safer and more prosperous economies is an uncomfortable by-product of the monetary flows of profit out of these markets and one of the 'blind spots of liberalism', a 'red-neck horror' of the West (Žižek, 1993: 211–12). Rather than distinguishing between seemingly contradictory moments of ethnic violence and liberalism in the Balkans, Žižek considers nationalisms and the streams of political refugees escaping the violence of civil war to be the uncanny mirror images of capitalism's universalist and liberalist logic of a global financial order and its concomitant culture: 'The emergence of ethnic causes breaks the narcissistic spell of the West's complacent recognition of its own values in the East: Eastern Europe is returning to the West the "repressed" truth of its democratic desire' (Žižek, 1993: 208). Writing during the height of the Balkans conflict, Müller deploys the Croatian migrant worker as an uncomfortable prefiguration of these uncanny processes and movements from West to East.

The scene does not stop there, however, as it transitions to another form of migration, this time with three well-dressed West German property developers arriving on the scene. The West Germans inflict a new form of inequality and violence on the landscape and its inhabitants, Müller suggests: if the widows were 'Blutadel' (blood nobility) lording it over the 'peasants', the 'Fortschritt' progress) of unification is merely a transformation of structural inequality and hegemony to a 'Geldadel' (nobility of money) (W5: 276). It is telling that the young West Germans hope to derive a profit from the castle and its ghosts of a violent German past: 'Was zählt ist der Bodenpreis. Wir könnten zum Beispiel einen Golfplatz anlegen hier oder einen Reiterhof ... für die neue Aristokratie aus Hamburg' (What counts is the price per square mile. We could create a golf course here, for instance, or start a riding school ... for the new aristocracy from Hamburg'). 'Wenn wir Glück haben, spuken sie noch' (If we're lucky the ghosts will still be active) (W5: 276). 'The guest-worker' thus initially develops a critique of western industrialisation and liberal economics prior to 1989 as itself haunted by the ghosts of violence, inequality and fascism, before presenting the process of German unification as an act of economic colonisation of the former GDR by precisely these same suspect haunted forces (Haas, 2004: 124). This is a sobering contrast to the more popular images of the celebrations that marked the fall of the Berlin Wall in 1989, a rejection of Helmut Kohl's promise to create a blooming landscape in the former GDR. From reproducing an emergent neoliberalist ideology, Müller's *Germania 3* has moved on to open up its workings to scrutiny.

The connection between the gothic and capital is not necessarily new in Müller's works – indeed, the global spread of western neoliberal ideology was already prefigured in his apocalyptic scenario of 1982, *Medeamaterial*, as a 'Parade / Der Zombies perforiert von Werbespots / In den Uniformen der Mode von gestern vormittag' (parade / Of zombies perforated by advertising / The uniforms of fashion from yesterday morning) (Müller, 2001b: 81). Müller, as a careful reader of Marx, is well versed in the phantasmagorical qualities of the commodity and consumerism in his analysis of capital, and indeed the undead and spectral figures in his works clearly recycle this analysis as a key argument. In interviews Müller speaks of people who define themselves primarily by abstract economic functions such as work, consumer goods etc. as being undead: 'koffertragende Zombies mit ihren leeren Gesichtern' (zombies with empty visages carrying suitcases) (Müller, 1990: 121). The deployment of the postdramatic form and its spectres in the 1990s now extends to a critique of capitalist ideology in general terms, however: the arrival of free-market economics in Eastern Germany is a source of haunting in and of itself. *Germania 3* is thus an early illustration of what Glennis Byron has observed in relation to the processes of expansion and ultimately globalisation of neoliberal ideology. In *Germania 3*, as in current discourses of globalisation, neoliberalism is 'facilitating the cultural exchanges that [are] producing new forms of gothic', and its discourses 'repeatedly turn to gothic tropes in articulating the social, cultural and economic impacts of a new world order' (Byron, 2013: 2–3).

Writing in 1995, Müller provides a first, tentative image of the transition to a late-capitalist economic order that generates a currency of gothic productivity. The ability of the two young men to derive a profit from the ghosts of the past in *Germania 3* is suggestive of a new intensity in this zombified economic logic. In this vision of post-socialist Eastern Europe, spectres are no longer merely the uncanny by-product of capitalism; the neoliberal world order imposing itself on the East now seems capable of turning the undead – and indeed the undead guilt and debts of the past – into a commodity with which further profit can be generated. This is a form of capitalism that is no longer threatened by the spectralising tendencies inherent to its patterns of production, marketing and consumerism, but that seems rather to exist quite comfortably with such figures – neoliberalism itself appears as a gothic manifestation. In Fredric Jameson's compelling account of finance capitalism, even crises and failing practices can be exploited for profit (as hedging and betting on defaulting nations demonstrate) and the 'free-floating', dematerialised nature of financial transactions generates 'a kind of cyberspace in which money capital has reached its ultimate dematerialization' and the spectralising tendencies of capital seem curiously normalised (Jameson, 2000: 259, 268). Similarly, Müller's vision is one of a post-socialist world order in which the gothic is no longer by necessity a transgressive formation. The uncanny, the haunting, the spectral and the undead seem to Müller to have become constitutive components of late capitalism, with which the gothic can rather comfortably survive.

Fred Botting has long since been interested in the question of whether the gothic has finished, highlighting 'the greater sympathy and stronger identification ... for figures once condemned as incarnations of evil' as gothic mutates into a sentimental mode (Botting, 2001: 3). If, as Jameson and others have remarked, neoliberalism itself not only seems entirely comfortable with spectrality and is a gothic formation in its own right, but in fact often trades willingly in spectres, then it is of interest that gothic seems to have become an infinitely marketable and consumable product within the transnational and corporate driven patterns and networks of consumption in globalised capitalism itself: 'another Coke, another McDonald's, another Nike ... with swoosh of bats encircling the globe, "GGI" – Global Goth Inc. – insinuates itself into every discourse' and replicates 'transnational flows of capital and commodities', as Botting recently playfully suggested (Botting, 2013: 189). Perhaps the academic acceptability and indeed success of familiar narratives of the gothic as a transgressive, subversive symbolic representation of modernity and its shadows are themselves a sign of this integration? Either way, in 'the dark and shadowy contours of a new world order that is mediated, networked, militarised and corporatised but offers no clear-cut image of itself, flickering between dissolutions and displacements', augmenting 'liminal and uncanny zones, making ephemeral spaces pervasive and generalised', the once disturbing articulations of liminal zones and figurations that enabled the gothic to dislocate and unsettle the binary ordering devices of modernity – the locked-room mysteries, subterranean passages, monsters, vampires and ghosts – are now the accepted structures of neoliberalism's 'mobile assemblages, complex clusters and nodal singularities' (Botting and Edwards, 2013: 18). Transgression and subversion mutate into marketable commodities in this world order: Müller's 'parades of zombies perforated by advertising' have relinquished life and its dignities to vampiric corporate powers, and haunted houses become marketable teasers and products for trading.

Of course this raises the question of how Müller, Žižek and, as I will suggest in the next section, Dea Loher offer a critical engagement with these increasingly dislocated forces. Žižek here provides a key in so far as his reading of Eastern Europe as sites of uncanny moments of shock, violence and suffering disrupts the strangely sanitised posthuman, dematerialised, 'free floating' cyberspace of Jameson's 'disembodied phantasmagoria' of global capital (Jameson, 2000: 273). As powerful as neoliberalism's self-representation as virtualised, placeless flows of ghostly signs and spectral values is, Žižek and Müller remind us that technology, production, trade, consumption and economics have real consequences for real bodies and real places. In this regard, it is of interest that Müller deploys the zombie as his figuration of consumption and capital, recalling the uneasy and underacknowledged opposition between the clean-cut, cosmopolitan smoothness of the vampire or posthuman cyborg as the epitome of the performative creative classes of Sennett's new world order and the brutally corporeal, lumbering and basic neediness embodied in the zombie in Rob Latham's otherwise persuasive account (Latham, 2002: 94–5, 249–50). Zombies, like the living dead in Müller's postdramatic performance of neoliberalism in Eastern Germany, represent the bodily suffering of the sweatshop workers making the products of global consumer culture; they represent the economic and political refugees, victims of terrorism, urban jobless and homeless all suffering under and attempting to free themselves from oppression and starvation. And here it is postdramatic theatre's performative dimension that is important: as a self-reflexive, conscious moment of bodily performance, postdramatic theatre places precisely such suffering, real bodies on stage while also reproducing the phantasmagorical moments of transnational, neoliberal capital; postdramatic theatre's insistence on bodily presence and on spatialised representations of the New Economy's phantasmagorical formations reintroduces that which neoliberalism's curiously sanitised version of gothic ignores: real moments of violence and suffering. This uneasy balance is at the centre of Dea Loher's *Manhattan Medea*.

Dea Loher and deals with the dead

The socio-economic transitions and frictions observed in *Germania 3* are also the background to Dea Loher's play *Manhattan Medea* (Loher, 1999),[12] first performed in 1999 and almost a summation of the expansion of globalised neoliberalism in the course of the 1990s, the beginnings of which her teacher Heiner Müller had also begun to address.[13] As its name suggests, Loher's play engages most obviously with questions of gender, alterity and patriarchal myths of rationalisation at the core of the Medea myth (Stephan, 2006), but it does so by anchoring these in contemporary questions of financial and political economy.

Despite this point of classical reference, it will become clear that an analysis of the play in gothic terms is possible because its formal features reproduce many of the self-reflexive, spectralising tendencies of postdramatic theatre sketched out above, not least in the manner in which the economic logic governing the relationship between Medea and Jason is in fact represented and determined by the haunting presences of Jason's and Medea's dead mother and brother respectively. *Manhattan Medea* thus provides an excellent example of the structural homologies between postdramatic forms of theatrical representation and neoliberal economic patterns, but in encapsulating the phantasmagorical moments of the New Economy in the kind of inherent violence identified by Walter Benjamin as lying at the core of capitalism's contracts and transactions, Loher's theatrical text opens these homologies up to view and hence to critique.

Manhattan Medea is less radically experimental than Müller's play and reinstates some of the diegetic, plot-based forms of representation rejected by his postdramatic theatre. Consisting of ten chronologically arranged 'scenes', or tableaux, of varying length and formal arrangement – ranging from dialogues to monologues, from a song to a fantastic intermedium in which a Valázquez painting is burned and mutates into Picasso's *Las Meninas* – Loher's play also distances itself from established forms of dramatic representation (Schößler, 2004: 19–20, 252–8). Medea's story is not told as part of a developmental plot; rather it is revealed through monologic and dialogic flashbacks and reports in the second (MM: 18–24) and the eighth (MM: 56–58) tableaux, and in a modernised setting (Macedonia rather than Colchis, immigrants in New York). This develops a similar chronotopic disruption to that which could be observed in *Germania 3*, as becomes visible in Medea's monologue in the eighth scene:

> Jason Sie ißt für zwei Mein Bruder Feines Paar Das sagt ihr jetzt Jason Nicht dein Geschäft Mein Bruder Wir sind zu dritt auf dieses Schiff gegangen Wir werden dieses Schiff verlassen zu dritt Ich sage Schwein Mein Bruder Wir haben nicht das Geld für vier Ich Ich habe es Mein Bruder Das reicht nicht für ein viertes Es reicht kaum für uns Du wirst es töten Ich sage Nein Mein Bruder Du wirst es müssen Hexe Ich sage Und wenn ich wüßte wie ich würde es nicht tun Mein Fleisch Mein Bruder Dann tu ich es Jason sagt Nein Mein Fleisch wird dieses neue Land sehen Unsere Zukunft ... Jason fällt den Mann von hinten an und faßt seine Arme Meine Hand sticht zu. (MM: 57)

> [Jason She's eating for two My Brother You're a fine pair You only say that now Jason Not your business My Brother Three of us went on-board this ship Three

of us will leave this ship I say pig My Brother We haven't enough money for four
I say I have it My Brother That's not enough for a fourth person It's only barely
enough for us You will have to kill it I say no My Brother You will have to you
witch I say and if I knew how I wouldn't do it My own flesh My Brother Then I'll
do it Jason says No My flesh will see this new land Our future ... Jason attacks
the man from behind and grabs his arms My hand stabs him.]

I will return to this scene in more detail below; here it is important to
note that Medea's dead brother gains a haunting presence through the
construction as a séance-like performance: as Medea's past is made present through her speech, the dead figure of his brother is brought back
to speak through her. In addition to such citational practices, rather
than being 'rounded' characters Medea and Jason seem aware that they
are intertextual revenants in a long tradition themselves. Talking to
Jason, Medea says 'Es heißt Jason und Medea seit wieviel Jahren' (It's
been Jason and Medea for so many years) (MM: 19). Medea, Jason
and the others appear to be the product of postmodern and postdramatic practices of citation and pastiche rather than realistic characters
with psychological depth; Medea's actions seem to be dictated as much
by the intertextual tradition depicting her as the murdering, spurned
lover; she herself seems to be aware of having an undead intertextual
status. Indeed, this formal instance of spectrality is a thematic concern
at the start of the play, where the doorman Velazquez describes Medea
as a spectre: 'Als ich die Augen aufschlug in der Morgendämmerung,
glaubte ich an ein Phantom. Ihr Umriß an derselben Stelle. Ist das
Fleisch und Blut' (When I opened my eyes in the twilight I believed it
was a phantom. Her outline in the same spot. Is that flesh and blood)
(MM: 9).

Manhattan Medea anchors Medea's story in a contemporary social
order that is dominated by an economic logic. Jason and Medea's relationship is based on the premise of managing a scarcity of resources: 'Die
Umstände ... Die Not' (The circumstances ... The poverty) brought
them together, not love (MM: 19). Impoverished in New York, they
turn the only property they have into capital: their bodies. Loher develops her version of Medea as the nadir of neoliberal privatisation where
the body is a medium and object of financial activity and Jason even
calls Medea's pregnancy a business transaction, 'ein Geschäft' (a transaction) (MM: 57). Jason concludes, 'Ja, ich würde dich immer wieder
betrügen, / mit jeder vielversprechenden Frau, / so lange, bis es sich
auszahlt. / Dieses Leben' (Yes, I would always cheat on you, / with
any promising woman, for as long as it pays off. / This life) (MM: 29).

According to this logic of an investment that yields a profitable return, people's lives are reduced to commodity status – goods to be consumed and marketed in a society that is more like a peep show and in which love has been degraded to prostitution.

On one important level *Manhattan Medea* is a postdramatic response to the financial and economic discourses of late capitalism and it achieves this by employing two main methods. *Firstly,* Loher develops a complex self-reflexive and intertextual form of composition that is constructed analogously to the increasingly abstract financial procedures, transactions and models of neoliberal business. She then *secondly* translates this abstract economic model into a performative dimension by employing the agonistic relationship between Jason and Medea as a means of representing these abstracts processes in the relationship between theatrical figures. This allows for the development of the kind of structural homologies between postdramatic theatre and the increasing spectralisation of financial and socio-economic discourses since the 1970s that were outlined above and are at the core of this chapter. From this basis, *Manhattan Medea* positions itself as a critique of these very mechanisms.

Loher focuses on one of the underpinning principles of neoliberal economics in this representation, namely the financial trading in synthetic or structured financial products such as asset-backed securities, futures trading and sub-prime papers, which culminated in the new economy bubbles around 2000 and in the asset inflation synonymous with the economic crises following the collapse of Lehmann Brothers in 2008 (Stadler, 2011: 230, 234). Ultimately, the ability to trade even in risks, debts and losses as a way of generating ever new sources of capital supported the belief in a completely liberalised market, as independent rating agencies seemed to rubber-stamp the financial health of these deregulated derivative markets. Such financial products tend towards a suspension of previously established measures of economic performance and the creation of capital, however (Vogl, 2011: 92–4). As the term 'synthetic' suggests, such products and their economic value function according to an uncoupling from the real economy and trading in 'real', biophysical products and goods (Vogl, 2011: 86–7). This absence of real points of economic reference was certainly no invention of the 1990s; ever since the abandonment of the gold standard in the early 1970s the demand for the convertibility of currency into real worth was loosened, a precondition for the development of derivative markets such as foreign exchange, hedge funds and futures trading. In short, this deregulation of the financial markets led to a progressively spectralised financial and economic sphere that functions according to the uncoupling from the real economy and concomitant processes of fictionalisation noted by Urs Stäheli (Stäheli, 2013: 66–75). Where Marx – especially as read through Derrida and indeed Žižek, although, as suggested above, also in his own terminology – was concerned with the spectralising tendencies of capitalism's industrial relations and consumerism, trading of synthetic products in modern finance takes this to a new level.

Jason's economic strategy is one based on financial models of futures exchanges and hedging. Where hedging is understood as offsetting future losses on the basis of present contracts, Jason too transforms the guilt over his mother's death into a symbolic currency with which he can wheel and deal in order to bind Medea and thereby create the preconditions for a secure future (Vogl, 2011: 93, 152). This is a contract founded on an economy of guilt, a clear reference to Walter Benjamin's understanding of capitalism's origins in a pseudo-religious cult of guilt/debt (the German *Schuld* meaning both) in a fragment entitled 'Capitalism as religion' (Benjamin, 1996).[14] Jason first gained Medea's trust by sharing the guilt at his act of matricide while escaping from civil war: 'Ich / nehme ihren Kopf in beide Hände sachte wie sie / es mir getan als Kind und ... halte den Kopf fest unter Wasser' (I / take her head softly in both my hands just like she / did with me as a child and ... hold her head tightly under the water) (MM: 219). Jason not only murders his mother, he subsequently transforms her body into a set of linguistic signs with which he can trade and secure Medea's companionship. This introduces the second, performative dimension of the structural homology between finance and theatre mentioned previously. Financial trading functions according to a performative logic: these are systems in which currency exchange, trading in futures, hedging risks and sub-prime deals all function on the basis of a *promise* to honour credit, generate profits and liquidate risks of debt. Such promises are actions that are fulfilled in performances by the financial agents/ actors involved, especially in those cases where the job of a trader is understood as a 'role' he or she plays/occupies (Pircher, 2011: 295–6). Medea accuses Jason of having placed her in his debt by playing a role through sharing the story of his mother's death with her, turning his guilt into part of an economic transaction: 'Deine Schuld hast du mit mir geteilt, sehr geschickt ... Heute denke ich, / du hast mein Mitgefühl gekauft, sehr geschickt ... Heute denke ich, / woher hast du gewusst, daß du mich so gewinnen / konntest ... du wolltest gar nicht mich / du wolltest nur das Geld' (You shared your guilt with me, very clever ... Today I think, / you bought my sympathy, very clever ... Today I think, / how did you know that you could win me / over ... you didn't want me at all / you only wanted the money) (MM: 23). Thus a performance is at the core of Medea and Jason's business arrangement in so far as he deploys his own culpability as an investment to secure his future well-being through (and, at least temporarily, with) Medea. This performance depicts the origins of complex derivative trading as a phantasmagorical transformation of people into financial products according to a spectral logic: through the act of narration, Jason transforms his mother into a phantasmatic presence capable of influencing Medea's actions, and hence a ghostly product with which he can trade and constitute his vision of a profitable future. This performative dimension is doubled, however, because Jason's original performance is actually being presented retrospectively in a dialogue between Medea and Jason as they both revisit the start of their relationship in a flashback, re-enacting a past event in the present. By these means the performative dimension of financial trading – a performative dimension that is depicted as based around a spectralising narrative – itself becomes the object of an equally hauntological, uncanny performance, postdramatic self-reflexivity opening up the performative dimension of financial trading to a critical view.

Interestingly, this entire transaction is repeated when the pair renew their original contract en route to America: Jason and Medea murder her brother. At the core of this murder is once again the management of scarcity. In a departure from Euripides' model, where Medea murders her brother in order to distract her father in the Black Sea, in Loher's version he is murdered in order to provide enough food to feed the pregnant Medea. Because 'wir haben nicht das Geld für vier' (we haven't enough money for four) (MM: 57), the brutal equation boils down to killing the brother or aborting her unborn son: 'Wir sind zu dritt auf dieses Schiff gegangen Wir werden dieses Schiff verlassen zu dritt ... Jason sagt Nein Mein Fleisch wird dieses neue Land sehen Unsere Zukunft' (Three of us went on-board this ship Three of us will leave this ship Jason says No My flesh will see this new land Our future) (MM: 57). This is no less an economic transaction based on futures and securities than was Jason's act of matricide: a brother for a son, one dead body for a future ('Zukunft' (future), MM: 57). In this brutal memory a life becomes a 'lebendes Pfand' (live deposit)

(MM: 49), and partnership is little more than a set of oral contracts that guarantee the risks of a shared future on the security of an unpaid debt. Now threatened by Jason with their separation, Medea invokes this guilt/debt in order to keep him by her side: '[das] verbindet. / Diese Nacht. / Und alle die Nächte danach, / in denen wir in dieser Schuld lagen, / die wir teilen' ([that] binds. / That night. / And every night since then, / in which we slept in this debt/guilt, / which we share) (MM: 30). Medea thus repeats Jason's model of trading, seeking to secure her future through a new contract of shared guilt, a contract by which he, however, refuses to be bound. Medea's credit rating appears to be in default.

The economic logic of the body that *Manhattan Medea* presents is a constitutive moment of precisely those haunting apparitional figures in gothic discourses of neoliberal capitalism set out above. As contemporary economic practice has been criticised for its increasingly phantasmagorical nature, its disconnection from any real, existing value and measurement, so too do Jason's mother and Medea's brother gain a phantasmagorical presence in this economy of guilt: transformed into a story, a set of signifiers, and hence a symbolic currency of transactions, they are an invisible presence defining their relationship. Medea's brother in particular takes on a ghostly presence, continually returning to haunt Medea's and Jason's memories and actions in New York. Speaking to Medea, Jason remarks of their son: 'Manchmal glaube ich / die Augen deines Bruders in dem Kind zu sehen. / Der Sterbende, der sich im Augenblick des Todes/ den ungeborenen Körper nimmt, / zum neuen Wohnsitz und zur Rache' (Sometimes I think I / see your brother's eyes in that child. / The dying one who in the moment of death / takes over the unborn body / for his new home and for revenge) (MM: 34). Shortly before murdering her son, Medea repeats these exact words to her son: 'Manchmal glaube ich / die Augen meines Bruders zu sehen / in den deinen ... zur Rache' (Sometimes I think I / see my brother's eyes / in your eyes ... for revenge) (MM: 56). Not only is this an example of the spectral repetitions in the play's postdramatic form (Jason's words resurfacing to haunt Medea's speech and hence denying her the individual elocution of a psychological character), it is also indicative of the logic of spectral haunting at the core of economic transactions invoked in Loher's play as a whole.

The transformation of both mother and brother into media of a financial transaction in Jason and Medea's shared prehistory means that they attain an uncanny, phantasmagorical status in the remainder of the play: the murders, the shared stories and the acts of storytelling all conjoin to depict an economic order driven by violence, suffering and haunting structures. *Manhattan Medea* also makes a point of focusing on acts of corporeal suffering and violence at the genesis of such phantasmagorical systems of finance and economics, however, thus deconstructing the supposedly peaceful legal basis of neoliberal economy: the contract ensuring co-operation between partners. The 'contract' between Jason and Medea is based on an act of violence, recalling a central idea in Walter Benjamin's 'Critique of violence' according to which 'like the outcome, the origin of every contract also points towards violence ... insofar as the power that guarantees a legal contract is in turn of violent origin even if violence is not introduced into the contract itself' (Benjamin, 1986: 288). One is reminded of Žižek's diagnosis of the violence in Central Europe in the early 1990s as the uncanny mirror of late-capitalist society in the West, as Loher's play dwells on the civil war in the Balkans as the violent origin of a contractual financial transaction later dominating personal and economic relations in the West. Just as Žižek identified the violence in the Balkans and the stream of migration from Eastern Europe in the 1990s as the uncanny mirror of late capitalism's liberalist ideology, so too does the violence of these refugees' story offer a brutally disturbing representation of the mechanisms of late capitalism.

As Joseph Vogl notes, 'Politische Ökonomie hat seit jeher eine Neigung zur Geisterkunde gehegt' (Political economy has always had a tendency to numinous qualities) (Vogl, 2011: 7). The post-1989 engagement with the political economy governing migration and consumerism in the plays by Heiner Müller and Dea Loher that have been considered here upholds this analysis. Müller's vision is one of a post-socialist world order in which the uncanny and the spectral, undead figures and the haunting are fast becoming constitutive components. Whereas the undead SS-soldiers and their widows are initially the undead remnants of Germany's violent past, in the course of 'Der Gastarbeiter' they also become products for trading. Loher's *Manhattan Medea* shares this sense that the gothic is no longer by necessity a transgressive formation in a late-capitalist world order. If Müller suggested that the core financial structures underpinning neoliberalism are inherently linked to numinous and spectral qualities, Loher's play represents an attempt to represent theatrically what are increasingly becoming abstract, spectralising financial practices in their own right. The postdramatic spectres and undead figurations generated by the complex formal experiments and citational practices in these plays are thus more than self-reflexive metaphors for theatrical practice itself; rather postdramatic theatre is able to both mimic *and* critically break with the spectralising and performative tendencies of late capitalism and neoliberalism. Hence *Manhattan Medea* ultimately focuses on the moments of corporeal suffering at the origin of these spectral financial models, enabling a disruption of neoliberalism's comfort with uncanny, numinous socio-economic practices, and suggesting that its trade in numinous, synthetic products is by no means as harmless as it would perhaps suggest. In its attempt to stage the abstract, numinous financial structures, postdramatic theatre capitalises on the ghosts of neoliberalism to ground its phantasmagorical formal experiments.

Notes

1 Lehmann (1999); an English translation was published in 2006 (Lehmann, 2006).
2 Although Lehmann prioritises theatrical practices in which a ceremonial or ritualistic moment of the performance itself is its key defining characteristic, the term 'postdramatic theatre' describes rather a panorama of different possible models of anti-representational theatre. In this regard, I depart somewhat from his more programmatic intention and align myself with more flexible models such as that described by Poschmann (1997).
3 All translations in the following chapter are my own.
4 Of course criticism of the spectral nature of trade is as old as the Aristotelian criticism of usury whereby money is used to produce more money. This criticism was no less prevalent in modern discourses surrounding paper money and early trading in stocks, as the Marxist critique of capital in the nineteenth century shows.
5 See Konrad Paul Liessmann's statement in Liessman *et al.* (2011), 281.
6 On the links between contemporary theatre and Debord see Etzold (2007), 230–57.
7 The following overview is indebted to Bernd Blaschke's excellent essay (Blaschke, 2009).
8 See Diedrichsen (2005) and Bergmann (2009).
9 See Pewny (2011).
10 On *Die Kontrakte des Kaufmanns* see Polt-Heinzl (2010) and Schößler (2011).
11 All further references are to this edition and will appear with the abbreviation WS and the relevant page number.
12 All subsequent references will be abbreviated as MM and the relevant page number.
13 Loher was enrolled in a creative writing course led by Müller and Yaak Karsunke at the Hochschule der Künste in Berlin in 1990.
14 On the relationship between guilt/debt and economics see Hamacher (2003).

References

Benjamin, Walter. 1986. 'Critique of violence'. In *Reflections: Essays, Aphorisms, Autobiographical Writings*. Ed. Peter Demetz, trans. Edmund Jephcoat. New York: Schocken, 277–300.

Benjamin, Walter. 1996. 'Capitalism as religion'. In *Selected Writings*. Ed. Marcus Bullock and Michael Jennings, Vol. I: *1913–1926*. Cambridge, MA: Harvard Belknap Press, 288–91.

Bergmann, Franziska. 2009. 'Die Dialektik der Postmoderne in Theatertexten von René Pollesch: Zur Verschränkung von Neoliberalismus und Gender'. In C. Bähr and F. Schößler, eds, *Ökonomie im Theater der Gegenwart: Ästhetik, Produktion, Institution*. Bielefeld: Transcript, 193–207.

Birringer, Johannes. 2003. 'A new Europe'. *Journal of Performance and Art* 25(3): 26–41.

Blaschke, Bernd. 2009. '"McKinseys Killerkommandos: Subventioniertes Abgruseln". Kleine Morphologie (Tool Box) zur Darstellung aktueller Wirtschaften im Theater'. In C. Bähr and F. Schößler, eds, *Ökonomie im Theater der Gegenwart: Ästhetik, Produktion, Institution*. Bielefeld: Transcript, 209–24.

Botting, Fred. 2001. 'Preface'. In Fred Botting, ed., *The Gothic*. Cambridge: D. S. Brewer, 1–10.

Botting, Fred. 2013. 'Globalzombie: From *White Zombie* to *World War Z*'. In Glennis Byron, ed., *Globalgothic*. Manchester: Manchester University Press, 188–201.

Botting, Fred and Justin D. Edwards. 2013. 'Theorising globalgothic'. In Glennis Byron, ed., *Globalgothic*. Manchester: Manchester University Press, 11–24.

Brecht, Bertolt. 2005. 'Anmerkungen zur Oper *Aufstieg und Fall der Stadt Mahagonny*'. In *Bertolt Brecht ausgewählte Werke in sechs Bänden*. Vol. VI: *Schriften 1920–1956*. Frankfurt am Main: Suhrkamp, 102–12.

Bröckling, Ulrich. 2007. *Das unternehmerische Selbst: Soziologie einer Subjektivierungsform*. Frankfurt am Main: Suhrkamp.

Byron, Glennis. 2013. 'Introduction'. In Glennis Byron, ed., *Globalgothic*. Manchester: Manchester University Press, 1–10.

Crouch, Colin. 2004. *Post-Democracy*. Cambridge: Polity.

Debord, Guy. 1983. *Society of the Spectacle*. Detroit: Black and Red.

Derrida, Jacques. 1994. *Spectres of Marx: The State of the Debt, the Work of Mourning, and the New International*. Trans. Peggy Kamuff. New York and London: Routledge.

Diedrichsen, Diedrich. 2005. 'Maggies Agentur'. In Aenne Quinones, ed., *René Pollesch: Prater-Saga*. Berlin: Volksbühne am Rosa-Luxemburg-Platz, 1–19.

Etzold, Jörn. 2007. 'Melancholie des Spektakels: Guy Debord'. In B. Menke and C. Menke, eds, *Tragödie, Trauerspiel, Spektakel*. Berlin: Theater der Zeit, 230–57.

Haas, Birgit. 2004. *Theater der Wende, Wendetheater*. Würzburg: Königshäusen und Neumann.

Hamacher, Werner. 2003. 'Schuldgeschichte: Benjamins Skizze "Kapitalismus und Religion"'. In Dirk Baecker, ed., *Kapitalismus als Religion*. Berlin: Kadmos, 83–120.

Jameson, Fredric. 2000. 'Culture and finance capital'. In *The Jameson Reader*, ed. Michael Hardt and Kathi Weeks. Oxford: Blackwell, 255–74.

Latham, Rob. 2002. *Consuming Youth: Vampires, Cyborgs and the Culture of Consumption*. Chicago: University of Chicago Press.

Lehmann, Hans-Thies. 1999. *Postdramatisches Theater*. Frankfurt am Main: Verlag der Autoren.

Lehmann, Hans-Thies. 2000. 'Zwischen Monolog und Chor: Zur Dramaturgie Heiner Müllers'. In Ian Wallace, Dennis Tate and Gerd Labroisse, eds, *Heiner Müller: Probleme und Perspektiven. Bath Symposion 1998*. Amsterdam and Atlanta, GA: Rodopi, 11–26.

Lehmann, Hans-Thies. 2002. 'Studien zu Heiner Müller: Müllers Gespenster'. In H. T. Lehmann, ed., *Das Politische Schreiben: Essays zu Theatertexten*. Berlin: Theater der Zeit, 283–300.

Lehmann, Hans-Thies. 2006. *Postdramatic Theatre*. Trans. Karen Jürs-Munby. London: Routledge.

Liessmann, Konrad Paul, Gerald Matt, Rudolf Scholten and Joseph Vogl. 2011. 'Kunst und Finanzwelt – Ein Widerspruch? Gespräch mit Konrad Paul Liessmann, Gerald Matt, Rudolf Scholten und Joseph Vogl'. *Jelinek[Jahr]Buch* 2011: 280–94.

Lilge, Thomas. 2012. *Du sollst: Kapitalismus als Religion und seine Performer*. Berlin: Merve.

Loher, Dea. 1999. *Manhattan Medea: Blaubart – Hoffnung der Frauen*. Frankfurt am Main: Verlag der Autoren.

Marx, Karl. 1976. *Capital*. Vol. I. Trans. Ben Fowkes. Harmondsworth: Penguin.

Müller, Heiner. 1990. *Gesammelte Irrtümer*. Vol. II: *Interviews und Gespräche*. Ed. Gregor Edelmann and Renate Ziemer. Frankfurt am Main: Verlag der Autoren.

Müller, Heiner. 2001a. *Die Hamletmaschine*. In *Werke*, Vol. IV: *Die Stücke 2*. Ed. Frank Hörnigk. Frankfurt am Main: Suhrkamp, 543–54.

Müller, Heiner. 2001b. *Verkommenes Ufer Medeamaterial Landschaft mit Argonauten*. In *Werke*, Vol. V: *Die Stücke 3*. Ed. Frank Hörnigk. Frankfurt am Main: Suhrkamp, 71–83.

Müller, Heiner. 2002 [1995]. *Germania 3: Gespenster am Toten Mann*. In *Werke*, Vol. V: *Die Stücke* 3. Ed. Frank Hörnigk. Frankfurt am Main: Suhrkamp, 253–96.

Murnane, Barry. 2011. 'Let's begin – again: History, rupture and intertexts in Heiner Müller's *Germania*-cycle'. In Gert Hofmann, Rachel MagShamhráin, Marko Pajević and Michael Shields, eds, *German and European Poetics after the Holocaust: Crisis and Creativity*. New York: Camden House, 180–99.

Pewny, Katharina. 2011. *Das Drama des Prekären*. Bielefeld: Transcript.

Pircher, Wolfgang. 2011. '… um fremd zu werden wie Geld …'. *Bemerkungen zu Elfriede Jineleks 'Die Kontrakte des Kaufmanns'*. *Jelinek[Jahr]Buch* 2011: 295–301.

Polt-Heinzl, Evelyne. 2010. 'Minus-Nichts, aber mündelsicher oder Besser eine Taube im Mündel als ein MEL-Zertifikat im Portfolio: Über Elfriede Jelineks *Die Kontrakte des Kaufmanns'*. *Jelinek[Jahr]Buch* 2010: 99–114.

Polt-Heinzl, Evelyne and Joseph Vogl. 2011. 'Wirtschafts- und Finanzkrise in Elfriede Jelineks *Die Kontrakte des Kaufmanns*: Ein Gespräch'. *Jelinek[Jahr]Buch* 2011: 316–26.

Poschmann, Gerda. 1997. *Der nicht mehr dramatische Theatertext: Aktuelle Bühnenstücke und ihre dramaturgische Analyse*. Tübingen: De Gruyter.

Schößler, Franziska. 2004. *Augen-Blicke: Erinnerung, Zeit und Geschichte in Dramen der neunziger Jahre*. Tübingen: Narr.

Schößler, Franziska. 2011. 'Die Arbeiten des Herkules als "Schöpfung aus dem Nichts": Jelinek's Stück *Die Kontrakte des Kaufmanns* und das Popkonzert von Nicolas Stegmann'. *Jelinek[Jahr]Buch* 2011: 327–40.

Sennett, Richard. 1998. *The Corrosion of Character: The Personal Consequences of Work in the New Capitalism*. New York: Norton.

Sennett, Richard. 2006. *The Culture of the New Capitalism*. New Haven: Yale University Press.

Stadler, Wilfried. 2011. 'Finanzkunst in der Krise'. *Jelinek[Jahr]Buch* 2011: 227–38.

Stäheli, Urs. 2013. *Spectacular Speculation: Thrills, the Economy, and Popular Discourse*. Trans. Eric Savoth. Stanford: Stanford University Press.

Stephan, Inge. 2006. *Medea: Multimediale Karriere einer mythologischen Figur*. Cologne, Weimar and Vienna: Böhlau.

Vogl, Joseph. 2011. *Das Gespenst des Kapitals*. Zürich: Diaphanes.

Žižek, Slavoj. 1993. *Tarrying with the Negative: Kant, Hegel and the Critique of Ideology*. Durham, NC: Duke University Press.

Part II

Biotechnologies, neoliberalism and the gothic

4

Katarzyna Ancuta

The return of the dismembered: representing organ trafficking in Asian cinemas

Introduction

There is perhaps no more poignant context for the discussion of the horrors of global neoliberalism than transplant medicine. Ever since the first successful transplantations were performed in the 1950s, the development of transplant medicine has run parallel with the rapid commercialisation and neoliberalisation of healthcare, globalisation of medical resources, and the promotion of the idea of 'the divisible body' comprising detachable organs that could and should be exchanged if no longer fully operational. Market economy, argues Nancy Scheper-Hughes, tends to 'reduce everything – including human beings, their labor, and their reproductive capacity – to the status of commodities that can be bought, sold, traded, and stolen' (2002: 62), and the increasing polarisation between rich and poor creates conditions for a thriving trade in biomaterials, often obtained illegally and by force. Additionally, if the 'miracle' of transplantation has successfully divided the human population into potential donors and receivers, the politics of global neoliberalism has ensured a steady supply of 'spare' parts from economically underdeveloped countries, whose citizens are frequently portrayed and conceived of as 'the living cadavers' (Moniruzzaman, 2012: 73), whose 'third-world bodies' are 'surplus bodies' containing 'extra' organs that can be better utilised when transplanted into their first-world recipients (Davidson, 2008: 201–2).

Michael Davidson argues that 'the organ sale narrative is *the* alle-gory of globalization', as it portrays commoditised bodies whose components are 'exchanged in a worldwide market that mirrors the structural inequality between wealth and poverty' (198). These com-ponents, notes Scheper-Hughes, follow 'the modern routes of cap-ital: from South to North, from Third to First World, from poor to rich, from black and brown to white, and from female to male' (2000: 5). Organ sale narratives abound in anthropological accounts of uneth-ical medical practices through which patients from affluent countries benefit from structural bio-violence against the underprivileged from the world's peripheries. The proliferation of research into the abuses of organ trade in such countries as India, Bangladesh, Pakistan, Brazil, the Philippines or Moldova (Cohen, 1999; Scheper-Hughes, 2000, 2002, 2004; Moniruzzaman, 2012) provides copious evidence that these practices are alarmingly common. These accounts get further reinforced through their popular representation in literature and film, situating organ trafficking 'within an ethnoscape of transnational labor flows, black market crime, and moral panic', or futuristic visions of eter-nal youth and immortality obtained through an inexhaustible supply of replacement parts (Davidson, 2008: 200–1).

Most cinematic narratives of organ trade dwell on the familiar motif of profit-oriented healthcare ruthlessly abusing the vulnerable. Films such as *Coma* (dir, Michael Crichton, 1978) or *The Ambulance* (dir. Larry Cohen, 1990) see the privatised hospital as potential ground for med-ical exploitation, where insignificant patients become unwilling sup-pliers of biomaterial to the wealthy. *The Island* (dir. Michael Bay, 2005) suggests that in the future people will be farmed for compatible parts. In *Repo Men* (dir. Miguel Sapochnik, 2010), transplant medicine operates akin to a bank loan scheme, with customers lured into upgrading their organs only to have them repossessed when they default on repayment. Migrant workers are dehumanised in *Dirty Pretty Things* (dir. Stephen Frears, 2002) as mere 'container[s] for labour exploitation, sexual abuse, rape and kidney removal' (Ewart, 2010: 11), while in *Turistas* (dir. John Stockwell, 2006) American backpackers are disembowelled to 'donate' organs to poor Brazilian children in a bizarre act of moral retribution.

The Asian continent is predominantly portrayed as the exploited per-iphery in such narratives, continuing the legacy of western colonial/imperialistic representation that saw it as the inexhaustible supplier of human and material resources. This chapter strives to counter this West–East dichotomy by eliminating the West from discussion to focus solely on intra-Asian relations. The chapter analyses the representation of organ harvesting and trade/trafficking in eight post-2000 Asian films. It discusses the films' consistent portrayal of transplantation as dependent on criminal networks and activities, and their critique of neoliberal medicine as responsible for deepening the economic divisions within Asian societies. The chapter argues that regional organ trade operates in accordance with the same principles as the global one, allowing for an identification of donor and recipient zones specific to Asia and directing the local organ flows towards the economically privileged Asian countries, such as Japan, Taiwan or South Korea, three countries identified as major beneficiaries in the films. Last but not least, the chapter offers a reading of the potentially gothic figures of vengeance appearing in the films (ghosts, resurrected neo-humans, victims-turned-abusers) in terms of a narrative strategy of resistance devised to empower the oppressed.

Neo-cannibalism in the age of market economy

A typical cinematic representation of organ trade situates it in the context of crime: organs are stolen from the poor to sell them at a profit to the rich. Since under late capitalism the divisible body and its detachable organs have become just another marketable commodity, they are distributed like any merchandise – 'sold to the highest bidder' (Blacker, 2007). To do so, 'a fiction of scarcity had to be instituted to simultaneously instil fear in potential organ consumers and a sense of opportunity and profitability in potential organ vendors' (Blacker, 2007). This scarcity, argues Scheper-Hughes, is created by the medical personnel involved in transplant surgery, and represents 'an artificial need, one that can never be satisfied, for underlying it is the unprecedented possibility of extending life indefinitely with the organs of others' (2000: 13). In reality, the medical discourse on scarcity serves to distract public attention from the overabundance of wasted organs left unprocessed because of a shortage of skilled technicians or equipment, or simply to spite the competition (Scheper-Hughes, 2002: 67). 'The real scarcity', concludes Scheper-Hughes, 'is not of organs but of transplant patients of sufficient means to pay for them' (2000: 14).

Sarah Blacker argues that in a market economy driven by consumer desire, the consumers rarely complain about the methods leading to the satisfaction of this desire (2007). The idea of the divisible body transforms a person into a 'life' that must be extended regardless of the cost, while the principle of consumerism demands that those who can afford to buy an organ should not be denied their right to do so (Scheper-Hughes, 2002: 62). As the sale of organs is illegal, this creates perfect conditions for criminal enterprise built around the supply of the parts in demand. Driven by market economy rather than ethics, neoliberal medicine sanctions sacrificing the disadvantaged for profit in the name of medical progress. After all, 'health is positioned as directly proportional to wealth, and suffering inversely proportional to ability to pay for medical treatment' (Blacker, 2007). The monstrosity of this arrangement is exposed in two Korean productions. Chanwook Park's *Sympathy for Mr Vengeance* (*Boksuneun naui geot*) (2002) is a harsh critique of the privatised health system in South Korea that discriminates against the poor and pushes them to deal with the black market. Jeong-beom Lee's *The Man from Nowhere* (*Ajeossi*) (2010) depicts organ harvesting as a by-product of crime, a convenient way of disposing of the bodies that pile up during regular activities of organised crime rings. Both movies strongly emphasise the class division within Korean society, against which backdrop their revenge plots are played out.

In *Sympathy for Mr Vengeance*, Ryu, a deaf-mute art school dropout, works double shifts in a metal factory to save money for his sister's (Han Bo-Bae) kidney transplant. In the absence of a social welfare system and public health coverage in Korea, like every patient suffering from renal failure, Bo-Bae and her family are expected to pay the full cost of dialysis, transplantation and follow-up treatment (Garden and Murphree, 2007: 220). While the hospitals in Korea are state-of-the-art institutions, they do not offer equal access to their procedures (225). Rejected as a donor for Bo-Bae, Ryu arranges to exchange his kidney for a compatible organ on the black market. Soon after that a match shows up on the hospital's donor list but by then Ryu has already been robbed of his life savings by the unscrupulous criminals. When he gets additionally laid off from work Ryu lets himself be talked into kidnapping his boss's daughter for ransom by his radically minded girlfriend Cha Youngmi, who convinces him that such an action stimulates the 'movement of capital [that] maximizes the value of money!'. Seizing an opportunity the two end up taking Yoosoon, the daughter of President Park, instead. Then things take a turn for the worse. Upon realising what a burden she has become to her brother, Bo-Bae commits suicide. Busy with burying his sister, Ryu does not notice Yoosoon drowning in the river behind him. This sets President Park off on a revenge mission that leaves everyone dead.

Behind the premise of the movie lies a basic formula that stipulates that 'human life has a cash value and circulates, accumulating value until it is consumed' (Garden and Murphree, 2007: 220) – whether sold for parts, or traded for ransom. This underlying capitalist logic motivates the film's critique of the ruthlessness of the system in which everything can be reduced to its exchange value (220). Despite its framing as a personal revenge story, Rebecca Garden and Hyon Joo Yoo Murphree argue that *Sympathy for Mr Vengeance* should be read as a socio-cultural allegory, as the film's theme was specifically constructed 'in reference to the commonality of trauma as the pith of social experience' (223). They compare the individual tragedies portrayed in the film with familiar social acts known from Korean history: group suicides of entire families ruined by the economic crisis in the 1980s, torture of political prisoners carried out by the Korean Government in the 1980s or self-immolations of intellectual radicals protesting against State repression in the late 1990s (223), and insist that the film cannot be separated from its socio-historical context determined by the logic of Korean capitalism (224).

The same logic justifies the actions of the gangsters in *The Man from Nowhere*, for whom getting involved with organ trade is synonymous with modernisation, as they expand their usual criminal repertoire in response to the needs of the market, and to compete with new groups threatening to replace them. Indeed, though the gangsters prey mostly on victims of opportunity – the weak, the poor and the vulnerable – their exchange value is calculated differently. Deemed too small for organ harvesting, children are kept as slaves instead, utilised as 'ants' transporting illegal merchandise without causing suspicion. Adults, however, having served their original purpose, inevitably end up as 'bodies without organs', functioning as a resource that can be broken into pieces and put to a better use someplace else (217). The plot of the film pits a quiet pawn-shop owner, Cha Tae-sik, against a ruthless drug-and-organ-trafficking ring, as he tries to save his neighbour's daughter, Jeong So-mi. An ex-secret service operative, Tae-sik is a 'man without soul', broken after the murder of his wife and his unborn child. In the film, he embarks on the mission to prevent So-mi from becoming another 'body without organs' like her heroin addict/prostitute mother, whose decision to steal from the gang set the action in motion.

The Man from Nowhere is first and foremost an action thriller, and its focus on organ trade is minimal, introduced by a close-up shot of

the eviscerated corpse of So-mi's mother, affirmed by a few explana-
tory lines of dialogue and glimpses of the underground operating theatre, and maximised through the appearance of gouged human eyeballs
(seemingly belonging to So-mi) in the climax scene – the final obstacle
that the hero must very literally step over to achieve his goal. The theme
of transplantation, with its context of uncaring hospitals and exploitative criminal networks, is integral for *Sympathy for Mr Vengeance*'s
depiction of Korea as a bleak neoliberal wasteland. The most direct references to the issue are repeatedly visualised as grotesque, bordering on
comical: a wide shot of four men in an act of synchronised masturba-
tion listening to loud moans from behind the wall – as the camera pans
through the wall we see Bo-Bae writhing in pain on the floor instead,
and Ryu helping a drug-addict 'doctor' to shoot heroin before she is
ready to remove his kidney – cut to Ryu waking up without the kidney or his clothes, forced to hitch-hike naked back to Seoul. Both films
depict the Korean medical market as driven by 'the artificial need' for
human organs, devaluation of cadaver organs and criminalisation of living donor transplants.

The introduction of local and international laws prohibiting the
trade in organs in the 1990s has pushed the procedure underground.
Most Asian countries, South Korea, Hong Kong and the Philippines
included, forbid the sale of organs for profit and demand that all dona-
tions be obtained from relatives and family friends. At the same time,
the underground market thrives because as long as 'class, race, and caste
ideologies' continue to contribute to the treatment of certain bodies as
'waste' (Scheper-Hughes, 2000: 34), a market for body parts will always
'[exploit] the desperation of the poor, turning their suffering into an
opportunity' (Scheper-Hughes, 2002: 78), because the poor can participate in such an exchange only as organ sellers (Moniruzzaman,
2012: 71) or victims of theft. Unless, that is, they choose to benefit
from the extortion scheme themselves.

The protagonists of Chi-Leung Law's *Koma* (*Jiu ming*) (2005), and
Ron Morales' *Graceland* (2012) fall into this category. The plot of *Koma*
is a combination of a love triangle and a crime story. Ching is a Hong
Kong socialite engaged to Raymond. She is wasting away as, despite
her wealth, she cannot buy a kidney her body would accept. Ling, her
underprivileged rival, makes extra money orchestrating kidney thefts,
acting on the popular but false assumption that each body contains
one 'surplus' kidney without which it remains fully functional. When
Ling realises that Raymond uses her for sex but remains in love with

Ching, she terrorises Ching, threatening to steal her organs. Upon learning about Ching's condition, however, Ling commits suicide and forces an unwanted 'gift of life' onto her rival, offering one of her own kidneys in replacement instead. The film problematises the concept of organ donation construed as a benevolent act, which effectively allows the medical personnel and organ recipients to hide that they are beneficiaries of a system exploiting social inequalities (Scheper-Hughes, 2002: 74). The 'donation' of Ling's kidney is reconstituted as her ultimate revenge on Ching, who is left alone with the enemy, very literally, inside.

Despite their obvious economic differences, Ching and Ling look surprisingly alike. When Ling is 'put in her place' by Raymond, who derides her lack of class, she seems like the victim of circumstance. But Ling's profiting from the illegal harvesting of organs makes her an ambiguous character, incapable of moral victory and difficult to empathise with. In this, she resembles Marlon Villar from *Graceland* – an impoverished driver of a rich politician in Manila who gets involved in the kidnapping of his boss's daughter for ransom in an act of revenge for getting unjustly fired and to raise money for his wife's kidney transplant. Throughout the film Marlon is made to look like a victim: he loses his job when he fails to cover up a scandal exposing his boss as a paedophile; his daughter, Elvie, gets taken when the kidnapping goes wrong and the other girl dies; he is bullied by a corrupt detective looking for a scapegoat, and is shown as unable to help his wife. Only the final scenes reveal his involvement in the scheme. Despite a semi-happy ending (Marlon's wife gets a new kidney, Elvie is back home and his boss loses all his ill-gotten gains) the film seems to lack closure: Marlon is still unemployed, his daughter resents him and his wife's chances of recovery are vague.

The protagonists of *Koma* and *Graceland* see the commoditised kidney in terms of an object of desire and a status symbol. The society is divided into those who can afford it and those who cannot. Turning against one's own class or trying to redress the imbalance by 'robbing the rich' is offered as a possible alternative but ultimately condemned in both films. It is also portrayed as a futile exercise, as the wealth and social status of the protagonists do not really improve. This is so because in highly hierarchical and economically polarised Asian societies such as South Korea, Hong Kong and the Philippines, bio-power and its derivative, bio-violence, are effective measures in place to ensure that the system benefits only the privileged.

Bio-power and bio-violence

Paul Farmer has argued that human suffering is 'structured by historically given (and often economically driven) processes and forces that
conspire ... to constrain agency' (1996: 263) and that human life
choices are severely hindered by 'racism, sexism, political violence *and*
grinding poverty' (263). The disadvantaged are 'not only more likely to
suffer, they are also more likely to have their suffering silenced' (280).
While globalisation has facilitated the spreading of transplant technologies, it has also promoted the identification of 'the poor, the naïve, the
medically illiterate, the displaced and the desperate' populations of the
less developed countries as 'surplus bodies' filled with 'spare' body parts
(Scheper-Hughes, 2004: 33). This is hardly surprising, as the reconsti-
tution of 'third world bodies' into raw material is a primary legacy of
colonialism, motivated by the historical relationship of conquest and
extraction, which continues to shape the dynamics of the developed
and developing worlds (Moniruzzaman, 2012: 70). Resignified as a
'negotiable surplus', the organs, which are seen as 'wasting away' in the
bodies of the third world paupers, can supposedly be better utilised by
the global elite, in whose bodies they can be 'mobilized to work towards
accumulation' (Blacker, 2007).

Inseparable from the global economy, the body becomes 'a site of
commodity extraction, piece by piece, moving from poor to rich where
bio-power consumes and redistributes itself' (Ewart, 2010: 1). In 1976,
Michel Foucault argued that the development of capitalism would not
have been possible without the controlled administration of bodies
and effective subjugation of populations to economic processes (1990
[1976]: 141). Such power over life, or 'bio-power', could be exercised
either through discipline (treating the body as a machine), or through
regulatory controls of various biological processes of the population
(139) leading towards the administration, optimisation and multiplica-
tion of life (137). This bio-power not only allowed for the steady supply
of bodies to be used in the machinery of production, but also ensured
that these bodies stayed submissive, available and easy to govern
(141). But bio-power, argues Moniruzzaman, is enabled through 'bio-
violence' – an instrument to transform bodies (dead or alive) into sites
of exploitation, harmed and manipulated more efficiently thanks to
the development of new medical technologies (2012: 72). Since transplantation always leaves organ sellers at a loss and frequently results in
their disablement (75–81), the systematic designation of 'third world

bodies' as donor bodies must be recognised for what it is: a structural form of bio-violence.

While most popular narratives of organ trade identify the buyers as westerners, Alexis Aronowitz notices that in recent years the market has substantially expanded, and lists Japan, South Korea, Taiwan, Hong Kong and Malaysia among the most common organ-recipient nations. India, Pakistan, China and the Philippines remain the primary organ-donor countries, despite the existence of local laws that limit or prohibit transplants to foreigners (Aronowitz, 2013: 78). Japan is strongly associated with transplant tourism in the region. In 2006, the *Independent* reported on a mass exodus of well-off Japanese transplant patients to China despite the controversy over the Chinese use of organs from executed prisoners (Coonan and McNeill, 2006). Three years later *The New York Times* wrote about the Chinese investigation of seventeen Japanese tourists for receiving illegal kidneys and livers, despite the fact that all transplants for foreigners were supposedly banned in China in 2007 (McDonald, 2009). In 2011, a Japanese newspaper *Manichi Shimbun* reported on the arrest of the members of a *yakuza* gang who orchestrated organ transplants from Philippine donors (Cook, 2011). Japan criminalises organ sales and does not recognise brain death as the end of life, therefore effectively limiting the possibility of transplant surgery within the country (Garden and Murphree, 2007: 225). The strict rules requiring that all potential donors must be related to the patient are, however, frequently circumvented, the most common schemes including fake marriages and adoptions, and transplant tourism (Cook, 2011).

Although not all transplant tourism is illegal or equivalent with organ trafficking,[1] the huge difference in prices at which the organs are bought from the donors and sold to the recipients[2] drives the market value of parts and exposes the lie that the exchange is mutually beneficial to the parties involved. The poor slum dwellers in India, Bangladesh or the Philippines, who by now have become accustomed to viewing their body parts as debt collateral, hardly ever manage to settle their debts with the compensation money they receive for their organs. Instead, they often wish they had more organs to sell (Cohen, 1999: 141). Chances are they may be allowed to do so, since at present, apart from kidneys, staple transplantations from living donors also include slices of liver, lungs and corneas (Moniruzzaman, 2012: 70). In 1989, Brian Yuzna's portrayal of the upper classes in *Society* (1989) concluded with the depiction of a monstrous carnal orgy during which the rich – whose individual bodies fused into one giant super-organism – very literally fed on the poor. Scheper-Hughes calls transplant medicine a form of 'neocannibalism', after Tsuyoshi Awaya, who in 1994 suggested that the current practices of utilisation of the human body will ultimately lead to its processing as food pellets in the future (Scheper-Hugues, 2002: 65).

Junki Sukamoto's *Children of the Dark* (*Yami no kodomo-tachi*) (2008) is a film portraying the flow of bodies and organs from Myanmar to Thailand and ultimately to Japan. The main plot of the film follows a Bangkok-based Japanese journalist investigating illegal organ harvesting from children. The recipient – a wealthy Japanese boy – is supposed to get the heart from a living donor, which means that to save one life, another one will be taken. Though deeply shocked by this unethical practice, the reporter, Hiroyuki Nanbu, stands firmly by his belief that the role of the press is to expose the truth rather than get involved. His sentiments are not appreciated by Keiko Otowa, a zealous Japanese volunteer for a Thai non-governmental organisation (NGO) fighting against the exploitation of children. The film focuses on two vaguely related cases – a semi-successful rescue of a Thai girl sold by her parents to a brothel in Chiang Mai, and an exposure of the killing of a Burmese girl, trafficked by the same gang, who becomes the heart donor for the Japanese child.

Little is known of organ trade in Thailand and Myanmar but this is not to say that it does not happen. In 2007, the International Organization for Migration expressed concerns about a dramatic increase in organ trafficking in all the less developed Southeast Asian countries, including Cambodia, Myanmar, Laos, the Philippines, Indonesia and Vietnam (Reuters, 2007). In 2014, the Office to Monitor and Combat Trafficking in Persons downgraded Thailand to the bottom tier of countries described as 'a source, destination, and transit country for men, women, and children subjected to forced labor and sex trafficking' (Office to Monitor and Combat Trafficking in Persons, 2014). The report estimates there are between 2 and 3 million migrants in Thailand, mostly from Myanmar and Cambodia, many undocumented. Reports of people being trafficked across borders and then sold into prostitution, or enslaved on boats and in factories, proliferate. Organ trafficking begins to make news in the region as well. In 2014, a Thai newspaper, *Bangkok Post*, reported on the rising organ trade in Cambodia with hints that the surgeries are also carried out in Thailand (Fernquest, 2014). A website that gathers global black market information lists the current price of buying a kidney in Thailand at 10,000 USD and selling one at

3,000–5,000 USD (Anon., 2014). Given Thailand's horrific record of exploiting its less fortunate neighbours (the Burmese, Cambodians and Laotians), the scenario offered in the film seems plausible.

The film paints a very disturbing picture of the complex, multi-level mechanism of exploitation. At one end of the spectrum we have an affluent Japanese middle-class family, introduced to the viewers in their immaculate suburban house. This image contrasts with the opening scene of the film showing the squalor of a Burmese village where two children are being sold to a Thai broker who takes them across the border. The Burmese children are certainly the ultimate victims in the movie, and indeed they both end up dead. Thai children rank slightly higher (they survive the ordeal although some get infected with HIV), but their fate is similarly determined by the grinding poverty of their families. Children's bodies, turned into living capital, satisfy the needs of a variety of consumers and are therefore exploited on a number of levels. Those who benefit from them most immediately are the gangsters, provided with a monetary reward for the children's services. The second group of beneficiaries are the paedophile clients who buy the right to sexually abuse and even kill them. As brothel customers and sexual perverts this second group are particularly reprehensible, the moral judgement clearly delivered in the depictions of their repugnant, shrivelled or morbidly obese bodies. The journalist who allows for the sacrifice of the child to abide by his professional rules is eventually also identified as a paedophile, even though he is allowed a degree of redemption through suicide. The eager NGO volunteer is criticised as patronising and judgemental, helping others in order to feel better about herself. Finally, let us not forget about the corrupt doctors and wealthy patients who benefit from the illegitimately procured parts.

Children of the Dark was shot on location in Thailand but the Thai Film Office reportedly denied the makers a filming permit. The film was also pulled out of the Bangkok International Film Festival 2008 line-up under pressure from the festival sponsors, the Tourism Authority of Thailand, and the Federation of National Film Association, who claimed that the movie was 'not appropriate for Thai society' (Rithdee, 2008). This is hardly surprising, since Thailand often comes across as a country preoccupied with keeping up appearances rather than tackling its problems directly. Besides, while the doctors and the organ receivers are given the benefit of the doubt in the film, and the Burmese parents are identified as economic victims, the film's portrayal of the uncaring ordinary Thai people – the middle-men – is by far the most disturbing, as some of them are shown to collaborate with the criminals for the price of a bowl of noodles in Bangkok. Trapped in a convoluted discourse of transplantation the film problematises the ethics of the procedure. The doctor kills an innocent child but he is also saving a life. The parents of the dying child, under the neoliberal imperative to preserve life, have an obligation to do whatever they can to save him. And if the lives of these two children are supposed to be measured solely by their economic value, then a wealthy Japanese boy is arguably more 'valuable' than an undernourished Burmese girl, regardless of how unethical this argument may sound.

Like the Japanese, South Koreans are increasingly reported to seek organs for transplantation abroad. Hong-seon Kim's *Traffickers* (*Gong-mo-ja-deul* 2012) identifies China as one of the most common transplant tourism destinations for Korean patients. The position of China on the international organ market remains dubious because of the country's long history of harvesting organs from executed prisoners, including prisoners of conscience. Budiani-Saberi and Delmonico estimate that in 2006, 11,000 organs were harvested from executed prisoners in China, counting 8,000 kidneys, 3,000 livers and 200 hearts (2008: 927), which constituted nine-tenths of China's entire organ supply (Fan, 2014). China has promised several times to switch to voluntary public donations,[3] but experts remain sceptical about the Government's commitment, given the growing demand. Confucian cultures are said to require that human bodies should enter the afterlife intact, which stops many people from donating their organs (Hosenball and Park, 2015). Additionally, harvesting organs from executed prisoners is not necessarily always seen as unethical, promoted as 'a form of public service, and an opportunity for [the prisoners] to redeem their families' honor' (Scheper-Hughes, 2000: 10).

Although in *Traffickers* the villains are unquestionably the Koreans, the film depicts China as an opportunistic country full of corrupt officials profiting from injustice. Such criticism earned it a ban from Chinese censors, despite the fact that the film's plot is predictably mapped out by its genre and the organ theft motive is but a convenient narrative device to justify the escalation of violence. The main protagonist, Yeong-gyoo, is an 'honest smuggler' operating a small drug-trafficking route between China and South Korea. Forced to harvest organs on a cruise ship, he risks his life to save the victim (young, beautiful, helpless and paralysed), whom he recognises as his dead friend's sister. He fails when the girl's loving fiancé, Sang-ho, is revealed to be the mastermind behind the operation – an ambitious insurance broker helping to procure the much sought-after organs for the Korean mega-rich. The sacrifice of Yeong-gyoo and his comrades, most of whom end up dead, is rewarded with a minor victory over the rival gang. The film, however, resists closure, leaving evil triumphant simply because it fits the monstrous neoliberal framework of Korean economy. In the final scene of the film we see Sang-ho in the roof garden of an impressive high-rise office complex making another transplant deal with a wealthy executive. Even though his gang has been disbanded, we have no doubt that the flow of organs will continue uninterrupted.

While *Traffickers* uses the theme of organ theft mostly for its graphic representation, the issue, and especially its Chinese connection, has been turned into an explicit political manifesto in a Taiwanese short film by Wu Derrick, *Declaration of Geneva* (2013). The film was made amidst perhaps the biggest controversy surrounding the Chinese transplantation practices, an accusation that China has methodically killed thousands of Falun Gong practitioners for their organs. The allegation was made public in 2006, in a report published by David Kilgour and David Matas based on the large discrepancy between the numbers of performed transplantations and of executed prisoners who were supposedly the source of organs. Falun Gong is a spiritual discipline that was criminalised in China in 1999. Its practitioners, incarcerated in large numbers, have been routinely blood-tested upon arrest (a procedure reportedly not performed on other prisoners), which may suggest that they are being matched as potential organ donors (Treasure, 2007). In 2012, the Taiwanese Parliament passed a resolution condemning forced organ harvesting in China. In 2014, Taiwan's Ministry of Health and Welfare rejected the Chinese Government's offer of organ supply and stated that Taiwan 'wouldn't accept organs from the mainland' (Su and Sun, 2014). It is also rather significant that Ko Wen-je, elected the mayor of Taipei in 2014, is the doctor credited with exposing Falun Gong organ harvesting to the world (Gutmann, 2014). At the same time, in 2013 the *Taipei Times* reported that 88 per cent of Taiwanese transplant patients undergo their operations in China (Hsiao, 2013).

Declaration of Geneva stands in stark contrast to the remaining movies discussed here because of its short format and its overall aesthetics. It is available on YouTube and its rudimentary IMDB credits make it seem more like a student film than a commercial production. The film introduces a happy middle-class Taiwanese couple: Grace has a heart condition and Peter, very conveniently, is a heart surgeon.

Peter makes money performing heart transplants in mainland China; Grace unknowingly makes friends with the ghosts of the people who were killed for their organs. The ghosts reveal their vengeful side and demand the couple's lives but are eventually dissuaded from doing so when Grace decides not to undergo her surgery and Peter repents for his sins. The film may be seen as overly moralising, aimed at protesting against the monstrous system that allows individuals and the State to benefit from bio-violence against others. But particularly interesting is that the fantastic framework of the movie allows for the introduction of an active (if non-human) figure of resistance. For, as evident in numerous gothic narratives, ghosts and monsters often dare to speak for the oppressed when humans choose to stay silent.

The return of the dismembered

In *Declaration of Geneva*, the harvested donors return as vengeful ghosts. In accordance with a greatly simplified Buddhist logic common in Asian horror, the returning ghosts represent the forces of *karma*, and an act of supernatural vengeance is seen as restoring balance to the universe. Having said that, in Buddhism ghosts are an aberration, as the dead are supposed not to dwell on their misfortunes but to let go of their suffering instead. Vengeful ghosts may act as the agents of *karma* but they cannot escape *karma* themselves and will remain trapped in the hell of their own making until they empty their minds of all emotions. The ghosts of Chinese donors enter the scene with a clear intention of punishing those who contributed to their demise. Within the narrative they function as revealers of secrets. They deliver a moral lesson and warn the audience of the dangers that may befall them. Organ sellers rarely have an opportunity to exercise agency, forced into the transaction 'out of economic desperation' (Blacker, 2007). Victims of state-orchestrated bio-violence robbed of their body parts have even less chance actively to resist their fate. Their return as vengeful ghosts, endowed with superpowers within the horror narrative is therefore significant and a clear call for action.

The power of narrative should not be disregarded. Narrative allows us to make sense of the world and convinces us that where there is a cause there will be an effect. The opening scene of *Koma* is a variation of a classic urban legend: a woman wakes up in a bathtub filled with ice in a hotel bathroom; a message written on the mirror advises her to call an ambulance, as she has just had one kidney removed and needs medical attention. Popular accounts track the origins of the 'kidney heist' tale to Europe in 1991, subsequently spreading to America and beyond. It has since been generally acknowledged to be a part of folk-lore and a hoax (Brunvand, 2002: 227–8). Anthropologists such as Scheper-Hughes argue that organ theft rumours 'are part of a univer-sal class of popular culture dating back to at least medieval Europe ... and they serve multiple ends' (2000: 20). Scheper-Hughes recalls the rumours circulating in Brazil in the 1980s, which spoke of American and Japanese 'medical agents' grabbing children from the streets and discarding their eviscerated bodies by the roadside. She argues that such rumours represent the collective fears of the population and express 'the chronic state of emergency ... experienced by desperately poor people living on the margins of the ... global economy' (19). She describes such rumours as an effective 'weapon of the weak', allowing the underclasses to mobilise their efforts to resist and interrupt the designs of medicine and the State (20). Whether legitimate or not, the sensational appeal of organ theft claims makes them popular with the media. As the stories gain momentum they may lead to the push for corrective legislature, or inquiries into local medical ethics (20). The 2014 announcement of the new government policy aiming to replace organ harvesting from prisoners in China with voluntary public dona-tions, came a year after the Chinese media reported a story of a six-year-old boy from Shanxi Province, Guo Bin, who was robbed of his eyes. Although ultimately the case may not have been motivated by organ theft (the eyeballs were found nearby with their corneas intact) it stimulated months of heated public debate on transplantation eth-ics within China and may well have contributed to the policy change (Fan, 2014).

Gothic figures of vengeance (be it ghosts, monsters or victims-turned-abusers) feature in many organ trade narratives. Their most dominant function is righting wrongs, since fantastic/supernatural creatures seem to do a better job of it than humans. The return of the dismembered is the premise of a Japanese manga-inspired science-fiction film, *Casshern* (2004), directed by Kazuaki Kiriya, offering a glimpse of a grim neo-liberal future. After a fifty-year war between the Eastern Federation and Europe, the Federation has gained control over Eurasia, but the victory has come at a price: the environment is polluted and the living popu-lation biologically degenerated. Dr Azuma proposes the use of Neo-Cells to regenerate human tissue. The cells can only be found in the genome of one ethnic group, currently fighting a rebellion in Eurasian

Zone 7, but the military readily obliges and supplies Dr Azuma with a large quantity of ethnically appropriate research material. A lightning bolt striking Dr Azuma's lab revitalises the dismembered body parts, which combine together into humans. Although most of the creatures are immediately executed, some manage to escape. They take over an abandoned castle with a robot army, assume the name of *Neo sapiens* and vow to destroy all humans. Dr Azuma's son, Tetsuya, who died as a soldier in Zone 7, is similarly revived when the lightning strikes. Unlike the *Neo sapiens*, however, he needs to be encased in an armoured suit that acts as his exoskeleton to survive. Predictably, Tetsuya rises as the hero to battle the *Neo sapiens* under the name of a local protective deity, Casshern.

The film problematises the relationship between the self, the body and society in the age of neoliberalism. The neoliberal ideal of the divisible body comes to life in the *Neo sapiens*, creatures regrown from the amalgamated body parts harvested from the victims of ethnic cleansing, who were mercilessly slaughtered for their Neo-Cells intended to prolong the lives of the military elite. Although the *Neo sapiens* are, in fact, resurrected humans, nothing in the film suggests that their dismembered bodies simply returned to their original configuration. In this sense, the creatures are closer to Frankenstein's monster, patched together from scraps of stolen cadavers, than to Lazarus (the Frankenstein connection is also suggested by their reanimation through a bolt of lightning). Reconceptualised as a commodity, the body raises a question of its ownership. *Casshern*'s extreme scenario, with its mass-harvesting of bio-material from a selected ethnic group rebranded as 'the war on terror', warns of the power of the neoliberal State run like a commercial corporation that ultimately owns its citizens' bodies and reclaims/redistributes their body parts at will.

Scheper-Hughes has argued that transplant surgery has largely contributed to the restructuring of subjectivities under late capitalism, as it has reconfigured 'social relations between self and other, between individual and society, and among the "three bodies" – the existential lived body-self, the social, representational body, and the body political' (2000: 4). The complexity of these relations is further illustrated in the example of *Casshern*'s main protagonist, whose body changes ownership several times throughout the film. Tetsuya's body belongs to the Federation, which sends him to his death in the line of duty; after his death, his body is returned to his parents, identified as secondary owners; and through his resurrection, his body is given to the entire nation/human race as its protector. While this predominantly collective orientation may be seen as derivative of Confucianism, the Confucian collective body is certainly not a collection of exchangeable parts, and Tetsuya's supernatural/technological upgrade makes him exactly that. The problematic multiple identification of Tetsuya as human/cyborg/god-Casshern may be seen as a remnant of postmodern flexible subjectivity, but it may also be an illustration of the neoliberal health ideal – a potentially immortal life-form put together through a combination of science and magic, with replaceable body parts and multiple personalities to choose from.

In the film, Tetsuya dies participating in the State-sanctioned massacre of the indigenous population for their bio-material. He returns to life thanks to the infusion of their Neo-Cells and the expensive military technology that builds his exoskeleton. In a sense, then, he is a direct beneficiary of the system powered by structural bio-violence. As a reanimated corpse, he may seem an unlikely champion of the human race, but then his opponents are the undead (revitalised bodies and body parts) and the unhuman (robots). The *Neo sapiens*, macabre reconfigurations of donor 'bodies without organs', are driven by the desire for revenge and intend to wipe out the entire human race, seeing that it has become inseparable from the monstrous economic processes that govern it. In this they differ from the ghosts of the Chinese donors who pursue individual wrongdoers, or characters such as Ling or Marlon, who channel their grudge against the system that failed them onto its select representatives. But their appearance in the narrative adds the possibility of an alternative ending to an otherwise depressing story of abuse and exploitation, and can be seen as a strategy of resistance.

Cinematic narratives of organ trade and harvesting have the power to work for change. They tell stories inspired by field research and media reports, and warn potential victims to stay alert at all times. By directing international attention towards the issue, they compel governments to change laws, or properly to implement the existing ones. They give a voice to those who have suffered and had their suffering silenced. Organ trade may have flourished under neoliberal globalisation, but structural bio-violence is predominantly used on a local or regional level. Asian ghosts and manga-inspired cyborg-warriors are appropriately local and iconic to become the symbols of much needed change.

Conclusion

Global neoliberalism is responsible for the commercialisation of medicine, inciting desire for the biological material of others, and designating economically disadvantaged populations as donor zones. As such it is often depicted as monstrous. Although discussions of the global organ trade tend to focus on the exploitation of 'third world bodies' for the benefit of western recipients, this neocolonial pattern of bio-material extraction also works to the advantage of wealthy Asian countries. Asian films have been quick to pick up on this, depicting local organ flows within Asia, and identifying donor and recipient countries, as well as the 'countries of procedure' where the operations take place. Unsurprisingly, these zones mirror the recognised economic centres and peripheries within East, Southeast and South Asia, with Japan, South Korea, Hong Kong and Taiwan identified as buyer-countries and India, Pakistan, Bangladesh, the Philippines, Myanmar and Cambodia as seller-countries. China and Thailand are often mentioned as the countries where organs can be bought but also as countries of procedure, as they offer access both to advanced medical facilities with trained personnel and to a large impoverished population desperate enough to sell their body parts.

Despite their varying genres, all the discussed films share the same concern: that as the traditional hierarchies in Asian societies get reinforced by the widening gap between wealth and poverty, the victimisation and dehumanisation of the poor become excessive. Commercialised hospitals and lack of affordable insurance coverage – a standard in both rich and poor Asian countries – effectively deny a large part of the population access to healthcare, forcing people to deal with the black market and underground, unlicensed clinics. This stimulates a growth of criminal enterprise and facilitates the abuse of the vulnerable. As the systematic acts of bio-violence are justified by the neoliberal State, which thrives on bio-power, the weak resort to weaving organ theft narratives as their strategy of resistance. All the films analysed in this chapter can be seen as an extension of this strategy, and the message they deliver is clear: while organ replacements can be bought at a price, our humanity cannot be saved through transplantation. Until countermeasures are introduced to prevent the escalation of State-sanctioned bio-violence, we will probably see more examples of neoliberal medical gothic, and the dismembered dispossessed will continue to return.

Notes

1 In 2007, Yosuke Shimazono estimated that between 5 and 10 per cent of kidney transplants worldwide were performed through organ trade (Shimazono, 2007).

2 In 2008, Karen Hudson estimated that a kidney can be bought from a donor at between 1,000 and 3,000 USD and sold at 40,000 USD (Hudson, 2008).

3 The latest policy announcement was made in December 2014, promising that 'Starting from January 1, China will end its reliance on the organs of executed prisoners for transplantation' (Hosenball and Park, 2015).

References

Aronowitz, Alexis A. 2013. 'Trafficking of human beings for the purpose of organ removal: Are (international) legal instruments effective measures to eradicate the practice?'. *Groningen Journal of International Law* 1(2): 73–90.

Budiani-Saberi, D. A. and F. L. Delmonico. 2008. 'Organ trafficking and transplant tourism: A commentary on the global realities'. *American Journal of Transplantation* 8(5): 925–9.

Brunvand, Jan Harold. 2002. *Encyclopedia of Urban Legends*. New York: Norton.

Cohen, Lawrence. 1999. 'Where it hurts: Indian material for an ethics of organ transplantation'. *Daedalus*, 128(4): 135–65.

Davidson, Michael. 2008. *Concerto for the Left Hand: Disability and the Defamiliar Body*. Ann Arbor: University of Michigan Press, 197–221.

Farmer, Paul. 1996. 'On suffering and structural violence: A view from below'. *Daedalus* 125(1): 261–83.

Foucault, Michel. 1990 [1976]. *The History of Sexuality*. Vol. I. Trans. Robert Hurley. New York: Vintage Books.

Garden, Rebecca and Hyon Joo Yoo Murphree. 2007. 'Class and ethnicity in the global market for organs: The case of Korean cinema'. *Journal of Medical Humanities* 28(4): 213–29.

Moniruzzaman, Monir. 2012. '"Living cadavers" in Bangladesh: Bioviolence in the human organ bazaar'. *Medical Anthropology Quarterly* 26(1): 69–91.

Scheper-Hughes, Nancy. 2000. 'The global traffic in human organs'. *Current Anthropology* 41(2): 1–59.

Scheper-Hughes, Nancy. 2002. 'The ends of the body: Commodity fetishism and the global traffic in organs'. *SAIS Review* 22(1): 61–80.

Scheper-Hughes, Nancy. 2004. 'Parts unknown: Undercover ethnography of the organs-trafficking underworld'. *Ethnography* 5: 29–73.

Treasure, Tom. 2007. 'The Falun Gong, organ transplantation, the Holocaust and ourselves'. *Journal of the Royal Society of Medicine* 100: 119–21.

Internet sources

Anon. 2014.'Organ Trafficking Prices and Kidney Sales'. *Havocscope*, 6 July. www.havocscope.com/black-market-prices/organs-kidneys/.

Blacker, Sarah. 2007. 'Corporeal capital: Theorizing the division of body parts under global capitalism'. *Politics and Culture* 2. http://politicsandculture.org/2009/10/02/sarah-blacker-corporeal-capital-theorizing-the-division-of-body-parts-under-global-capitalism/.

Cook, Michael. 2011. 'Black market organ trade uncovered in Japan'. *BioEdge*, 25 June. www.bioedge.org/index.php/bioethics/bioethics_article/black_market_organ_trade_uncovered_in_japan.

Coonan, Clifford and David McNeill. 2006. 'Japan's rich buy organs from executed Chinese prisoners'. *Independent*, 21 March. www.independent.co.uk/news/world/asia/japans-rich-buy-organs-from-executed-chinese-prisoners-470719.html.

Ewart, Chris. 2010. 'Kidneys to go: Dis-ordering the body in a pretty dirty economy'. *Shift: Queen's Journal of Visual and Material Culture* 3: 1–20. http://shiftjournal.org/wp-content/uploads/2014/11/ewart.pdf.

Fan, Jiayang. 2014. 'Can China stop organ trafficking?'. *New Yorker*, 10 January. www.newyorker.com/news/news-desk/can-china-stop-organ-trafficking.

Fernquest, Jon. 2014. 'Cambodia–Thai kidney trafficking: Fears of new organ market'. *Bangkok Post*, 27 October. www.bangkokpost.com/learning/learning-from-news/439887/cambodia-thai-kidney-trafficking-fears-of-new-organ-market.

Gutmann, Ethan. 2014. 'Ethan Gutmann responds to allegations from Taiwan'. International Coalition to End Organ Pillaging in China. http://ethan-gutmann.com/ethan-gutmann-responds-to-allegations-from-taiwan/.

Hosenball, Alex and Cho Park. 2015. 'China's new year's resolution: No more harvesting executed prisoners' organs'. *ABC News*, 1 January. http://abcnews.go.com/International/chinas-years-resolution-harvesting-executed-prisoners-organs/story?id=27947524.

Hsiao, Alison. 2013. 'Stop using illicit Chinese organ transplants: Experts'. *Taipei Times*, 28 February. www.taipeitimes.com/News/taiwan/archives/2013/02/28/2003555919.

Hudson, Karen A. 2008. 'Globalization and the black market organ trade: When even a kidney can't pay the bills'. *Disability Studies Quarterly* 28(4). http://dsq-psds.org/article/view/143/143.

McDonald, Mark. 2009. 'Report of "organ tourism" stirs new Japan–China controversy'. *The New York Times*, 7 November. www.nytimes.com/2009/02/17/world/asia/17iht-organs.1.20242560.html?_r=0.

Office to Monitor and Combat Trafficking in Persons. 2014. '2014 trafficking in persons report'. www.state.gov/j/tip/rls/tiprpt/countries/2014/226832.htm.

Reuters. 2007. 'Rising trade in human organs is alarming: IOM'. 7 June. www.reuters.com/article/2007/06/07/us-crime-trafficking-philippines-idUSMAN28233220070607.

Rithdee, Kong. 2008. 'Bangkok fest removes "Children"'. *Variety*, 19 September. http://variety.com/2008/film/news/bangkok-fest-removes-children-1117992548/.

Shimazono, Yosuke. 2007. 'The state of the international organ trade: A provisional picture based on integration of available information'. *Bulletin of the World Health Organization* 85(12): 955–62. www.who.int/bulletin/volumes/85/12/06-039370.pdf.

Su Rong and Sun Bai. 2014. 'Taiwan says "no" to importing organs for transplant from China'. *Minghui*, 26 December. http://en.minghui.org/html/articles/2014/12/26/147465p.html.

Filmography

The Ambulance. 1990. Dir. Larry Cohen. Epic Productions/Esparza/Katz Productions.

Casshern. 2004. Dir. Kazuaki Kiriya. Casshern Film Partners/Tatsunoko Productions/ Shochiku.

Children of the Dark (*Yami no kodomo-tachi*). 2008. Dir. Junji Sakamoto. Geneon Entertainment/Sedic.

Coma. 1978. Dir. Michael Crichton. MGM.

Declaration of Geneva. 2013. Dir. Wu Derrick. Production company uncredited.

Dirty Pretty Things. 2002. Dir. Stephen Frears. BBC Films/Celador Films.

Graceland. 2012. Dir. Ron Morales. Imprint Pictures.

The Island. 2005. Dir. Michael Bay. DreamWorks/Warner Brothers.

Koma (*Jiu ming*). 2005. Dir Chi-Leung Law. Camera Media/Filmiko Entertainment.

The Man from Nowhere (*Ajeossi*). 2010. Dir. Jeong-beom Lee. Cinema Service/Opus

Repo Men. 2010. Dir. Miguel Sapochnik. Universal Pictures/Relativity Media.

Society. 1989. Dir. Brian Yuzna. Society Productions Inc./Wild Street Pictures.

Sympathy for Mr Vengeance (*Boksuneun naui geot*). 2002. Dir. Chan-wook Park. CJ Entertainment/Studio Box.

Pictures/United Pictures.

Traffickers (*Gong-mo-ja-deul*). 2012. Dir. Hong-seon Kim. Che Um/Zio Entertainment/ Asian Palm Film.

Turistas. 2006. Dir. John Stockwell. Fox Atomic, Stone Village Pictures.

5

Linnie Blake

Catastrophic events and queer northern villages: zombie pharmacology *In the Flesh*

Dominic Mitchell's BAFTA award-winning three-part series *In the Flesh* was first broadcast on BBC3 in March 2013, with a second six-part series following in May 2014. Focusing on the return of the rehabilitated zombie Kieran Walker to his village in the rain-swept north of England, the series proffers a distinctively British take on the globally ubiquitous popular-cultural trope of zombie apocalypse. For unlike dramas such as *The Walking Dead* (AMC, 2010–), which focuses on a group of vastly outnumbered survivors subsisting in the ruins of an infrastructurally devastated nation, Mitchell's undead are the minority, who have been pharmacologically returned to sentient consciousness and, at the drama's opening, are in the process of being reintegrated into their communities. As the traumatised living struggle to adjust to an unsettling new world in which 'the Risen' not only walk but also work and socialise amongst them (enacting their fear in prejudicial words and deeds), the Risen wrestle with their own traumatic memories, pariahs in the communities they once terrorised. Both groups are afraid, not least of the matrix of bio-power that now encompasses all aspects of contemporary life – from government, the law, law enforcement, the military and the media to the living, working and leisure practices of individual subjects, both the living and the Risen being insistently interpellated by neoliberal ideology. In his depiction of a village in the north of England in the months following the emergence of the dead from their graves, Mitchell undertakes therefore a sustained interrogation of the networks of power that characterise our own neoliberal UK, here exemplified by the biotech industry on whose commercialised products the new social order rests. In so doing, he voices significant concerns regarding national inequalities in the United Kingdom of the present, specifically the legislative dehumanisation of entire swathes of the population at the hands of welfare reform and policies relating to immigration and asylum, the ongoing privatisation of the NHS, regionally differential cutbacks to public services, and the mainstream media's promotion of a governmentally sponsored politics of hate. In this, I argue, the series participates in the contemporary mass-cultural deployment of the zombie as a means of exposing and exploring the impact of neoliberal economics on the social and cultural organisation of the world and, in turn, the models of subjectivity available to its inhabitants.

Set in the fictional Lancashire village of Roarton, *In the Flesh* looks back to 'the Rising', when those who died in the year 2009 rose from their graves to consume the brains of the living.[1] Reflecting both the swingeing cutbacks enforced on the communities of the poorer north by the Coalition Government, and indeed the historic underresourcing of rural areas, the inhabitants of Roarton had received no governmental assistance in fighting off the undead.[2] So, in an ironic reference to David Cameron's now abandoned 'Big Society' initiative, they banded together to do the work of the State, forming an armed militia called the Human Volunteer Force (HVF) that protected the villagers from the local Risen. At the opening of the series, the village has clearly survived the onslaught and remains a proud, independent and quite freakishly insular place.[3] With public understanding of recent events mediated by Vicar Oddie's hellfire fundamentalism, which proclaims the Risen 'agents of Satan' (1.3), the community now lives in fear of all that lies beyond its bounds. In the belief that leaving the valley is to 'take your life in your hands', Roartonians affirm that 'you'll pay the price if you go gallivanting' (2.1), not least because foreigners are said to 'do their business in a hole' (2.1). Huddled against the elements and with their backs to the outside world, the villagers thus proclaim themselves 'proud to be rotter-free', socialise predominantly at the Royal British Legion social club and decry the 'lying bastard Government' (1.1) at every turn.[4] In the second series they even put up a fence to ensure that any straggling brain-eaters stay out. Even with the series' Victus Party championing the rights of the living at a national level and exerting a phenomenal degree of control over local policies and practices, the Roartonians are, by their very nature, isolationist. Theirs is Fortress Roarton, the fence evoking contemporary British efforts to stem mass migration to the country, even in the face of humanitarian crisis beyond our borders.

For all its zombie apocalypticism, then, Roarton is a world very like our own: the resistance of the living to the influx of rehabilitated undead being pointedly reminiscent of the immigration hysteria that has gripped the public imagination in the UK over the course of the past five years or so, as rising food and energy prices, high unemployment and wholesale governmental attacks on the welfare state have seen a significant fall in the standard of living for the majority, with the most defenceless members of society, such as the unemployed and the disabled, suffering most at the hands of both Government and media alike.[5] The rise of the Victus Party thus echoes *both* the success of the well-funded, right-wing, anti-EU and anti-immigration party UKIP in the local government elections of 2014 *and* the growing popularity, at street level, of unashamedly racist organisations such as Britain First and the English Defence League. Troublingly, it also evokes the contemporary administration, Victus deploying an election slogan familiar to Britons from the Conservative election campaign of 2010. Here a smiling white nuclear family is captioned with the words 'I've never voted Victus before but their policy against … integration will make us safe.'[6] For just as Victus abhor the Risen and justify socially divisive policies through an insistence on their dangerous alterity, our own Conservative Party (which won only 16 per cent of the ethnic minority vote in 2010) has been widely criticised for its own inherent racism, frequently justified as a necessary response to the threat of Islamic terrorism within and without the island (Heath and Khan, 2012). The Home Office's 'Go Home' campaign of 2013 (comprising vans driven about the streets of London enjoining illegal immigrants to return whence they came) was widely seen to typify attitudes to ethnic and cultural difference that have led the party's sole black peer to affirm that 'racism is endemic in the Tory Party' (anon., 2014). Clearly, Mitchell's UK is no more hate-filled than our own, and its leadership no less sectarian.

But although the central locale of the series is Roarton, other locations are narratologically and symbolically significant – specifically the derelict and boarded-up Greater Manchester (the blighted post-Rising estates of the series having been filmed in contemporary Salford) and the military camp in Norfolk where the pharmaceuticals company Halperin and Weston conducts experiments on the undead. Delightfully named for the director and writer of the 1932 classic *White Zombie*, Victor Halperin and John Weston are entrepreneurial pharmacologists who have formulated the regenerative drug Neurotriptyline.[7] When injected into the spines of the Risen, it brings about a return of consciousness; a restoration of speech and memory; and, in turn, a restored sense of individuated selfhood. In an act of governmentally sponsored nominative determinism[8] designed to allay public fears and facilitate the reintegration of the undead into their communities, moreover, the Risen are even renamed – becoming 'Partially Deceased Syndrome [PDS] sufferers'. Thus pathologised, they find themselves within a new post-Rising matrix of discursive power that combines the might of the State and the invasive inventiveness of emergent biotechnologies to position them as British-born but somehow less than human. They are taught how to perform their new identities, being reminded repeatedly that they are not responsible for anything they did in their 'untreated state' (1.1) and are not to blame for having risen from the dead in the first place. Under armed guard, they are re-educated – learning to intone 'I am a PDS sufferer, and that is not my fault' (2.1). They remain, however, entirely dependent on the drug company's ongoing provision of Neurotriptyline for their continued functionality and, in turn, their very personhood as it is recognised by the State.

In this, *In the Flesh* explores the ways in which neoliberal societies position the body as the central object of bio-power – becoming a complex field on which are written the economic and political imperatives of the present as they impact upon our conceptualisation of life itself. In their 'untreated state', for example, the Risen may be 'someone's family' (2.3) but they cannot be thought of as persons. They have no self-control, no capacity to reason and no stability as subjects. Being unable to consent to their treatment, they therefore have it imposed upon them in the interests of the public good. Once treated with Neurotriptyline, however, they come to possess once more their intelligence, reason, reflection, self-consciousness, speech and the ability to value their own life – all foundational characteristics of personhood as the philosopher John Locke defined it (Locke, 1690). Personhood, in Mitchell's world, is thus contingent on access to the commercialised products of a profit-driven health industry. The same is true in ours – the National Health Service having been so progressively marketised by the Coalition Government that it has effectively passed into private hands (Chand, 2014), with profitable areas being opened to tender whilst 'Cinderella services' such as mental health languish, underfunded by Government and unattractive to private healthcare providers driven purely by the profit motive (British Medical Association, 2014). So just as the

Risen of *In the Flesh* have their personhood defined by their access to Neurotriptyline, our own world disavows the personhood of those to whom it denies appropriate medical services and pharmacological supplies.[9] One is reminded of Big Pharma's insistent refusal to develop appropriate antimalarial drugs because of the poverty of the target market, and the death of 25 million people from AIDS, the vast majority of these in countries too poor to afford the cost of anti-retroviral treatments (Petryna and Kleinman, 2006: 1). Roarton may boast of its independence from government, but it is interpellated and indeed penetrated at every turn by the matrix of bio-power that circumscribes the globe.

Mitchell's pharmacological solution to the complex emergency of the walking dead echoes, of course, neoliberalism's securitisation of the biological sphere. Led by the United States, where George W. Bush undertook a strategic investment in 'biodefense' as a means of revivifying an ailing biotech sector, securitisation is a quintessentially neoliberal move. On the one hand, it allows for a disinvestment in public health – whether that takes the form of a local under-resourcing of Cinderalla services or a global commitment to prevent, treat and eradicate disease through bodies such as the World Health Organization. On the other, it enables a disingenuous insistence that the mass investment of public funds in the products of private pharmacology is vital to our survival as a species. In Mitchell's world as in our own, the Keynesian consensus that disease could be globally eradicated through quarantine, vaccination and treatment has been replaced by a model of illness as a permanent and immanent hazard that can only be tackled by purchasing, at market price, the wares of the drugs companies and accepting, at face value, the claims they make for their efficacy. The year 2009, when the Rising occurred, exemplifies the paradigm. It was then, in our own world, that the World Health Organization declared swine flu (a strain of the H1N1 virus responsible for the decimation of world populations in the years following the First World War) to be a global pandemic, resulting in billions of pounds of public expenditure on the antiviral drug Tamiflu®, despite the fact that its manufacturers had sponsored all trials assessing its value and had consequently suppressed the evidence that it was entirely ineffective in reducing the spread or severity of the illness.[10] Like the Rising, swine flu was an apocalypse that never happened, but in both cases public funds were channelled in their billions into the coffers of the corporations as the mass media hysterically propounded that Big Pharma would save us all.[11] Assuming the role of deliverer from the global threat of disease, privatised global pharmacology has thus attained the capacity to alter 'both the meaning and function of other public institutions such as states' (Petryna and Kleinman, 2006: 21) and, in turn, to redefine what it means to be a person by predicating personhood on the ability to access Big Pharma's products. Mitchell's depiction of the zombie pandemic is a powerful allegory of this real-world scenario.

Certainly, Mitchell's depiction of the biotech company Halperin and Weston is characterised by a highly gothic suspicion of science as a hubristic endeavour inimical to the interests of humanity. In this he echoes the concerns of texts such as Mary Shelley's *Frankenstein* (1818) and H. G. Wells' *The Island of Dr Moreau* (1896). Mitchell's is, though, an insistently contemporary vision that links the activities of the 'mad scientist' with the insanity of the post-9/11 world to explore the ways in which bioscience has come to impact on identity formation in the neo-liberal age. Being the site to which those liminal subjectivities deemed a threat to the public good are rendered, the Norfolk rehabilitation camp clearly evokes Guantánamo Bay. In Norfolk, as in Guantánamo, individuals are subject to acts of torture that are deemed necessary in the interest of national security and considered acceptable because the victim's personhood has been disavowed.[12] This is exemplified by Simon, one of the original test subjects for Neurotriptyline and the first to respond positively to its regenerative properties. Having withdrawn his consent to torturous 'treatment', and having had his wishes ignored, Simon is progressively radicalised – hearing the voice of the Undead Prophet as he lies shot through with electricity and mutilated by surgical instruments. Such imagery underscores the assertions of Amnesty International's General Secretary, Salil Shetty, that 'since the so-called war against terrorism, the use of torture, particularly in the United States and their sphere of influence ... has got so much more normalized as part of national security expectations', generating in turn increasing incidences of 'justifiable torture' scenarios in contemporary popular culture (Agence France-Presse, 2014). Simon's human rights, like those of torture victims across the globe, have been denied not simply in the interests of national security (which is bad enough) but in the interests of corporate profitability. In Mitchell's world, as in our own, the two are inextricably entwined.[13]

The Risen thus come to experience many of the infringements of civil liberties to which the neoliberal self is subject. They are rounded up in their 'untreated state' both by the military and by outsourced sub-contractors and are detained in camps. They are subject to experiments that resemble torture and on release have their right to freedom of movement revoked by the confiscation of their passports. They are told where to live and are prevented from choosing their occupation, being debarred from returning to their previous professions.[14] As such, their situation echoes that of those seeking asylum in the UK, who may be kept for an unlimited period in prison-like conditions and whose treatment has been described by the human rights lawyer and Labour peer Baroness Helena Kennedy as 'a source of profound shame' to the nation.[15] In a Series 2 initiative, moreover, the Risen are forced to work in any capacity the State decrees whilst wearing orange tabards emblazoned with the words 'I'm PDS and I'm Giving Back', this evoking the 'Community Payback' vests worn in the UK by those subject to Community Service orders following conviction for crimes that do not warrant a custodial sentence. More troublingly, such outfits further evoke the workfare programmes of the Coalition Government, which force benefits claimants to work unpaid in both the public and private sectors on a range of privately administrated schemes.[16] Such is the nature of freedom in the age of the so-called free market, where the putative security of the State is seen as justificatory of gross infringements of human rights whilst the welfare of human beings consistently comes a poor second to corporate profitability. It was not Victus, we note, but the contemporary Conservative Party that proposed withdrawal from the European Convention on Human Rights as a means of curbing the appeal rights of some 70,000 immigrants and asylum seekers who face deportation from the UK every year.[17]

Unsurprisingly, the Risen dissent. The voice of the Undead Prophet, a quasi-supernatural anti-establishment visionary is heard by Simon as he lies strapped to a gurney being shot through with electricity in the interests of corporate science. 'They are lying to you', says the Prophet, 'don't trust them' (2.5). In time, the Risen will recognise that the PDS label is nothing more than an invention of the 'vile pulse-beating scum' (2.6) that persecute them, proclaiming themselves instead to be both 'chosen ... redeemed' (2.1) and standing at the vanguard of a Second Rising when the dead will inherit the earth. Following the all-out war between the living and the dead in the year of the Rising and the uneasy peace that is depicted in the series, a further clash seems inevitable. On one side are the living, whose lack of acceptance of the new world order is underscored by their ongoing use of the terms 'rotter', 'rabid' and 'deadun'. On the other are the Risen, whose difference is underscored by the rather-too-orange-to-be-flesh-coloured mousse they are instructed to wear to disguise the pallid mottling of their skin, and the Government-issued contact lenses that hide the fractured whiteness of their eyes. For, like the use of the term 'PDS', both make-up and contacts position the Risen as a new kind of quintessentially neoliberal subjectivity, defined by both pharmacology and strategies of statist control. In time, of course, they will create their own organisation to protect them from the hostilities of the living – the Undead Liberation Army (ULA) – proffering an intriguing illustration of the ways in which the disenfranchised may be radicalised to acts of violence by those who speak to their disempowered condition. Pledging allegiance to the Undead Prophet (whose grainy videos and scriptural proclamations echo those of online jihadists), they enact their rejection of the living's heterodoxies by consuming two drugs of their own. The first is a self-made chemical that functions like Neurotriptyline but returns no profits to the corporation, and the second is Blue Oblivion. This challenges the pharmaceutical industry's control over undead subjectivity by temporarily blocking the effect of Neurotriptyline and precipitating a temporary reversion to a brain-eating state. In stepping outside pharmaceutical definitions of their selfhood and in repudiating the language in which that selfhood is couched they seek a kind of authenticity that in itself challenges the matrix of bio-power through hideous acts of indiscriminate slaughter.

The ULA have a significant membership in the derelict and boarded-up city in which the second season opens with a Blue Oblivion-fuelled massacre on a tram. Self-consciously echoing the London suicide bombings of 7 July 2005, when four British Muslims killed 52 people and injured over 700 on the London Transport network, the massacre illustrates how socially marginalised and media-persecuted groups may opt to become the monsters that society believes them to be.[18] And just as Muslim community leaders in our world unequivocally repudiate all terrorist activities as un-Islamic, so do Mitchell's assimilationist 'undead organisations' set about 'distancing themselves from ... extremist factions' (2.1) such as the ULA. In both worlds, of course, the fear of radicalisation provides a ready justification for a retrenchment of highly regressive conceptions of national identity and a concomitant curtailment of the civil liberties of those who are deemed 'other' to the national 'self'. As the Victus MP Maxine Martin puts it, 'You'd be amazed at what I can do to your sort ... and what you can do sod all about' (2.1). Roarton too is replete with sectarian imagery. For just as the very term 'the Rising' is drawn from the Irish Republican struggle against British colonial rule, so is Roarton's HVF, with its berets and graveside gun salutes, highly evocative of Ulster during the years of the so-called Troubles. Then, Nationalist and Republican paramilitaries of predominantly Catholic descent (such as the Irish Republican Army) and Protestant Unionist paramilitaries (such as the Ulster Defence Association) contested Ulster's national status through acts of extreme violence both on the island of Ireland and in the United Kingdom.[19] The same kind of contestation is visible here, the heroic status of the HVF in Roarton echoing the increasing valorisation of the military in British culture in recent years. Here, the centenary of the outbreak of the First World War has been greeted not with a period of mourning for the deaths of 37 million people, but as a noble, inspiring and entirely justifiable national effort. Established in the year of the series' Rising, moreover, National Armed Forces Day aims to increase public support for the forces by running hundreds of events nationally, many offering a fun day out for all the family. As the Government seeks to embed support for the military within our civilian institutions, Territorial Army reservists are encouraged to wear their uniforms to their workplaces (Uniform to Work Day) and on visits to schools (Camo Day). This is assiduously reinforced by the promotion of a 'military ethos' in said schools and the production of the 'Armed Forces Community Covenant' and 'Corporate Covenant', whereby local authorities and major businesses sign up to support the armed forces and encourage recruitment to their ranks. Meanwhile, the actualities of combat coupled with a withdrawal of funds from welfare provision mean that 12 per cent of the nation's homeless are veterans, many struggling with addiction and mental health issues that underfunded 'Cinderella services' simply cannot address.[20] This is echoed in the series' highly sympathetic depiction of Kieran's sister Jem, a teenage HVF hero who finds it near impossible to return to any kind of normality following the restoration of order, her emotional turmoil manifesting in nightmares, flashbacks and alcohol abuse. In the conflict of the living and the Risen, the divisions that lie at the heart of the United Kingdom are manifested in the damaged lives and broken psyches of the survivors. It is a situation exacerbated by a moribund economy and a politics of austerity that pits interest groups against each other whilst demonising the weakest members of society. Notably, in both Mitchell's world and in our own, nationalist signs and symbols proliferate as a means of imparting the illusion of social cohesion whilst justifying economic expansion through military means.

In Melinda Cooper's words, 'Neoliberalism and the biotech industry share a common ambition to overcome the ecological and economic limits to growth associated with the end of industrial production, through a speculative reinvention of the future (Cooper, 2008: 13). For whilst classic economic models once invested in the present in order to generate a profit at some point yet to come, neoliberalism affirms the 'purely speculative existence of a future profit' as true and, 'investing in the after-life of a life that has not yet been lived', views the present merely as 'the past of production' (Cooper, 2002: 96). Such an overweening focus on an envisioned future is dangerously absurd, as the collapse of so-called futures markets in 2008 attests. And *In the Flesh* interrogates this model of futurity through an insistent textual queering of the paradigm. Roarton is, after all, an avowedly heteronormative society. It enforces its customs, practices and values through the social exclusion of those who fail to conform. It transmits them to the next generation by having children and raising them to think and act in a particular manner. In Roarton, as in our own world, the nuclear family is the pre-eminent institution for the transmission of such values, but the church, the school and social spaces such the Royal British Legion social club play a role, as does the media – Mitchell's television, radio and press all being seen consistently to reinforce the dominant ideologies of the post-Rising world order. Thus the solidarity of the Roarton community is bolstered by ritualised cultural practices that range from the marching and shooting of the HVF, to the bunting-festooned village fete, to the ancient English practice of 'beating the bounds' that quite literally reaffirms the separation of those of 'us' who live within and those 'others' who live quite literally beyond the pale. In attaching the privilege of membership to those whose behaviours and relationships validate the norm, and in stigmatising, marginalising or harming those who do not, the community therefore beats the bounds of regional selfhood. But as the conflict that breaks out on the day of the village fete between villagers-wielding-sharp-implements and the ULA-supporting-undead illustrates, the Rising has rather queered the pitch.

The controversial work of the queer theorist Lee Edelman is significant in this context. Asserting that 'queer can never define an identity, it can only ever disturb one' (Edelman, 2004: 17), Edelman affirms the Freudian death drive as 'the negativity opposed to every form of social viability' (9). Thus, he argues, the political sphere insistently opposes the death drive by proffering a 'fantasy of a viable future' (11) through a celebration of the figure of the child. For Edelman, queerness ruptures

the reproductive futurism of heternonormativity and, as such, proffers a challenge to politics itself. In embracing the negativity ascribed
to queer by heteronormative cultures, in aligning queerness with the
death drive, Edelman argues against the possibility of a queer politics per se in a manner that resonates strongly with the queerness of
Dominic Mitchell's text. For throughout *In the Flesh*, the protagonist
Kieran Walker's homosexuality is inseparable from his Risen status.
For Kieran was always 'different', marked out by his artistic aspirations,
his desire to escape the confines of Roarton and his relationship with
the hyper-masculine Rick Macy. It was this 'difference' that led him
to kill himself in 2009 when Rick was killed in Afghanistan, having
joined the army in the belief that Kieran was leaving town for college.
Thus, both Kieran and Rick rise again, the former to feast on brains
in the local supermarket, the latter to roam the Afghani countryside
before being caught, drugged, re-educated, slathered with mousse and
returned home. Masquerading as living, though fooling nobody, Rick
will ultimately be killed by his homophobic and rotter-hating father
when he 'comes out' as PDS. In the second series, Kieran will enter into
another relationship, this time with Simon, who significantly killed his
own mother in his 'untreated state'. This conceptual alignment of being
Risen and being gay is fabulously realised in a tortuously embarrass-
ing Sunday lunch with Kieran's family when Kieran 'comes out' as an
undead cannibal to his father, who has somehow convinced himself
that his son had avoided feasting on human brains. In a room decorated
with masks, Kieran removes his own – in much the same way as he
removes the Government-issued cosmetic mousse in several significant
scenes across the series. 'I rose from the dead', he says, 'and then I ripped
people apart' (2.4). Only Kieran's father is surprised. His mother has
always known of his queerness, as does his sister, having witnessed him
feeding on brains in a significant scene in the local supermarket that
opens the series in flashback and returns on two subsequent occasions
(1.1, 1.3, 2.1). It is only when Kieran takes public ownership of the terrible things he did during the Rising (when his very subjectivity was
defined by the death drive) that he liberates himself from his past and
begins to live in the now. In Kieran's words, it is only if we 'stop pre-
tending' (2.4) that a meaningful present can be born. And this present
is of significantly greater value than a speculated future we can never
inhabit. For Kieran's future does not shape up as he imagines, and he
reverts, albeit temporarily, to his brain-eating state, having been forced
to consume Blue Oblivion by HVF sergeant Gary. Gary too is a man

who needs to make peace with his past, the Rising having consumed the best years of his life and left him feeling untethered to the contemporary world. For Kieran, at least, the ability to heal appears to lie in an authentic acceptance of self and a personal assumption of responsibility for one's actions. Notably, it is the hideous sight of Kieran in his 'untreated state' that enables his father to set aside his habitual emotional repression and affirm his love for his son: 'no matter who you are' (2.6). His statement effectively puts an end to the standoff between the living and the Risen on the day of the village fete and enables Kieran to remain voluntarily in Roarton.

As for the future, that remains unknown. In time, Kieran's friend Amy Dyer will be restored to full biological functionality, her heart beating briefly before she is shockingly murdered by the Victus MP Maxine Martin, buried and later disinterred and returned to Norfolk for further experimentation by Halperin and Weston's polyester-clad middle management. The heteronormative community of Roarton may wish, therefore, to cast off the Risen in the same way as it disavows those men it catches having sex with undead prostitutes – Amy teasing the guilty Philip that he faces 'some sort of lynching or socio-ostracism' (2.4) for his transgressive sexual activities – but its future has been irreparably altered by their presence. The only named child in the narrative is notably dead – Danny, the young brother of the Victus MP Maxine Martin, lying long-buried in the churchyard and failing, like other denizens of the non-emergent Second Rising, to live again. The living may seek to lay claim to the future in the face of the undead's ostensible and illusory immortality but the Rising has changed everything. In embracing their own abjection and affirming their undead personhood, the Risen will bring forth a hitherto unimaginable future. For just as the term 'PDS sufferer' proffers an attempt at resignifying the more negative 'rotter' or 'deadun', so does the very existence of the Risen proffer a resignification of the human, the family, the social and indeed the temporal. The terms 'living' and 'dead' are no longer binaristically opposed but are mutually constitutive in Mitchell's narrative. It is a highly gothic paradigm that forces, I would argue, a significant reconsideration of what it means to be human at all.

As I have argued elsewhere, the metaphor of the zombie apocalypse enacts and embodies a range of contemporary fears that relate specifically to the ideological machinations, material workings and socio-cultural ramifications of neoliberal economics. For like the 'civil strife, ethnic violence, guerrilla rebellions, and *coups d'états*' that have

come to characterise the neoliberal age, the eruption of the undead
from their graves is a 'non-normalizable event or complex emergency'
that tears through 'the fabric of social and biological reproduction
(Cooper, 2008: 64). In our neoliberal world, which 'legitimates a ruthless Social Darwinism in which particular individuals and groups are
considered simply redundant, disposable' (Giroux, 2011: 2), the figure
of the risen undead allows therefore for a visceral reconsideration of
neoliberal ideology that 'posits capitalism as the only viable system for
social organization and geopolitical relations as well as for economic
exchange' and renders even the biologically living 'zombies, or zombie-
like' (Webb and Byrnand, 2008: 9). In the pharmacologically penetrated bodies and ideologically interpellated selfhoods of Mitchell's
Risen, then, we witness a pronouncedly gothic exploration of the ways
in which neoliberal economics challenge the personhood of the citizen and, in so doing, deprive him or her of fundamental human rights.
Indicted here are the economic changes of the past thirty years and
their more pressing incarnations in the domestic and foreign policies of
the UK's Coalition Government. Here too is an affectionate yet broadly
satirical evocation of the rural communities of the north of England,
depicted in a manner that evokes the socially critical British film and
television drama of an earlier age.[21] And yet, *In the Flesh* remains a
highly gothic entity – its undead protagonists shifting between life and
death in entirely new ways, its narrative marked by dreams, visions and
flashbacks that take us far beyond the concerns of a Ken Loach or an
Alan Bleasdale. In its deployment of mad science, its depiction of the
dungeons of Big Pharma's contemporary torture-house and the bleak
wildness of the rain-lashed northern moors, in its broken urban estates
and hellfire-preaching villages, *In the Flesh* undertakes a highly gothic
queering of neoliberal England, interrogating both the contemporary
state of the nation and the rights, responsibilities and subjectivity of
us all.

Notes

1 It is a significant year, of course. For in 2009, the leaders of the twenty most economically powerful nations met not once but twice in response to the global
   financial crisis of the previous year and, far from retreating from the neoliberal
   consensus, assumed even greater control over world economies. As the economist
   David Kotz has argued (2009), the financial crisis of 2008 may have begun with
   the collapse in mortgage-related securities in the United States that led, in turn, to
   the collapse of the US and in turn the global financial system. But this was coupled

with a global recession in the non-financial sector characterised by a fall in output and employment. For Kotz, 'the crisis was not therefore an isolated incident but a systemic crisis of a particular form of capitalism, namely neoliberal capitalism' (1).

2 Hilary Benn, the Shadow Communities Secretary, illustrated in 2014 how public spending cuts for poorer councils, many of them in the north, are up to sixteen times higher than those levied on the more affluent Conservative-voting councils of the south. See Sparrow (2014).

3 Propounded, in neoliberal mode, as a counter to a State that had become too big and too bureaucratic, the Big Society initiative purported to link the work of families; neighbours; and community organisations, from churches and charities to libraries, schools and hospitals, in the provision of services that had, hitherto, been centrally funded and administered by the State. By 2014 it had disappeared from the Conservative agenda as the party fought off the threat from UKIP on the right. See Helm (2014).

4 Parallels could be drawn here between Mitchell's Roarton and the small towns of the Southern Gothic tradition of the United States, replete with dark secrets from the past, sexual perversity, highly idiosyncratic characters and low Protestantism, tinged with a superstitious fear of strangers and propensity for violent retribution.

5 Recent changes, by the Conservative–Liberal Democrat Coalition Government, to the ways in which benefits are assessed and paid have had a marked impact on social welfare in the United Kingdom. These include the introduction of Universal Credit, which combines six means-tested benefits into a single payment, capping the amount in benefits that working-age people can receive; cutting benefits for social housing tenants with spare bedrooms; and capping rises to most working-age benefits and tax credits at 1 per cent, instead of increasing them in line with inflation. As Nicholas Watt has reported (2014), this led twenty-seven Anglican bishops and sixteen other clergy to condemn publicly the culture of 'hardship and hunger' such measures had caused.

6 In a popular social-media counter-campaign on *knowyourmeme* that came to be known as 'airbrushed for change', such posters were subject to merciless satire. This ranged from a simple reaffirmation of the popular perception of the Conservatives as 'the nasty party' ('I've never voted Tory before but Cameron said he'd kill the puppy if I didn't') to accurate predictions of the cost of a Conservative election victory ('I've never voted Tory before but I believe in halting the economic recovery', and 'I've never voted Tory before but losing my job and house looks like fun').

7 The name of the drug echoes, of course, that of Amitriptyline, a tricyclic antidepressant that is now commonly prescribed (as to the author) to tackle neurological pain.

8 See Butler (1997) for an exploration of such naming practices.

9 Writing on the day the Health and Social Care Act came into force, the doctor, journalist and writer Max Pemberton affirmed in the *Telegraph* that 'the NHS's strengths – resources, expertise and the united focus on the patient – are being replaced by a fragmented and atomised service, bound not by a duty of care but by a contract and driven, not by what is best for the patient, but by the cost of the encounter' (Pemberton, 2013).

10 By 2009, the British Government had already spent £473 million of public funds on the drug Tamiflu®. See Gallagher (2014).

11 As the Tamiflu® debacle attests, moreover, the drug companies' motives have little to do with the public health – flawed clinical trials, the suppression of unfavourable results, poor regulation, the invention of diseases purely for profit, inflated marketing budgets and the unethical incentivisation of healthcare professionals having become so commonplace as to undermine the credibility of the entire industry (Goldacre, 2012).

12 Asking whether 'such insufferable policies such as the indefinite detention of people, sometimes without charge, [can] be tolerated [by] countries that entertain such notions as habeas corpus and the need for a fair trial?', Binoy Kampmark's 2014 article for the Centre for Research on Globalization explores the status of Guantánamo as 'a reminder that indefinite detention is a species of population control that is here to stay'.

13 As Lucia Ortiz has illustrated (2014), as instances of human rights violations by transnational corporations escalated, the UN Human Rights Council in Geneva voted in June 2014 to start passing legally binding international legislation that holds not individuals but corporations responsible. It is notable that both the United States and the United Kingdom opposed the resolution.

14 Echoing David Cameron's disingenuous affirmation at the 2013 Conservative Party Conference that the National Health Service was 'safe in our hands', whilst reinforcing fears voiced by the right-wing press that doctors qualified overseas pose a danger to patients, Mitchell had a Victus Party campaign poster proclaim 'The government wants to let PDS sufferers carry on with their previous professions. Would you trust them?' – this over a picture of a heavily moussed and decidedly sinister man in white coat and stethoscope.

15 Baroness Kennedy was commenting on the report produced for Women for Refugee Women: Girma *et al.* (2014). See Morrison (2014). As Andy Keefe, Director of National Clinical Services, Freedom from Torture has commented, on the Anglican Community News site, the Home Office's decision to retain the 'breadline level of support' of £36 a week for a single asylum seeker means that they are condemned to 'a continuing day-to-day struggle with destitution … [without] enough money to eat three times a day, or to buy toiletries or over the counter medicines, or do laundry, or catch a bus or phone a friend' (2014).

16 At the time of writing, a number of schemes exist: Mandatory Work Activity, the Work Programme and the Community Action Programme. Targeting different groups of unemployed people, each demands that individuals must work for benefits or risk being 'sanctioned' and losing them. The programmes have been challenged on grounds of both effectiveness and rights – private companies profiting from the free labour of individuals who have no right to withdraw that labour without economic sanction. The ensuing controversy has resulted in several big-name employers withdrawing from the schemes.

17 Travis (2014). It is notable, writing from the perspective of 2015, that these attempts failed because of the activities of Conservative peers in the House of Lords, indignant that the postwar human rights legacy of their hero Winston Churchill would be obliterated should such legislation go through.

18 For parallels to Muslim youth see Briggs and Birdwell (2009).

19 Between the late 1960s and late 1990s, this conflict terrorised communities and reinforced a rigid adherence to sectarian models of identity whilst killing some three-and-a-half thousand people. See Rogers (2010).

20 In 2014 the website of the charity Help4HomelessVeterans explained: 'They are on the streets because of a variety of factors, PTSD or post traumatic stress disorder is one. Adjusting to civilian life is also very difficult as the structure they once knew has now gone. These people have served queen and country for what? Having left the army suffering from PTSD and coped with it by abusing alcohol, many ending up homeless living on the streets of Britain'. Notably, a recent update of the site has removed all such contentious information.
21 I am thinking of films such as *Kes* (dir. Ken Loach, 1969), and television programmes such as *Cathy Come Home* (dir. Ken Loach, 1966) and *The Boys from the Blackstuff* (dir. Alan Bleasdale, 1982).

References

Agence France-Presse. 2014. 'Torture spreading as "glorified" by TV series like 24: Amnesty'. 13 May. www.thejakartaglobe.com/international/torture-spreading-glorified-television-series-like-24-amnesty-intl/.

Anglican Community News Service. 2014. 'UK anti-torture charity: "Home Office decision will mean asylum seekers struggle"'. 14 August. www.anglicannews.org/news/2014/08/uk-anti-torture-charity-home-office-decision-will-mean-asylum-seekers-struggle.aspx.

Anon. 2014. 'Racism row hits Tory leadership battle'. *Daily Mail*, 27 August. www.daily-mail.co.uk/news/article-69970/Racism-row-hits-Tory-leadership-battle.html.

Briggs, Rachel and Jonathan Birdwell. 2009. 'Radicalisation among Muslims in the UK'. Brighton: MICROCON (Micro-level Analysis of Conflict) Policy Working Paper 7. www.microconflict.eu/publications/PWP7_RB_JB.pdf.

Butler, Judith. 1997. *Excitable Speech: A Politics of the Performative*. New York and London: Routledge.

Chand, Kailash. 2014. 'Privatisation is ripping the NHS from our hands'. *Guardian*, 6 August. www.theguardian.com/healthcare-network/2014/aug/06/privatisation-ripping-nhs-from-our-hands.

Chomsky, Noam. 1999. *Profit over People: Neoliberalism and Global Order*. New York: Seven Stories.

Cooper, Melinda. 2002. 'The living and the dead: Variations on *De anima*'. *Angelaki: Journal of the Theoretical Humanities* 7(3): 81–102.

Cooper, Melinda. 2008. *Life as Surplus: Biotechnology and Capitalism in the Neoliberal Era*. Seattle: University of Washington Press.

British Medical Association. 2014. 'Doctors warn on "Cinderella" mental health service'. 5 March. www.bma.org.uk/news/2014/march/doctors-warn-on-cinderella-mental-health-service.

Edelman, Lee. 2004. *No Future: Queer Theory and the Death Drive*. Durham, NC and London: Duke University Press.

Gallagher, James. 2014. 'Tamiflu: Millions wasted on flu drug'. BBC News, 10 April. www.bbc.co.uk/news/health-26954482.

Girma, Marchu, Sophie Radice, Natasha Tsangarides and Natasha Walter. 2014. 'Women asylum seekers locked up in the UK: Detained'. http://refugeewomen.com/wp-content/uploads/2014/01/WRWDetained.pdf.

Giroux, Henry A. 2011. *Zombie Politics and Culture in the Age of Casino Capitalism*. London: Peter Lang.

Goldacre, Ben. 2012. *Bad Pharma: How Drug Companies Mislead Doctors and Harm Patients*. London: Fourth Estate.

Grey, Alexander. 2011. 'Airbrushed for change'. http://knowyourmeme.com/memes/airbrushed-for-change.

Heath, Anthony and Omar Khan. 2012. 'Ethnic minority British election study: Key findings'. Runnymede Trust. www.runnymedetrust.org/uploads/EMBES briefingFINALx.pdf.

Helm, David. 2014. 'David Cameron "has devalued the big society idea" says his former adviser'. *Observer*, 4 January. www.theguardian.com/politics/2014/jan/05/tories-cameron-big-society-danny-kruger.

Kampmark, Binoy. 'Indefinite detention without charge: Habeas corpus and the continuing role of the Guantánamo Bay Prison'. www.globalresearch.ca/indefinite-detention-without-charge-habeas-corpus-and-the-continuing-role-of-the-guantanamo-bay-prison/5399777.

Klein, Naomi. 2007. *The Shock Doctrine*. London: Penguin.

Kotz, David M. 2009. 'The financial and economic crisis of 2008: A systemic crisis of neoliberal capitalism'. *Radical Political Economics* 41(3): 305–17.

Locke, John. 1690. 'Of identity and diversity'. In *An Essay Concerning Human Understanding*. Ed. Jim Manis. The Electronic Classics Series. Hazleton, PA: Pennsylvania State University, 311–33. www2.hn.psu.edu/faculty/jmanis/locke/humanund.pdf.

McNally, David. 2011. *Monsters of the Market: Zombies, Vampires and Global Capitalism*. Leiden: Brill.

Morrison, Sarah. 2014. 'Handling of female asylum seekers "puts UK to shame"'. *Independent*, 29 January. www.independent.co.uk/news/uk/home-news/handling-of-female-asylum-seekers-puts-uk-to-shame-9091856.html.

Ortiz, Lucia. 2014. 'UN to outlaw corporations' human rights abuses'. *Ecologist*, 1 July. www.theecologist.org/News/news_analysis/2459002/un_to_outlaw_corporations human rights_abuses.html.

Pemberton, Max. 2013. 'NHS reforms: From today the Coalition has put the NHS up for grabs. Health cutbacks endangering public health'. *Telegraph*, 1 April. www.telegraph.co.uk/health/healthnews/9962195/NHS-reforms-From-today-the-Coalition-has-put-the-NHS-up-for-grabs.html.

Petryna, Adriana and Arthur Kleinman. 2006. 'The pharmaceutical nexus'. In Adriana Petryna, Andrew Lakoff and Arthur Kleinman, eds, *Global Pharmaceuticals: Ethics, Markets, Practices*. Durham, NC and London: Duke University Press: 1–33.

Quiggan, John. 2010. *Zombie Economics; or, How Dead Ideas Still Walk Amongst Us*. Princeton: Princeton University Press.

Rogers, Simon. 2010. 'Deaths in the Northern Ireland conflict since 1969'. *Guardian*, 10 June. www.theguardian.com/news/datablog/2010/jun/10/deaths-in-northern-ireland-conflict-data.

Sparrow, Andrew. 2014. 'Councils in poorest areas suffering biggest budget cuts, Labour says'. 25 August. www.theguardian.com/society/2014/aug/25/councils-poorest-areas-biggest-cuts-labour-says.

Travis, Alan. 2014. 'Conservatives promise to scrap Human Rights Act after next election'. *Guardian*, 30 September. www.theguardian.com/law/2013/sep/30/conservitives-scrap-human-rights-act.

Watt, Nicholas. 2014. 'Bishops blame Cameron for food bank crisis'. *Guardian*, 20 February. www.theguardian.com/politics/2014/feb/20/bishops-blame-cameron-food-bank-crisis.

Webb, Jen and Sam Byrnand. 2008. 'Some kind of virus: The zombie as body and as trope'. *Body & Society* 14: 83–98. http://bod.sagepub.com.ezproxy.mmu.ac.uk/content/14/2/83.

6

Rebecca Duncan

Gothic vulnerability: affect and ethics in fiction from neoliberal South Africa

Gothic as it is being written in postmillennial South Africa is a particularly engaged, particularly politically aware form of fiction-making. The monstrous, the horrifying and the weird – hallmarks of gothic narrative – are being mobilised in the post-apartheid culture of letters as one literary means through which to negotiate dissonant relationships with the neocolonial operation of neoliberal capital. Each of these terms will be examined in more detail in the pages that follow. For now, it suffices to say that the extent to which post-apartheid South Africa has embraced free-market economics has, in the wake of the nation's shift to democracy in 1994, not worked by and large to produce the social transformations necessary to undo the divided socio-economic geographies cultivated under old, racist regimes. Instead, the enthusiasm for neoliberal policy-making has, as in other postcolonial contexts, participated in the perpetuation of historic inequalities. Henrietta Rose-Innes' *Nineveh* (2011), which forms the textual focus here, is one gothic narrative from neoliberal South Africa invested in horror as a possible form of thinking through resistance to the stratifying processes of capital. It is in the conjuring of fearful, affective images of the body that the novel looks to realise this potential. The text presents the human entity not simply as an enclosed, quantifiable organism, but as an open, flexible agglomeration of the self and its conventional others, and this more diffuse body is shown to resist economic processes of capture through which people are assigned values as commodities and consumers. This location of dissenting potential in the body as a changeable web of multitudinous connections emphasises the extent to which the disruption of neoliberal power configurations begins from a sense of the world that is cognisant not simply of the broad lineaments of oppression, but also of the smaller, less discernible back-and-forth interactions these belie. It is from just such a vision, significantly, that the text also implies we might begin to derive an ethical mode of being under neoliberal conditions. In so far as gothic seeks to occasion intense, sensory engagements with its readers and audiences, to the extent that it positions these as vulnerable or *affectable*, fictions of this kind might offer us a means by which to begin a rerouting of the dehumanising principles of self-gain on which the logic of neoliberal capital is founded.

Post-apartheid South Africa, neoliberalism and the neocolonial operation of global capital

Writing of South Africa's transition out of official apartheid and into an age shaped by the principles of inclusive, representative democracy, Neil Lazarus notes that 'the single most striking feature of the African National Congress's performance in power over the course of the last several years is the about-turn that it has enacted in its macroeconomic policy' (2004: 612). The country's ruling party, still at the governmental helm in the second decade of the new millennium, negotiated its accession to leadership via a series of economic amendments to the social democratic agenda that had informed its manifesto throughout the long years of resistance, and that would serve to bring the 'new' South Africa into a position amenable to the flows of global capital. This, critics such as Lazarus have noted, has largely worked to undermine the egalitarian vision that was the African National Congress' polestar in the time of struggle. 'If one looks closely at the demographic distribution of wealth and privilege in South Africa now', Shaun Irlam remarks, 'it would be difficult to decipher any significant change'. 'The society remains deeply divided racially', he goes on, 'and the gulf between rich and poor gapes ever wider' (2004: 696, 697). Segregations cultivated under the apartheid State linger on, in other words, having been reforged in the democratic present as economic inequalities proliferating in the wake of an enthusiasm for the neoliberal programme.

This David Harvey defines in terms of a fundamental emphasis on the rights of the individual, and on an extension and intensification of the privatising capitalist impulse to accrue profit:

> Neoliberalism is in the first instance a theory of economic practices that proposes human well-being can best be advanced by liberating individual entrepreneurial freedoms within an institutional framework characterized by strong private property rights, free markets and free trade. The role of the state is to create and preserve an institutional framework appropriate to such practices. (Harvey, 2005: 2)

This is achieved largely through a curtailing of public institutions. In a bid to facilitate the free flow of capital, neoliberal governments are geared towards the erecting of 'those ... structures and functions required to ... guarantee, by force if necessary, the proper functioning of markets' (2). As a result, they are distinguishable by '[d]eregulation, privatization and the withdrawal of the state from many areas of social provision' (3). Neoliberal policy advocates a surrendering, to the greatest possible extent, of responsibilities to do with labour conditions, with basic resources and with healthcare. These become, not matters of state, but of enterprise: wages are determined by markets in order to maximise surplus value, access to infrastructure is subject to purchase, and recourse to medical care and education becomes equally contingent on individual financial solvency. The result of all of this is a maximisation of the opportunities for private accumulation, a never-ending extension of the market into new areas, including those previously circumscribed by state control. These are some of the means, then, through which the neoliberal administration seeks to realise its sense of 'human well-being' as a corollary of the liberty to pursue profit; it opens the way at every turn to the possibility of individual gain.

At the same time, however, the equation of personal freedom with the freedom to accrue wealth also generates conditions of heightened vulnerability. It results, Harvey points out, in the State's 'determination to transfer all responsibility for well-being back to the individual': 'As the state withdraws from welfare provision', he writes, 'it leaves larger and larger segments of the population exposed to impoverishment' (76). The neoliberal emphasis on the individual thus works to facilitate circumstances of *mass* deprivation. It potentiates the creation of dramatic and wide-scale divisions between the manner in which those with means exist and the conditions under which those without are driven to live their lives. 'Neoliberalization ... has succeeded remarkably well in restoring ... the power of an economic elite' (19), Harvey observes, an action he later discusses as 'the momentous shift towards greater social inequality' (26). Even as it theoretically opens up possibilities for great personal gain, then, the neoliberal dispensation also works to configure one instance of what Gilles Deleuze and Félix Guattari term the 'great molar aggregate' (Deleuze and Guattari, 2005: 195), a massive, uniform organisation (at least superficially) determined along 'well defined, segmented line[s]' of difference (217). Neoliberal policy does not simply have purchase at the level of the individual; it also shapes, in powerful ways, the broader contours of society. It carves out uneven geographies characterised by sharp material divisions, by just that widening chasm between rich and poor of which Irlam writes with reference to South Africa. Unable to afford access to progressively privatised resources, the latter are left in conditions of increasing desperation, becoming ever more vulnerable to exploitation at the hand of deregulated enterprise, which in turn profits from an increasingly malleable labour force.

Thus, the economic gulf widens and the post-apartheid nation, as a postcolony, is by no means alone in this plight. It is precisely neo-liberalism's stratifying potential that has given rise in diverse fields of postcolonial studies to the notion of the *neocolonial*, a term used to designate 'the continuing economic control by the West of the once-colonized world' (Boehmer, 2005: 9). In post-imperial contexts – and post-apartheid South Africa among them – poverty is a historically cultivated condition. The post-independence failure of the neoliberal State to alleviate deprivation in any decisive way is thus experienced as consistent with an extension of the material conditions of domination. Old oppressions are kept alive through the operation of new economic administrations; 'in a world order powered by multinational companies', Elleke Boehmer writes, 'colonialism is not a thing of the past' (2005: 10).

The production of 'dividuals': Neocolonial capital and the commoditisation of life

Significantly, the divisive action of capital extends, for Deleuze and Guattari, beyond the level of mass formations such as 'rich' and 'poor' to have purchase, too, on the bodies from which these larger categories are constituted. In their bid to accrue profit ever more efficiently, neocolonial, neoliberal economies seek to mark out and define isolated human entities as potential resources or as target markets – as commodities or consumers – in a way that shapes the individual itself as a molar entity, an enclosed, quantifiable mass of matter organised in relation to the aggregate to which it is ascribed as belonging: 'Not only are the great molar aggregates segmented (States, institutions, classes) but so are people as elements of an aggregate ... they are segmented ... to ensure the control of the identity of each agency, including personal identity (Deleuze and Guattari, 2005 [1987]: 195).

Capital's bid to render individuals as clearly definable molar entities is cast here as an exercise in control. Classifications of life within the market economy exert a force of capture, working to impose sharply demarcated lines of difference and definition not simply on a grand demographic scale, but also at a more intimate level that pertains to the identities of independent bodies. In his 'Postscript on the societies of control', Deleuze conceptualises this process of simultaneous isolation and massing together as one through which 'dividuals' are generated. Under conditions of late capital, he argues, '[w]e no longer find ourselves dealing with a mass/individual pair. Individuals become "dividuals".' They are 'samples, data, markets, or *banks*' (Deleuze, 1992: 5 (emphasis in original)); their worth is determined according to those economic criteria that also shape clearly defined mass demographics. Patricia T. Clough reiterates this thought in a way that emphasises the extent to which capital's manufacturing of dividuals produces imposed segmentations among isolated human elements of the wider aggregate. '[C]apital accumulation', she writes, 'is seeking at a deeper level to measure ... the human body and "life itself" ... such that equivalencies might be found to value one form of life against another' (Clough, 2010: 221). Dividuals, as definable, molar elements in the aggregate, are thus subject to imposed relationships of difference that allow them to be separated out from other single entities within the wider configuration, *and* they are determined according to their place in this broad category. All of this, significantly, has a bearing on postcolonial contexts. If it is the processes of the market economy that reanimate the broad conditions of segregation that obtained under the imperial – or the apartheid – administration, then they do so via just these processes, drawing lines among racialised economic classes *and* among the individuals from which these are made up. Historically charged divisions between mass categories of rich and poor in postcolonial societies are – because they arise through the operation of capital – bound up with more intimate insistences on the isolation and segmentation of life, which is quantified and captured to serve the ends of profit. Neocolonialism is thus a process through which dividuals are generated; great neocolonial molar aggregates – economic hierarchies inscribed over older cultural and racial hierarchies – belie and depend on the treatment of individual bodies as molar, as enclosed wholes that might be cleanly divided from each other, defined and thus controlled.

Writing of the neocolonial operation of global capital, Boehmer emphasises the extent to which its reinscription of the divides that characterised the imperial programme necessitates, with no small degree of urgency, the continuation of engagements from fields of post-colonial studies (Boehmer, 2005: 10). This critical territory she out-lines in terms of an active disruption of the mechanisms of (ongoing) colonial domination: 'Postcolonial', she writes, 'is generally defined as that which critically or subversively scrutinizes the colonial relation-ship' (3). In the neocolonial context such resistances might consist in engagements with the dividualising action of neoliberal capital. An alternative to the vision of bodies as molar might, in other words, pro-vide a point from which to begin to formulate strategies of postcolonial dissent, modes of thinking that go some of the way towards a disrup-tion of the logic of neocolonial capital control.

Monstrosity and 'becoming': beyond the molar body in the gothic text

It is at this point that gothic becomes particularly salient. Fictions of this kind present us with one imaginative means through which to access a sense of the body not as a cleanly defined unit, but as a more diffuse entity, one that might be resistant to the molarising action of dividualisation. This potential shifts into especially sharp focus if we consider the extent to which, since its inception, gothic has evinced a deep suspicion of boundary-driven thought. While the gothic aes-thetic has witnessed various changes throughout its two-century-long history, the destabilising strategy underpinning such fictions has per-sisted, and it is this that opens gothic in the millennial moment – as in earlier periods – to the possibility of dissonant, even resistant, appropriation. Indeed, gothic has always been sensitive to the condi-tions under which structure of the status quo might break down. In its eighteenth-century iterations, as Fred Botting argues, gothic figures of unease 'reflect the anxieties of a culture defining itself in diametri-cally opposed terms' (2012: 14). Enlightenment Britain, the context within which the first gothic novels emerged, was in profound ways a culture characterised by a sense of its own modernity – an identity that, as Botting suggests, rests on the postulation of a temporal break, on the setting up of a boundary between the civilised rationalism of the 'now' and the savagery of a primitive past. This distinction is registered in early gothic texts, which, from Walpole to Radcliffe, are populated by menacing figures who loom – or so it seems – from the shadows of a barbarous, medieval history. Gothic is thus witness to that which is conceived as threatening to a particular social configuration; its avatars of monstrosity are shaped by a sense of what has been rejected or overcome in order for more civilised forms of cultural identity to cohere. At the same time, however, as the antiquated lexicon of these narratives is imprinted by an impulse to establish a dividing line between the order of the present and the perceived violence of the past, gothic fictions of the eighteenth century – and beyond – also admit of less clearly discernible fears. There is a sense, as Robert Miles – for one – has pointed out, in which eighteenth-century figures of medieval unease attest to anxieties that come, not from the annals of a history that has been surmounted, but from the heart of the moment in which gothic texts are produced (Miles, 2002: 55).[1] Clear here, then, is a sense in which, since their earliest iterations, figures of gothic unease have been constructed according to self-conscious and culturally specific discourses of threat; their eighteenth-century medievalism remains testament, after all, to enlightenment modernity's deliberate break with an apparently violent past. At the same time and more incipiently, however, gothic narratives also reveal that what is conceived of as dramatically other does not assail from some external zone beyond the contemporary social fold, but rather inheres in it, emerging covertly at its core.

This programme, which simultaneously registers impulses to distance and reveals these in arrest, constitutes, for Botting, the prevailing dynamic of gothic production (1996: 4). Even as they reflect attempts to draw a line between past and present – which is fundamentally a line between self and Other – gothic fictions and their images of the intolerable also always undermine that division. Figures of emphatic otherness give way to ambiguity; they throw the binary into crisis, insisting that, in all its iterations, the logic of opposition is at best precarious. This destabilising strategy, which begins with the early gothic, is persistently evident throughout the history of the mode. Frankenstein's monster, Dracula, Bertha Rochester, Mr Hyde, Dorian Gray: these nineteenth-century gothic icons conflate various permutations of the self–Other opposition (science and alchemy, human and beast, familiar and foreign, male and female, good and evil), and this confounding action is discernible, too, in diverse gothic offerings over the last hundred years, which, into the twenty-first century, continue to dismantle the polarities through which we habitually construct our cultural worlds.[2]

It is this simultaneous witnessing and dissolving of clearly defined, oppositional relationships that has opened gothic to appropriations, both critical and literary, within fields of postcolonial thought. To the extent that fictions of this kind dramatise the disintegration of imposed and politicised paradigms of otherness, they might participate in that programme of scrutinisation in which, Boehmer has suggested, the postcolonial consists. Hybrid gothic forms might, in other words, be mobilised to contest the implementation of segregating colonial and neocolonial power; they might work to trouble imperialist codings of the world, gesturing to a less clearly segmented reality in which binaric discourses of race and culture cannot obtain. Various critics have explored this potential; there exists a growing body of scholarship dedicated to the postcolonial possibilities of the gothic text. Notable in particular for its foregrounding of gothic's transgressive dynamic is Tabish Khair's *The Gothic, Postcolonialism and Otherness* (2009), in which he points to the mode's characteristic emotive excesses – its tendency to perforate limiting boundaries – as a means through which to gesture to a world where colonially inflected oppressions lose their purchase: one, he writes, 'in which all of us can claim ... I am an*other*' (Khair, 2009: 4 (emphasis in original)).

While there is clearly value for the postcolonial programme in this conception of gothic as a discourse in which polarised categories fall in on one another, such a reading does not exhaust its potential as a dissonant fictional mode. Recent critical engagements with ambivalent figures of gothic unease have begun to view the boundary-resistant characteristics of monstrosity in terms that emphasise not the violation of classifying lines, but a sense of accretive, fluid identity-formation that is not constrained by the apparently monadic nature of the material body, and less by the normative requirements of conventional moralities or rational sense. On this view, hybrid gothic figures are constructed through a dynamic and indiscriminate agglomerative process, standing as a mode of being that is realised in the unpremeditated and disorganised forging of temporary connections with elements of the organic and inorganic world. This, as Anna Powell notes, is a vision of monstrosity predicated on notions of what Deleuze and Guattari call 'becoming' (Powell, 2012: 266), a kind of processual being-in-the-world that entails, not the awkward conjoining of conventionally oppositional molar categories, but 'an exploding of ... heterogeneous series', a dissolution of the one element into others in a way that reveals each to be itself not unitary, but constituted through the confluence of multiple, smaller linkages and intersections (Deleuze and Guattari, 2005 [1987]: 10).

Deleuze and Guattari conceive of this dissolution as 'molecularisation' (196), a term that seeks to emphasise the extent to which becoming is discernible only through an attuning of the perceptual apparatuses to the microscopic. At this level there can be no circumscription or uniformity. The world is shown to be a mass of individually different, mobile particles; what have appeared to be lines are only those places in which molecules have collected more densely, and the shape of these apparent limit-zones is ceaselessly, if minutely, altered by the osmotic movements that facilitate incremental transformation, or becoming. Collections of particles constantly lose and gain components, and the trajectories of these rogue elements – their 'lines of flight' (202) – chart connections across molar segregations, revealing the body as a set of relations that modulate as it moves through its world. 'Such entities are not fixed, but in perpetual motion', Powell confirms, 'maintaining transformative potential as they become' (2012: 268).

Salient here is the extent to which monstrous iterations of becoming present an alternative to the vision of the body as molar on which the stratifying action of neocolonial capital depends. If, as Clough has written (2010), neoliberal dispensations treat of the bodies existing in their purviews as fleshy units of measurable matter, and if this action works in postcolonial contexts to extend the experience of oppressive imperial hierarchies, then gothic as a mode in which these lines are dissolved into relations might begin to provide us imaginative access to a kind of dissent. Molecular visions of the monstrous body enable encounters with alternatives to the grid-world of neocolonial control; they show that alongside this molar universe, there exists another, more diffuse zone on which the congealing, dividualising operation of neoliberal power can have little definitive bearing.

Gothic affect: conjuring the molecular body

If gothic fictions present us with visions of the body caught in molecularising processes of becoming, then they also, significantly, explore this state of dissolution in a less representational, more immediate way. As we have seen, gothic is distinguishable, not simply for its evocations of hybridisation, but also for its indexing of the anxieties circulating within a particular historical moment. Fearful sensation is thus fundamental to the gothic text; monstrous iterations of becoming work to evoke in the reading body thrills of unease. It is Botting, again, who confirms this definitive characteristic, writing that horrifying gothic texts 'deal primarily ... in the production of extreme affects' (2010: 180). 'In its most general sense', Claire Colebrook remarks, '"affect" is what happens to us when we feel an event' (2002: xix). It designates the sensory fluctuations stimulated in the interaction of living bodies with animate and inanimate elements of the world. These are pointedly emphasised in engagements with the gothic, which seeks, as Botting suggests, to engender in its readers heightened sensational states.

Notably, for Deleuze and Guattari, affective experience is integral to their notion of the processual self. For them, sensory relations between body and world draw into focus the extent to which these exist, not chiefly in opposition to one another, but as a kind of dynamic interface. For them, '[a]ffects are becomings' (Deleuze and Guattari, 2005 [1987]: 256). They are testament to the minute, molecular shuttlings that connect us to the world beyond what Melissa Gregg and Gregory Seigworth call our 'skin-envelope' (2010: 2). Affects show us bodies as imbricated in their environments, and not separated from them, and to the extent that they are occasioned through the gothic mode, this kind of fiction might be seen to proffer lived access to a realm beyond the clasp of the molarising dispensation. Gothic, then, not only presents us with images of bodies in flux; it also works, through the emphatic sensory reactions stimulated by these monstrous figures, to highlight the extent to which the reading body itself exists as an affectable element in a molecular human-text relation. 'A book is an assemblage', Deleuze and Guattari confirm (2005 [1987]: 4); through the affective fluctuations occasioned in the experience of narrative – and amplified in the hyper-emotive gothic mode – we might come to find ourselves, not cleanly separable from the world on the page, but situated, as Gregg and Seigworth suggest, 'in the midst of *in-between-ness*' (2010: 1 (emphasis in original)). We might access a sense of ourselves, not as monadic units, but as affective agglomerations of 'intensities that pass body to body' (1), and it is from the potentiating of such momentary encounters that gothic might work to extend the resistant possibilities already inherent in its representations of monstrous becoming. Fictions of this kind might, in other words, offer an immediate experience of that body

which materially eludes the congealing, segmenting action of neocolonial, neoliberal capital.[3]

Becoming-plague: dissolving neo-apartheid molarities in Henrietta Rose-Innes' insectal South African gothic

It is precisely to a sense of the body in process that certain, politically
engaged fictions produced in South Africa have begun to turn since the
millennium. The novels of Lauren Beukes and S. L. Grey, for example,
and the films of Neil Blomkamp each draw on gothic's hybrid and affective lexicon in order both to represent and to conjure moments of dissolution and multiplicity, all of which are deployed, in one way or another,
to destabilise the segregating and apparently immoveable lattice of neoliberal power. In her 2011 novel *Nineveh*, Henrietta Rose-Innes capitalises on gothic's potential in just this way; visions of monstrosity that
treat of hybridity as molar disintegration work, in this text, to evoke a
web-world of affective imbrications and becomings, and it is from this
molecular zone, the narrative suggests, that we might begin to extrapolate strategies of resistance to neocolonial power. *Nineveh* is written in
and for a neoliberalising South Africa, a South Africa in which redis-
tribution has yet to come to any kind of definitive fruition and where
an enthusiasm for privatisation and the elusive trickle-down effect has
ensured that the poor – by and large – remain poor while only a select
few prosper, and do so overwhelmingly at the expense of the vulnerable and the destitute. Rose-Innes' characters are, variously, wealthy
business people, squatters and vagrants. The text swings between gated
Cape Town communities – leafy islands of privilege – and the fringe
spaces on which the homeless congregate and from which they are
moved on. In these last, Rose-Innes' protagonist Katya Grubbs – 'a
white woman' – tells us she 'doesn't fit' (Rose-Innes, 2011: 93): old segregations live on, the novel insists, and have been reanimated under contemporary capital. Narrative emplotment is organised by the attempts
of a high-end property developer to build a potentially incredibly profitable luxury housing complex (named 'Nineveh') on a coastal wetland,
an unstable, marshy 'urban bush' (107), dotted with the 'shackland'
of informal settlements (93). In contrast to these heterogeneous and
ramshackle impoverished collectives, Nineveh is both thoroughly ser-
viced and, as Katya puts it, 'sterile as a swabbed out surgery' (63). The
development is a static, commoditised and significantly white architectural avatar of molar power: a heavy, solid, luxurious imposition, an

'immaculate blankness', in the protagonist's own words, 'a place of such lustrous surfaces' (113).

It is, in fact, with a shoring up of this division between Nineveh and the living landscape on which it stands that the narrative is chiefly concerned. Katya is in the pest-control trade: action turns on her attempts to capture – and significantly not to exterminate – a mysterious plague of insects that, swarming destructively and unpredictably, apparently from the wetlands, has been hampering the housing estate's construction. These creatures come to emblematise the organic energy of the marshy territory, and Katya's bids to catch them – an exercise undertaken, significantly, as a job, an economic transaction – work as an especially literal metaphor for the processes of capital capture for which Nineveh's commoditised blankness also stands. In all its iterations, however, this controlling endeavour fails: the insects continue to swarm, and the fortifications of the housing estate, which seem so cleanly to mark it off from the slum-wilderness outside, prove useless as a defence. In the following lines, Katya witnesses the disintegration of the historically loaded division between architecture and environment, and describes it as a transmogrification of the estate into plague:

> Nineveh is breathing, flexing in a complex new rhythm that is alien to her: it is not the rhythm of a heartbeat, it is nothing warm-blooded … What are those things catching the light? They're moving. Swarming. Between her and the walls of Nineveh, the mud is alive. It whispers and it clicks … Things scuttle over her feet. The whole surface is alive with tiny creatures, stirring, swarming. (Rose-Innes, 2011: 173)

If previous depictions of Nineveh as sterile, silent and demarcated have evoked a controlling molar configuration – the sharp, racially and historically inflected separation of the privileged from the deprived in South Africa – then this passage, in which we begin to discern the novel's engagement with the gothic, presents us with a different vision. It shows us the housing estate as a species of hybridising, shifting monster, involved in an unsettling process of becoming: its architectural contours, no longer cold, smooth and even, are now morphing, coming 'alive' in ways that Katya describes as both 'new' and 'alien'. The swarm – a concept, significantly, to which Deleuze and Guattari themselves have recourse in their articulations of the molecular body (2005 [1987]: 241) – allows us to perceive the imposed construction anew, not as a deadening monolith, but as a moving assemblage of mud, walls and insect vitality – a teeming, if frightening, world that confounds the operation of demarcation and control.

This sense of a world of diffuse multiplicities is realised, not just in terms related to the landscape, but to the human entity as well. It is Katya's father, in fact, who eventually offers us a vivid and literalised image of the individual-becoming-swarm. Len Grubbs, it turns out, is responsible for the plague's continued invasion; he has been cultivating the beetle larvae in one of the estate's empty homes. He is thus the locus from which the disruption of Nineveh's capital-driven molarisation of the wetland proceeds, and in the novel's climactic chapter, the transformation of the architectural monolith into insectal assemblage is replicated as Katya watches the unity of her father's body literally dissolve into molecular process:

> At the wooden table sits a figure, quite still and upright. There is something wrong with his skin, his hair … A human shape, perhaps, but built of insect wings. Beetles crawl across his skin … The insects flutter off him and for a moment … she thinks they are flying away with parts of him, that those lightly grasping feet have somehow drawn away from him an outer layer of skin. (Rose-Innes, 2011: 187)

The skin envelope encasing the clearly defined, molar individual is dissolved in these lines, which also work to affirm Len's gothic figuration. Imagined as swarm, he presents us with an especially clearly rendered exploration of that molecularising potential of the monster to which Powell has drawn attention: Katya's father is, in this moment, a hybrid formation of insect and human worlds, and yet, even as he conflates categories of beetle and person, of familiar and foreign, human self and insectal other, he is also presented explicitly as a dissolving whole. He ceases to be a sharply differentiated unitary being and becomes instead a shifting collection of mobile parts, parts that fly off and come back in a way that resembles the affective vision of the body as assemblage. All of this, furthermore, is marked by gothic's characteristic frisson of unease, a reaction that, as it is conjured in the reading body, is dramatised through Katya's own panicky response ('Oh shit, Dad, shit' (187)).

It is thus with recourse to gothic imaginings of hybridity as dissolution that the unitary body is decomposed in Rose-Innes' text, and this disintegration gives rise in the narrative, significantly, to an undoing of the greater neocolonial molar aggregates of historically inflected classes of rich and poor. Following the swarming in which Len becomes plague, the boundaries of Nineveh collapse in a symbolically loaded

way: on returning to the estate after the insects have gone, Katya finds
it populated not by the wealthy for whom it was intended, but by those
who had previously lived in the informal settlements outside its walls.
This breaking open of the divisions inscribed over old racial lines by the
operation of neocolonial capital has been enabled by insistent pressure
on the molar configurations of power from a gothically realised insectal
world of dynamic molecular becomings: Len, as the narrative's clearest
example of the human caught in flexible process works to dissolve segmenting lines that exist not simply between dividualised entities, but
also between the broader demographic categorisation. His unleashing
of the insects – a swarm from which his own body is ultimately shown
to be inseparable – sets in motion a molecularising diffusion of dividing barriers that ultimately serves redistributive ends. Unable to complete construction in the wake of the damage Len has conspired to do,
the developers abandon the project and, acting as one, the community
appropriates and transforms it in a way that points up the beginnings
of an undoing of neocolonial difference. As informal occupants of the
luxury estate, after all, Nineveh's new inhabitants constitute a community that is not reducible to any clearly rendered category of rich
or poor. It is thus to the diffuse, non-unitary body that *Nineveh* attributes the potential for resistance and transformation in neoliberal South
Africa: in a world where bodies are not measurable quantities, but less
easily defined assemblages, Rose-Innes implies, the circumscribing
action of dividualisation breaks down, halting the production of wider,
historically trenchant demographic classifications that are derived from
it, and it is chiefly with recourse to gothic visions of monstrosity that
this dissenting programme is advanced in the text.

Towards gothic vulnerability: ethics and the affective encounter

Indeed, the unsettling nature of Rose-Innes' dark lexicon – in which
threatening insectal life pours forth from dank, egg-filled chambers,
in which we seem to witness the body flayed as it becomes teeming
beetle-assemblage – works to suggest that, while it is from a sense of
the body in uncapturable process that we might begin to extrapolate
resistances to the wider operation of neocolonial control, these dissenting becomings cannot be arrived at by any easy path. In one sense,
then, Rose-Innes' engagement of gothic forms might be read to imply
that change in post-apartheid South Africa will necessitate an openness

to that which might initially appear unacceptably uncomfortable. The ending to which the author subjects Katya is, in fact, testament to this. In another redistributive manoeuvre, the novel concludes with the protagonist giving up her flat to her father and to Derek, one of the vagrants on her street. Notably, her previous attitude to Cape Town's homeless has been less benign. At the beginning of the novel she meditates on her imperviousness to their condition: Never 'in all her years of living in this house', she tells us, has she 'taken anything to Derek and his friends, never really tried to speak to them, never given them more than an empty coke bottle to return for deposit' (Rose-Innes, 2011: 30).

Relinquishing her home to the vagrants, then, constitutes a dramatic change in attitude for Katya and one that is bound up with a new sense of herself gained after witnessing the diffusion of Len's body into plague: 'Even human skin', she tells us at the novel's close, 'is porous and infested, every second letting microscopic creatures in and out. Our own bodies are menageries. Short of total sterility, there is no controlling it' (207). In these lines, the protagonist imagines the body in terms that echo both those horrifying scenes of swarming transformation, and Deleuze and Guattari's vision of the affective assemblage. Katya's human menagerie is not an enclosed entity, starkly separated from the world around it, but is rather a shifting, multiple being caught in the flux of becoming; it modulates, uncontrollably, as it is affected by encounters with that which appears to lie beyond its external surface. Such a body is imbricated in the environment through which it moves. It operates in a molecular world, where, like its own skin, barriers of all kinds are not impenetrable but porous; they are seams of interface where osmotic particles, or 'tiny creatures', have collected more densely, but where these continue, as the protagonist indicates, to let elements 'in and out'. Indeed, Katya's self-imposed vagrancy signals an affirmation of this borderless territory. The relinquishing of her home constitutes a rejection of stable, enclosing parameters, and the way of life she adopts instead reiterates and emphasises this point: rather than seeking out another fixed abode, Katya makes a travelling home of her van, choosing a wandering mode of existence that entails a ceaseless traversal of the historically and economically segregated Cape Town geography. For the menagerie body, the implication here is that these divisions are not impermeable: beginning from a sense of herself as assemblage, Katya comes to navigate a world of 'overlap … where things get mixed up' (207), where molar segmentations of all kinds lose their solidity.

Once again, then, Rose-Innes suggests that transformation in post-apartheid South Africa might begin from a reconceptualisation of the human entity, one that highlights the extent to which bodies are not quantifiable units of matter, but dynamic, menagerie-like constellations inhabiting worlds of porous, permeable contact zones. At the same time, however, as Katya reiterates this potential of the assemblage body, her situation also begins to intimate a sense of unavoidable risk that is attendant on it. If her new, wandering lifestyle signals an affirmation of an unsegregated molecular geography, then it is also, as she explicitly points out, especially 'dangerous in a place like Cape Town' (205). Becomings, in which *Nineveh* has located the possibility for postcolonial change, are neither simple nor safe, the text seems to suggest. A dissolution of the differences that have given the world its molar shape, and which begins from the body in interface, might entail encounters that threaten even as they potentiate transformation. Deleuze and Guattari themselves draw attention to this difficult possibility; they write that the dispersal of unifying boundaries, and the concomitant affirmation of a world of shuttling affects, opens the way for relationships that might be empowering to a certain body, but that might also work 'to destroy that body' (Deleuze and Guattari, 2005 [1987]: 257). The human menagerie is, as Katya puts it, a 'soft' entity (Rose-Innes, 2011: 14), one vulnerable to interactions that may serve to weaken rather than to strengthen; even as its porous skin lets in innocuous particles, it might also be the conduit through which infection and parasites invade. An opening up to a world of affective connections offers the possibility of empowering transformation, then, but it also always entails a susceptibility to potential danger, even to death.

And yet, it is from this exposed condition that Rose-Innes' text begins to develop an alternative to the neoliberal logic of individual gain that underpins the action of neocolonial capital control. In her *Precarious Life* (2009), Judith Butler proposes that places of vulnerability constitute points from which an ethical mode of being might be projected. 'That we can be injured', she writes, 'that others can be injured, that we are subject to death at the whim of another, are all reasons for both fear and grief' (Butler, 2009: xii). At the same time, she suggests, the possibility of injury draws into focus the webs of interconnection that – for her as for Deleuze and Guattari – link bodies together in relationships of mutual determination. It reveals the contingency of all lives: just as 'there are others out there on whom my life depends', Butler writes, so the lives of others are subject to my actions. This realisation, she argues, might lead to ways of existing that do not reproduce violent, defensive strategies of self-preservation, but that instead work towards 'arresting cycles of violence to produce less violent outcomes' (xii). 'To be injured means that one has the chance to reflect upon injury', she writes, and thus consequently 'to start to imagine a world in which that violence might be minimized, in which an inevitable interdependency becomes acknowledged' (xii–xiii). Apprehensions of the extent to which we might be affected – to empowering or disempowering ends – offer us the opportunity to meditate on the ways in which we might affect others in turn, and, further, might prompt the development of behaviours that reduce the violent fallout of these encounters.

This is just the thought with which *Nineveh* leaves us: Katya is cast as an affectable body in a shifting molecular geography, and she is also an ethical figure in Butler's sense. Having given up her home to those whose desperation in the neocolonial context is especially acute, she participates, if only on a micro scale, actively in the minimisation of persistent economic violence. Working from a sense of herself as an especially vulnerable, porous menagerie, she reassesses her previous lack of receptivity to the dispossession of others in neoliberal South Africa, and relates to them instead in a way that seeks to redress their persistent impoverishment, thus accounting for the sense in which they – like herself – are affectable, capable of suffering. These final actions have purchase, too, on the narrative's dissenting agenda, working to disrupt the accumulative, self-serving principles that inform the neoliberal programme. Far from seeking out personal gain, Katya actively engages in a process of loss; she proceeds in a way that is not in sync with a profiteering capitalist logic, and her actions are connected, as we have seen, to a sense of herself as affectable, existing as a web of interdependencies with others.[4]

It is here, significantly, that we might, in conclusion, return to the gothicised vocabulary on which Rose-Innes has drawn throughout the novel. At the same time as the text's dark imaginings of becoming work to suggest something of the threat inherent in breaking up the molar body, they also function to instantiate just that sense of the human entity as *affectable* from which Butler's ethical mode of being is derived. Gothic, as we have seen, is a sensationally charged brand of fiction-making; in the shudders of unease engendered, for example, as we read of Len's body flayed as it becomes swarm, or in which we witness the clean lines of Nineveh dissolving into insectal mass, there consists the potential for an experience of interdependency, one in which the body is rendered vulnerable to that which plays out on the page. In their production of discomfort, then, gothic forms work to situate readers in positions not unlike the one Butler has described. We are physically changed, even injured, by the gothic text, and, as a result, such narratives offer us the opportunity to reflect on the extent to which we exist, not simply as individualised, self-sufficient bodies-in-skins, but in webbed relationships of interconnection. Through its particularly intense conjuring of sensory fluctuations, then, gothic might be deployed, not simply to represent the body as an affectable entity, but to generate a lived sense of this body, from which, Butler writes, an ethical mode of being might be pursued. Rose-Innes' gothic visions work in precisely this way. Her uneasy delineations of becoming produce experiences of an affectable assemblage-self, one that might – significantly – be resistant to capital-driven dividualisation, and that works to align readers with Katya's transformation into vulnerable menagerie. Prompted by the protagonist's own empathic response to this condition, furthermore, we ourselves might begin to account ethically for a world of interdependencies, in which we are both acted upon and have the capacity to act.

Notes

1 Miles shows that William Godwin's *Caleb Williams*, for example, deploys gothic vocabulary of medieval monstrosity in order to explore contemporary tensions that have to do with the French Revolution, and specifically with a fear that 'the mob and the state' (2002: 55) were taking root in Britain.

2 Here we might think, for example, of Henry James' ambivalent articulation of childhood innocence and Du Maurier's hybrid visions of gender, and later of Angela Carter's brutal fairytales, Stephen King's possessed psychologies and Sarah Waters' unsettling of contemporary class hierarchies.

3 If this notion of a fluid assemblage body appears to replicate the collapse of subject and object within postmodern consumer identity, as Fredric Jameson, for example, has conceived of it (1998: 52), then this is because capital partially depends on the human entity's infinite capacity for connection in order ceaselessly to market commodity objects as new and tantalising forms of selfhood. However, for Deleuze and Guattari, capital seeks not to unlock the potential for becoming, but to close this down. It imposes what they term 'axiomatics' (Deleuze and Guattari, 2005 [1987]: 436) on bodies and commodities: fixed but temporary relationships between consumers and objects, the determining lines of which work to channel connective affective flows towards certain items, and thus ultimately to correlate the ungovernable molecular body to a clearly defined, molar commodity identity. Affect retains its dissonant charge, however: because particular axiomatics are dissolved so that new ones might be imposed, the assemblage body remains integral to the

continued operation of the economy. It is in harnessing residual affective potential to forge connections that are not in sync with conventional axiomatic relations that the possibility for a resistance to capital from within its ambit might begin.

4 There is a sense here in which Katya's actions resonate with religious doctrines, and notably with Christianity's emphasis on charity and self-sacrifice. This association is problematic in the post-apartheid context, not least because the ideology of apartheid was itself deeply invested in Christian paradigms. While this uneasy consonance exists, however, Katya's actions are also distinguishable from the Christian programme to the extent that they are not undertaken as part of an organised or teleological discourse; the loss to which the protagonist subjects herself is not, in other words, a measure taken in the interest of ultimately securing greater gain (admittance to paradise, everlasting life), but is rather a spontaneous response, one that is not produced within the organising structures of predetermined morality.

References

Boehmer, Elleke. 2005. *Colonial and Postcolonial Literature: Migrant Metaphors*. Oxford: Oxford University Press.

Botting, Fred. 1996. *Gothic*. London and New York: Routledge.

Botting, Fred. 2010. 'A-ffect-less: Zombie, horror, shock'. *English Language Notes* 48(1): 177–90.

Botting, Fred. 2012. 'In gothic darkly: Heterotopia, history, culture'. In David Punter, ed., *A New Companion to Gothic Literature*. Chichester: Blackwell, 13–24.

Butler, Judith. 2009. *Precarious Life: The Power of Mourning and Violence*. London and New York: Verso.

Clough, Patricia T. 2010. 'The affective turn: Political economy, biomedia and bodies'. In Melissa Gregg and Gregory J. Seigworth, eds, *The Affect Theory Reader*. Durham, NC and London: Duke University Press, 206–25.

Colebrook, Claire. 2002. *Understanding Deleuze*. Crows Nest: Allen and Unwin.

Deleuze, Gilles. 1992. 'Postscript on the societies of control'. *October* 59: 3–7.

Deleuze, Gilles and Félix Guattari. 2005 [1987]. *A Thousand Plateaus: Capitalism and Schizophrenia*. Trans. Brian Massumi. London and Minneapolis: University of Minnesota Press.

Gregg, Melissa and Gregory J. Seigworth. 2010. 'An inventory of shimmers'. In Melissa Gregg and Gregory J. Seigworth, eds, *The Affect Theory Reader*. Durham, NC and London: Duke University Press, 1–25.

Harvey, David. 2005. *A Brief History of Neoliberalism*. Oxford: Oxford University Press.

Irlam, Shaun. 2004. 'Unravelling the rainbow: The remission of the nation in post-apartheid literature'. *South Atlantic Quarterly* 103(4): 695–718.

Jameson, Fredric. 1998. *The Cultural Turn: Selected Writings on the Postmodern*. New York and London: Verso.

Khair, Tabish. 2009. *The Gothic, Postcolonialism and Otherness: Ghosts from Elsewhere*. Basingstoke: Palgrave Macmillan.

Lazarus, Neil. 2004. 'The South African ideology: The myth of exceptionalism, the idea of resistance'. *South Atlantic Quarterly* 103(4): 607–28.

Miles, Robert. 2002. 'The 1790s: The effulgence of the gothic'. In Jerrold E. Hogle, ed., *The Cambridge Companion to Gothic Literature*. Cambridge: Cambridge University Press, 41–62.

Powell, Anna. 2012. 'Unskewered: The anti-Oedipal gothic of Patrick McGrath'. *Horror Studies* 3(2): 263–79.

Rose-Innes, Henrietta. 2011. *Nineveh*. Cape Town: Umuzi.

Part III

The gothic home and neoliberalism

7

Karen E. Macfarlane

Market value: *American Horror Story*'s housing crisis

Ain't that America
Home of the free …
Little pink houses
For you and me

John Cougar Mellencamp, 'Pink houses' (1983)

It is *unbelievably* difficult to get accurate information about a haunted house.

Jackson (1959)

No one can own this house.

(Constance, *American Horror Story*. 'Open House'. 2011)

At the heart of the American Dream, as the outward and visible sign of upward mobility and prosperity that are its most basic principles, is the house. In a recent article published on the National Public Radio website, Ari Shapiro notes that the American Dream 'suggests an underlying belief that hard work pays off and that the next generation will have a better life than the previous generation' (Shapiro, 2012). The belief in this Dream is a fundamental element of the construction of American national identity. Perhaps even more significantly, descriptions and elaborations on the concept of the Dream, as Shapiro and others note, lie in distinguishing the upward mobility of Americans from the social and economic positions of any other country or national or political system. In popular culture, the Dream is generally constructed around a single image: the family home. But with the US mortgage crisis of 2008, certainties about how achievable the terms of the American

Dream actually are began to slip away as the bottom fell out of the housing market and families lost their homes to banks and lenders. *American Horror Story* was first aired in the immediate aftermath of this real estate crisis.[1] The series' focus on the house as a monstrous trap for spirits, the upwardly mobile and unwary investors alike makes it, I argue, a commentary on the anxieties generated by the unravelling of the narrative of the American Dream. In light of the spiralling number of foreclosures and forced sales in the USA since 2008, driven largely (if not exclusively) by neoliberal policies of privatisation and deregulation, David Harvey's notion that contemporary neoliberal politics are characterised by 'accumulation by dispossession' has a truly gothic ring to it. My argument here is that the tenets of neoliberalism that focus on privatisation and on an unfettered free market have their gothic manifestation in the representation of the relationship between the house and the family in the first season of *American Horror Story*.

To read the house in *American Horror Story* is to read a web of interconnected ideological positions that the house – as concept, as construct – represents in American culture. It is a home, yes, but in the first season of the series it is also a place of business, a commodity, a relic and a trap. It represents, to draw on Harvey, the simultaneity of (dis) possession. But this series' focus is not on the conventional anxieties about the unfettered accumulation of territory through the dispossession that haunts the national narrative of the United States: that of the displaced Native population whose prior claim to land is most often represented by the synecdochal 'Indian Burial Ground' or the obvious exclusion of the always already dispossessed multi-generational poor. It is, instead, about the violent death of the American Dream itself: the loss of a clear sense of unhindered upward mobility and the sense of bourgeois economic and social stability.

If the house in 'Murder House' is the centre of the horror in the first season of *American Horror Story*, it is because that horror is not only located in the murders for which it is famous or the ghosts that haunt it. The horror comes from the house's precarious position in the American marketplace. It is a symbol of the American position in the shattered global economy. It is a sign for affluence, American history and entrepreneurial spirit. It is the stuff of 'house porn' (Stack, 2011): originally owned by 'a doctor to the stars', it has genuine Tiffany fixtures; is lovingly restored; and boasts an expensive, fully renovated kitchen. It is simultaneously the gothic house, full of secrets, transgressions and endless instabilities. And, perhaps most importantly, it is also a symbol of the empty burden that the house has become in American culture: not a 'home', not a site of remembrance (of times past) or return (for family celebrations in the present), but a bizarre object of exchange in the American economy. The Montgomery house, also known as the 'Murder House',[2] stands, in many ways, for the 'house' as a concept in American culture in the neoliberal age, in which foreclosed houses are bought and taken back and sold again and again: over and on the financially dead bodies of the previous owners.

The Montgomery house is, we learn in the final episode of the series, Vivien's dream house. In the flashback that opens the episode, Ben tries to convince Vivien that a move to Los Angeles will help to save their marriage. Showing her the real estate advertisement for the house, he says that it is one of the 'big mansions from the twenties. You always wanted a house like this' (Ep. 11). Ben is further enticed by the price of the house, which is, as Marcy tells them when they tour it, 'half the price of every other house in the neighbourhood' (Ep. 1). Ben admits that the price is 'a stretch', but the Harmons are seduced by the house and convince themselves that it is a good investment: it is, as Ben says confidently, 'worth about four times what we paid for it' (Ep. 1). The Harmons, like many other Americans who fell prey to the investment-driven rhetoric of home ownership, realise quickly that they are in a financial trap. As Ben notes, 'We are not broke. We have money. It's just tied up in this house. Once we sell it, we can take it out' (Ep. 3). But 'taking things out' of the Montgomery house is never an option in this series: people and items are seen going in but almost never (until the final episode, and with the exception of Constance) is anything or anyone taken 'out'.

The neoliberal economic policies that precipitated the mortgage crisis in the USA do not need to be rehearsed or elaborated on here. They are, as Herb Wyile has recently pointed out, 'that familiar cocktail of deregulation, privatization, reduction of taxes and diminution of social programs, emphasis on the bottom line, efficiency, competition, private property rights *et cetera* that has been the drink of choice since the 1980s' (2013: 29). The tangle of cause and effect that resulted in the mortgage crisis in the USA is an almost impenetrable labyrinth of buying and selling, and of backroom trading and financial manipulation that resulted in millions[3] of American families losing their homes to banks and other financial institutions that, in turn, failed, putting the housing market into a downward spiral from which it has yet to recover. The decidedly gothic terminology[4] in mainstream discussions of neoliberal policies is echoed in the ways in which the predatory system that fuelled the mortgage crisis and, ultimately, the economic downturn are characterised.

It is the gothic nature of the residue of neoliberal policies that shapes the horror in the first season of *American Horror Story*. The effects of those policies kill off the ideal of the American home, leaving instead only its spectre, which haunts its replacement: the real estate investment. For Dawn Keetley, the repetitions and doubling that make up the circling, entropic plot of the first season of the series are enmeshed in questions about the future of the American dream and the series' investment in uncanny pregnancy and dead children (Keetley, 2013). Similarly, Gary Hoppenstand suggests that the series depicts 'ultimately nihilistic representations of home and family in twentieth century America, where past crimes of illicit sex and passion never die, but continue to haunt the present' (2012: 2). That the global recession and the mortgage crisis in the United States reduced the American Dream to a haunted relic of its former self has become a truism in recent years. The Dream is not only haunted by the ghosts of its own white bourgeois ideals but by the exclusions upon which those ideals were built: the dispossession of Native people from their lands, the ongoing segregation and disenfranchisement of people of colour, the hypocrisy inherent in discourses of immigration and upward mobility. And it is the truism of these hauntings, the cliché, that *American Horror Story* capitalises on throughout the series: unhappy marriages, obsessive extra-marital affairs, disgruntled teenagers, strange neighbours and unattainable – or all too attainable – properties. In fact, the structure of the first season establishes this anxiety as something that has always been part of the American ethos by projecting the anxieties generated by neoliberal policies backwards into all of the representations of the historical moments and characters associated with the Montgomery house. In *American Horror Story*, the Dream has always already been shattered, its pieces have never been anything but quaint remnants in the false memory of the national myth that informs the 'entropic' (Keetley, 2013) nature of the series' gothic repetitions.

Contrary to the earnest protestations of the series' producers and actors, who characterise this series as 'An American story … of a family at a crisis point' and as 'an exploration of fear and loss … [about] about the choices we make that lure us into bad decisions and dark places versus the choices we make that keep us strong and keep us safe',[5] I have always read the first season of *American Horror Story* as a critique of the middle-class dream of an ideal family, upward mobility and the possibility of being able to live out the American Dream in twenty-first-century America. Part of this reading, I think, lies in thinking about the house itself as a trap not only for the ghosts that reside there but also for the living owners who, as a result of the persistence of depressed housing markets, are as trapped in their real estate investment as effectively and as irrevocably as the ghosts. The series uses the trope of the haunted house as a palimpsest in which attempts at achieving the Dream are played out over and over again, each attempt written over the next, with the previous attempts always present, always influencing those that succeed them. But while the 'evil' in the house manifests itself in the recognisable guise of horror (dismemberment, murder, suicide) for its early owners, the most recent residents are victims of another kind of horror. Even before their gruesome deaths, the post-2006 owners of the house are trapped within its walls. Like the ghosts of the previous owners, their plight echoes that of Eleanor in Shirley Jackson's *The Haunting of Hill House*, who feels that she is 'disappearing inch by inch into [the] house' (Jackson, 2006: 102). Chad and Patrick, and Vivien and Ben, are unable to leave: their money, as Ben notes in 'Murder House', is '*in* the house'. Until the house is sold – a gothic impossibility in the spiralling economic decline – its owners are held captive by their investment.

If the house, in the contemporary version of the American Dream, is characterised primarily as an investment and a symbol of economic success, then it is, in this sense, primarily a gesture towards the future. It is something that will provide for its owners in their old age: something to pass down to their children. The house, for Barry Curtis, embodies a 'conspiracy between the grandeur and narrative complexity of the house and the aspirations and susceptibilities of those who are attracted to it' (2008: 37). In American culture the house 'is [the] primary marker of class and [America's] central symbol of domesticity' (Bailey, 1999: 7). When the house is haunted, it reverses ideal notions of domesticity, revealing instead what Bailey calls the 'fault lines in familial relationships' (5) and the destructive nature of America's obsessive cultural investment in real estate. The haunted house becomes 'a symbol for what has gone fatally awry with the American Experiment' (9). For Curtis, the haunted house is a 'powerful metaphor for persistent themes of loss, memory, retribution and confrontation with unacknowledged and unresolved histories' (2008: 10). Curtis, like Bailey and others, notes that the representations of haunted houses in contemporary television and film are 'increasingly reminders that the forces of history and the economy ... create restless spaces whose uses and meanings are constantly being repurposed, each time displacing and marginalizing disturbed spirits' (2008: 12).

In her discussion of what she insightfully calls the 'Entropic Gothic' in *American Horror Story*, Keetley argues that the 'Gothic house has often ... contained explicit fears about the viability of the American Dream and of futurity more generally' (2013: 102). My reading of the American Dream as defunct and derelict in the series – not a dream of upward mobility but a futile striving for an unattainable stability[6] – leads to a characterisation of a breaking down or reversal of the relationship between the house and its owner. The shift to neoliberal economic policies has transformed the relationship between Americans and their houses: They are not so much 'homeowners' (with the emphasis on the concept of 'home' as a place of belonging) as they are 'property owners', and it this distinction that is at the heart of the horror in *American Horror Story*. In spite of the series' ostentatious displays of buying and selling, its emphasis on successive owners' obsessive restoration and redecoration, it is the *owners* who are owned and controlled by the house: they are not only 'house poor' after they purchase the Montgomery house, they are its captives. What haunts the Montgomery house, I would suggest, is not as simple as the actuality of the acts that were committed there or some accident of construction or location. It is possessed by the remnants of the American Dream and haunted by the spectre of the house itself, which continues to compel its owners to believe in it, to revive it, to see it not as the derelict that appears in the opening shot of the pilot episode but 'for its potential': as alluring, desirable, real. As with Moira's ghost, the house's owners and potential owners see what their desire for the Dream makes them see.

Although beautiful and well appointed, the Montgomery house is a commodity first, and a residence second ... or maybe even third. The house is up for sale, being inspected, improved, its features and values discussed for most of the series. Indeed, it is put up for sale within months (three episodes) of the Harmons moving in. The 'For Sale' sign that appears in a disproportionate number of the external shots of the house signals this explicitly. As 'house porn' (Stack, 2011) the house is an object of desire for potential buyers and the audience[7] alike. The attributes of its features are recited over and over. The cameras linger on the woodwork, on the play of light through the Tiffany glass, and caressingly follow the curve of the staircase to the expansive entryway. The focus of these expositions is less to establish the details of the setting than it is to reinforce the house's status as a commodity whose value is simultaneously constructed and reinforced through this cataloguing. In the same vein, the house is a stop on the commercial 'Eternal Darkness Tour': the object of the curious, covetous gaze of the tourists who pay to see it and hear its story, and the prized commodity for the tour's owners. In a supplemental video on the DVD of the first season the audience is invited to participate in a tour of the interior of the house (something that does not happen in the series). Stan, the tour guide, leads a group of tourists through the house, pointing out the locations of some of the characters' deaths. But Stan's tour, like the rest of the series, conflates the horror of the murders with the imperatives to renovate and restore the property when he says 'you know what is really scary about this kitchen? What it cost to renovate it!' ('Murder House: Presented …').

The house's multilayered relation to the marketplace is a significant element in its palimpsestic representation. As with its position as an investment – the notion that the house will pay for itself *and* make the owner money – the Montgomery house is further caught between the fantasy that it is a home and the imperative of its market value because it is always a place of business. For all of the owners of the Montgomery house there is no separation between their investment and their income. The house, paradoxically, must pay for itself by straddling the line between its commercial and its residential status. From Charles Montgomery's medical practice ('doctor to the stars' and illegal abortionist) through its time as a boarding house for nursing students, to Ben Harmon's psychiatric practice, the characters are dependent on the house for the income that will, presumably, pay its mortgage. For Ben and Vivien, this means that Ben cannot leave the house after they decide to sell because Ben depends on the house for his income: 'My office is here', he says, 'People see me here. Patients see me here' (Ep. 3). The horror of the family's entrapment is compounded by this undifferentiated relation between home and work: between living and professional expenses in the Harmon's finances. Ultimately, the house cannot pay for itself and so the owners pay with their lives.

In the series, the images of entrapment that shape the descriptions of the relations between the house and the ghosts are acted out in the characters and actions of its current inhabitants, as social systems break down and the Harmons are trapped not only by their investment, but by their social isolation. One of the central tenets of neoliberalism is its focus on independence and its rejection of social networks and support systems. As David Harvey argues, neoliberalism 'holds that the social good will be maximized by maximizing the reach and frequency of market transactions and seeks to bring all human action into the domain of the market' (2005: 3). This, as with the play on the economic imperatives of neoliberalism's focus on 'possession', is taken to its gothic extreme as the Harmons are increasingly removed from any external networks and are driven inexorably back into the house. In Vivien's case, she is literally forced back into the house after she has decided to leave when she goes into labour. She is denied access to her expensive obstetrician and instead placed in the nightmarish care of a gothic version of medical care in the form of the house ghosts. By the end of the series, they have no social resources except those who 'come with' the property. In 'Birth', the penultimate episode of the first season, Vivien gives birth in the house, with only the house ghosts (a doctor, a dentist and two nursing students) to aid in the delivery. The family, at this stage, has been completely isolated to the point where the electricity is cut off, the car has been destroyed by the ghosts of Troy and Bryan, and Ben's cell phone has no reception. This moment, the birth of the child, would conventionally signal an unambiguously positive futurity[8] in the conventions of the American Dream and, indeed, in most western narratives. Instead, it signals the completion of the process of the family's isolation and entrapment in the house. Ben and Vivien are dependent on the house ghosts for the (still) birth of their American Dream.

The claustrophobic, anti-social side of the neoliberal ideal is thus played out in the life and death of the family. As the season progresses, the Harmons' interactions with anyone besides the residents of the house are focused almost exclusively on commercial transactions. The first non-resident to enter the house, Leah, believes she is going to buy drugs from Violet, and the rest are either Ben's patients or people who seek to buy (or in the case of Marcy, help to sell) the house.[9] Larry Harvey's frequent visits, for example, are primarily motivated by his attempt to extort money from Ben and to assert his prior claim to the house. Luke, the security guard, is an employee, but perhaps most significantly, he represents a specific, commercial relation to the 'house in particular and to property in general. His position reinforces the sanctity of private property and the exclusion of anyone who would try to take it. The world outside the house disappears as the action in the episodes becomes increasingly insular and inward-looking, locking out every possibility for community.

The moments when the house's past is revealed follow a similar pattern: with the exception of the intrusions of the copycat murderers (Ep. 2), the historical residents of the house also limit their interactions with outsiders to those with whom they have an economic relationship. As noted earlier, contemporary anxieties generated by the effects of neoliberal economic and social policies are projected backwards into the house's history and colour the representations of the past in the series. Almost without exception, the previous owners of the house are represented as being in the throes of economic hardship. In spite of her privileged upbringing, for example, Nora Montgomery is forced to turn to brokering illegal abortions in order to maintain her standard of living (Ep. 3), and in the flashback introduction to 'Birth', Constance is shown in the living room of the house, surrounded by unpaid bills and 'past due' notices. In both cases, the change in circumstances is accompanied in these episodes by a clear connection to the house and its power. In this sense, the house swallows the families who inhabit it 'whole [like] a monster' (Jackson, 2006: 29).

As the idealised outward sign of the American Dream in mainstream narratives, the house-as-home is represented in terms of prosperity and stability. It is both a reality and a symbol: standing for a sense of material and physical security and for an idealised connection to, and fulfilment of, the imperative for material success and upward mobility that characterises the myth of American 'progress'. Crane shots of neighbourhoods with rows of spacious, identical houses and children running, biking, and playing on the streets have become standard in American television and film. And, like many of these representations, the instability of this ideal has become the standard stuff of horror and comedy alike.[10] In contrast, the Montgomery house's first appearance in the series (Ep. 1) as derelict, open to intrusion, corpse-like and associated with death reflects its role in the series. In this sense, the spectre of the house's previous (and eventual) ruin haunts – like the images of the corpses that become ghosts throughout the series – the lingering 'house porn' scenes throughout the season. Each of the ghosts appear alternately as they were at the moment of their deaths – mutilated, bloodied – and as they appeared in their prime: Vivien never looks better than she does when she is a ghost. The house's miraculous restoration is itemised by Marcy as she leads the Harmons on their tour of the property, and later by Nora when she tours the house, posing as a prospective buyer. The 'real Tiffany fixtures' (Ep. 3) imported from a studio in New York, the chestnut panelling, the 'Lois Comfort Tiffany glass'

(Ep. 6) and the details of the restoration are recited over and over like a mantra that seems to conjure the features even as it describes them. In spite of Chad and Patrick's careful restoration, however, there remain apparently 'original', 'untouched' spaces in the house: spaces such as the attic, the basement and the crawl space that contain relics of the house's former inhabitants. The attic, in particular, yields a box of photographs of the Montgomery family to Violet, and Patrick and Chad's 'Rubber Man' suit to Vivien and Ben, while Charles Montgomery's shelves and sometimes his specimen jars, and Dr Curran's dentist's chair, appear and disappear in the background of basement scenes.

As Dawn Keetley has argued, repetition is a key element in the construction of *American Horror Story*: 'all the characters become their own twin, their own clone. The characters die and persist, becoming their own undead "perfect clone, an identical copy of their formerly mortal self" (Baudrillard, 'Final Solution': 5–6)' (2013: 97). The doubling, or redoubling, of events and characters in the series, she says, marks the house as the space of 'primitive entropy, of the death drive' (102). As I have suggested here, though, the house is not only or simply a symbol for what Keetley calls 'the dream of salvation' (2013: 93). As the 'Murder House', the house in *American Horror Story* participates actively in the doublings and redoublings that Keetley describes. In this way, the house, I would argue, is, itself, a ghost: or at least ghostly, spectral. It, too, is its own clone: regenerated and reconstructed using some of its original parts and others that are copies. As the opening scene of the series asserts, it has, like the characters, been a corpse, and its appearance in subsequent episodes always carries with it the spectral repetition of those opening moments. Its features, we are repeatedly, obsessively assured, are restored, doubled, apparently returned to their former states and indistinguishable from the original. Nora, for example, is not able to tell that the Lois Comfort Glass in the hall is not the glass that was purchased to match her eyes (Ep. 6). The house's immaculate restoration is always haunted by the memory of its introductory ruin. The persistence of the house's derelict status, I would suggest, represents the true state of economic affairs in the series: a state that, like neoliberal economic policies, belies and confounds linear temporality.

The house's restoration is less about newly acquired prosperity or stable ownership than it is about a nostalgia for the possibility of a *dream* of prosperity: the illusion that the kind of prosperity that a house such as the Montgomery house represents could, in fact, exist.

As the series illustrates, however, the dream of prosperity and stability that drew the Montgomerys and Constance and others to Los Angeles was always illusory – always unattainable and idealised. The homeowner – who sees the house as a home, the sign of economic and social stability – is replaced with his/her gothic counterpart in the series: the developer. Unlike Marcy, who buys and sells existing houses, Joe Escandarian's plan is to buy the Montgomery house and tear it down in order to build affordable housing on the property. The horror of this plan for Constance and the house ghosts is the loss of a stable space to haunt. In terms of the neoliberal politics, the horror is embodied by the unscrupulous developer who will, presumably, profit from those who have lost their homes in the crisis by building the 'affordable' housing into which they will be forced to move. His predatory and undisguised desire to accumulate through dispossession is, initially, indistinguishable from the desire of a 'legitimate' buyer looking for a cheap way into the Dream. Escandarian's desire, though, is for profit rather than for access to the layered 'histories' that the house represents for Constance and, to a lesser extent, the other owners. This makes him only the most extreme, but not the only, clear manifestation of the impulses that drive the neoliberal marketplace in the series. His focus on the house as 'inventory' (Ep. 6) contrasts sharply with the house ghosts' persistent desire to be 'at home' there: to realise the Dream through and in the house.

The moment that plays out the gothic elements of this desire most effectively is the penultimate scene of the series, as the Harmon family – Ben, Vivien, Violet, their housekeeper Moira and the newborn baby – stand around a beautifully decorated Christmas tree in the picture window of the house. This moment consolidates the ideals of the American Dream: family, prosperity, a stable home. But the fact is that the series is clear that this ideal is only attainable in death.[11] The ghostly, harmonious Harmons represent an ideal of prosperity and futurity: a futurity that has been oddly enacted but also curtailed. The future that the Harmons and the baby represent is suspended: always promised but never having to be delivered. Like the introductory image of the house, this image of the Harmons telegraphs a truth about the place of the family in contemporary American culture. The image of their gruesome deaths persists even as the image of the ideal family is foregrounded in the scene. Ben, Vivien, Violet and the baby are happy because they finally fully possess the house but they are not financially enslaved by it. In their ghostly state, they are ideal because they are free of the economic tyranny that trapped them there as its living owners. Now, oddly, gothically, death and their continued presence in the house are, at last, a release from the nightmare of their mortgage crisis: an awakening into the only possible version of the reality of the Dream that can exist in the wake of the financial meltdown.

The bleak futurity that the Harmons represent is reinforced when, in the final scenes, they drive the Ramoses out of the house: dispossessing another family of their part in the American Dream. This part of the final episode of the season is, I think, especially telling. That the white resident ghosts band together to drive the recently arrived Hispanic family from the house suggests that the final, definitive move in the gothic re-vision of the American Dream is working through the racially fraught anxieties at its core. In this sense, the act of forcing the Ramoses out of the house simultaneously critiques some of the more horrific policies of sub-prime lending practices, even as it reinforces the politics that underwrite them. As Jacob S. Rugh and Douglas S. Massey have illustrated, in the time of the 'housing boom' that preceded and pre-cipitated the mortgage crisis, 'lenders [were] substantially more likely to deny loans to people of color, regardless of their income' (2010: 1), and as a result, a disproportionate number of black, Hispanic and Asian Americans applied for sub-prime mortgages. In fact, Emily Badger points out, minority clients tended to be pushed towards taking on sub-prime mortgages because this sort of loan, with its higher interest rates and fees, was more profitable for the lenders who targeted minor-ity communities in the ads and literature: 'In 2006, at the height of the boom, black and Hispanic families making more than $200,000 a year were more likely on average to be given a subprime loan than a white family making less than $30,000 a year' (Badger, 2013). That there was a racial bias in the distribution of the high-cost loans is not surprising. Nor is the way that this imbalance plays out in the gothic narrative of the mortgage crisis in *American Horror Story*.

The Ramos family is a double of the Harmons: attractive parents of a teenaged child who, almost as soon as they have taken possession of the house, decide that they would like to have a baby. But, unlike the Harmons, their race is foregrounded from the moment they appear on screen. As Marcy invites the Ramoses in to view the house, she com-ments on Miguel Ramos' name: 'Miguel, what an exotic name! I have to confess that I have always been fascinated by things south of the bor-der' (Ep. 11). Later, she notes that 'you folks tolerate the heat better than us gringos'. With her ongoing commentary about the 'superiority' of 'European Hispanics' and her assumptions about 'your' habits and preferences, Marcy's sales patter keeps Stacey and Miguel's 'Otherness' at the forefront of their representation. Marcy plays out the same racist script as those who sold the sub-prime mortgages to minority home-owners during the housing boom: selling – regardless of the conse-quences – to the Hispanic family what she (presumably) can no longer sell to Euro-Americans.

The ostensible rationale that the 'innocent, blameless, kind' house ghosts give for driving Stacy, Miguel and Gabe out of the house is that, as Vivien states, 'They can't have a baby in this house' (Ep. 11). But the reason that the Ramoses are, ultimately, the only family to get out of the house alive is, perhaps, darker than this would suggest. The devalu-ation of the property – from its building by a prominent doctor for his socialite wife to ultimately being sold to a Hispanic family – takes the racist implications of the property's devaluation to a gothic extreme. As with the depiction of Joe Escandarian, the danger of a racial minority's or immigrant's[12] intervention in the housing market reflects fears of racial and cultural displacement and dispossession in the destabilised American economy. Taking over the house, that symbol of American domesticity and stability, whether to inhabit it or to tear it down, plays out every 'there goes the neighbourhood' and 'they are buying up all of our property' cliché that haunts the mythologised ideal of white America.

While the ghosts in the house vie for possession of Vivien's white baby, they refuse to allow the Ramos' Hispanic child to be born, as stated explicitly, 'in this house'. Presumably, Vivien's statement ties dir-ectly into the narrative that the house is an inherently dangerous place for infants (see Keetley, 2013), but it also reflects cultural anxieties about illegal immigration and the rights of the American-born children of immigrants. The fact that the Ramoses don't, like all of the previous owners, die in the house is undercut by the reality that they are also the only owners of the house who will suffer the financial consequences of its decreased market value. Like the conclusion that 'subprime lend-ing disparities become foreclosure disparities' (Institute on Race and Poverty, 2009: 2), the minority owners of the Montgomery house con-tinue, as the series ends, to be possessed, even in their absence, by the house: ejected from the American Dream but still, somehow, subject to the impossibility of its terms.

To paraphrase Harvey's terms in his discussion of neoliberalism, the Ramoses, like the other owners of the house, are dispossessed by their possession. The Montgomery house is the grandiose illusion of the attainability of the American Dream in the wake of the fulfilment of neoliberal economic policies and practices. Characterising the sought-after 'dream house' that is the symbol of the Dream as a conflation of commodity, fetishised object and spectral reminder of the past, and as a space that can be invaded and potentially possessed by anarchic and terrifying 'Others', destabilises the narrative of a secure, desirable centre that the house represents. Even as the Montgomery house continues to be put up for sale, sold and resold, its market value declining with every failed owner, the persistence of the ghostly heteronormative family who have become its idealised centre is a marker of the unattainability of the American Dream in contemporary culture.

Notes

1 The pilot episode aired in the USA on 5 October 2011.
2 The house is known as the 'Murder House' in the commentary provided on the 'Eternal Darkness Tour'. I am using its more formal designation, the 'Montgomery house', in this chapter as a way of distinguishing the house itself from the title of the episode 'Murder House' (aired 19 October 2011), which eventually also became the title of the first season of the series.
3 *Democracy Now*. www.democracynow.org/2007/4/4/subprime_lending_crisis_ millions_of_families.
4 Words such as 'uncertainty', 'insecurity', 'deterioration', and even 'fear' and 'horror' (Kaklamanidou, 2013: 6, 124). It is 'a hungry beast' (McMullen, 2013).
5 *Behind the Fright: The Making of 'American Horror Story'*. 2011. DVD. Twentieth Century Fox.
6 Everyone who has lived in or owned the 'Murder House' is acting on the assumption that 'upward' mobility is a viable option.
7 Sites like Hookedonhouses.net focus on the details of the Rosenheim mansion (the basis for the Montgomery house in the series and one of its locations) based on listing photos and real estate websites. http://hookedonhouses.net/2011/10/31/ the-real-american-horror-story-house-in-l-a/.
8 See Keetley (2013) for a full and provocative discussion of futurity, 'never-born babies and slaughtered children' (94) in *American Horror Story*.
9 The exception to this is the trio who seek to replicate the 1964 murders of the nursing students. Their entry into the house is, for Keetley, another of a series of repetitions. In the context of this argument, though, their actions are focused not on financial gain, but on the other side of the Hollywood manifestation of the Dream: fame.
10 Films such as *The Burbs* (1989), *American Beauty* (1990) and *Neighbors* (2014), among others, parody and portray the panic and obsession with the idealised

sense of home ownership and 'respectable' neighbourhoods, while films such as *Halloween* (1978), *Poltergeist* (1982), *Dawn of the Dead* (2004 remake) and *The House at the End of the Street* (2012) play on the inherent 'un-homeliness' and horrific impossibility of attaining the dream of the idealised house and home.

11 Almost every conversation I've had about the series, with a variety of people, has mentioned the Christmas scene, and the general comments were always in the vein of the initial conclusion about the impossibility of the ideal family that I repeat here. Thanks to the friends and colleagues who participated in these discussions!

12 Joe Escandarian is Armenian-American.

References

Bailey, Dale. 1999. *American Nightmares: The Haunted House Formula in American Popular Fiction*. Madison: University of Wisconsin Press.

Curtis, Barry. 2008. *Dark Places: The Haunted House in Film*. London: Reaktion Books.

Harvey, David. 2005. *A Brief History of Neoliberalism*. Oxford: Oxford University Press.

Hoppenstand, Gary. 2012. 'Editorial: The horror of it all'. *Journal of Popular Culture* 45(1): 1–2.

Institute on Race and Poverty. 2009. *Communities in Crisis: Race and Mortgage Lending in the Twin Cities*. Minneapolis: University of Minnesota.

Jackson, Shirley. 2006 [1959]. *The Haunting of Hill House*. New York: Penguin.

Kaklamanidou, Betty. 2013. *Genre, Gender and the Effects of Neoliberalism: New Millennium Hollywood Rom Com*. New York: Routledge.

Keetley, Dawn. 2013. 'Stillborn: The entropic gothic of *American Horror Story*'. *Gothic Studies* 15(2): 89–107.

Rugh, Jacob S. and Douglas S. Massey. 2010. 'Racial segregation and the American foreclosure crisis'. *American Sociological Review* 75(5): 629–51.

Wyile, Herb. 2013. 'Neoliberalism, austerity, and the academy'. *English Studies in Canada* 34(4): 29–31.

Internet sources

Badger, Emily. 2013. 'The dramatic racial bias of subprime lending during the housing boom'. *Citylab*, 16 August. www.citylab.com/housing/2013/08/blacks-really-were-targeted-bogus-loans-during-housing-boom/6559/.

Institute on Race and Poverty (2009). 'Communities in crisis: Race and mortgage lending in the twin cities'. Minneapolis: University of Minnesota Law School.

McMullen, Jeff. 'The new land grab'. 2013. *New Internationalist Blog*, 29 August. www.newint.com.au/blog/the-new-land-grab/.

Shapiro, Ari. 2012. 'American Dream faces harsh new reality'. 29 May. www.wbur.org/npr/153513153/american-dream-faces-harsh-new-reality.

Stack, Tim. 2011. '*American Horror Story*: Ryan Murphy talks the game-changing season finale'. *Entertainment Weekly*, 22 December. http://insidetv.ew.com/2011/12/22/american-horror-story-ryan-murphy-season-finale/.

Filmography

American Horror Story: The Complete First Season. 2011. Dir. Ryan Murphy and Brad Falchuk. Twentieth Century Fox Home Entertainment.

Behind the Fright: The Making of 'American Horror Story'. 2011. DVD. Dir. Dylan McDermott. Twentieth Century Fox.

8

Tracy Fahey

Haunted by the ghost: from global economics to domestic anxiety in contemporary art practice

> There is something disappeared, departed in the apparition itself as re-apparition of the departed.
>
> (Derrida, 1994: 5)

It is October 2010. In the gathering twilight of a country evening in Leitrim, in the northeast of Ireland, a lone house is suddenly illuminated, blazing light from every window. The light disappears into darkness, and then flares on again. This is *On/Off States*, a video piece by Irish artist Elaine Reynolds. In this work the comforting signifier of lit windows is negated as the viewer becomes aware that the house is missing its windows and doors. Worse still, as the lights flash on, then off again, a familiar pattern emerges – three long flashes, three short, three long – the classic distress signal. Reynolds writes of the programming of this piece – 'It was significant that action was automated rather than a manual intervention, therefore the S.O.S can be perceived as coming from the house itself' (Reynolds, 2010). The flares of light are less alarming than the void that the darkness between the flashes reveals. For the duration of that long October night in 2010, the abandoned house, without human agency, frantically and repeatedly telegraphs its distress call to the world. It signals a crisis that runs to the heart of what home means in contemporary Ireland. Animated by its own distress, this house semaphores the contemporary crisis of Irish gothic suburbia to the world. For this is not an isolated house. It is part of a *ghost estate*: a term coined by Irish economist and broadcaster David McWilliams in his prescient blog entry 'A warning from deserted ghost estates' (McWilliams, 2006). Reynolds chose this small ghost estate in a Leitrim village quite deliberately as the site for her project. This site is one of twenty-one such estates in the county of Leitrim, its houses deemed not viable for completion and scheduled for eventual demolition by the National Assets Management Agency (NAMA), an agency established by government in 2009 to handle the housing crisis. It is therefore a doomed estate, built as part of the unregulated free-falling development in Ireland during the 'Celtic Tiger' economic boom that lasted from 2000 to 2008, but now populated only by the forlorn ghosts of a future that will never take place.

This chapter sets out to examine the ghost estate as the most compelling trope of the post-Celtic Tiger housing crisis in Ireland. It views these estates as *revenant spaces*, as a recurrence of the Irish gothic home in contemporary culture, and examines the fine-art response that this situation has provoked – an art of documentation, of articulation and of protest. It focuses on the uneasy relationship between neoliberal economic policy and the Irish ghost estates. and how this relationship is exposed through the fine-art practice of Elaine Reynolds, Valerie Anex, Dominic Thorpe, Aideen Barry, Anthony Haughey and Eamonn Crudden. It examines how this crisis of home exacerbates existing postcolonial anxieties around housing and security in Ireland to create these haunted estates, sites of anxiety that recall older Irish cultural memories of dispossession and ruin. To quote Fintan O'Toole: 'When the past is "now", the artistic genre that cannot be escaped is the gothic. It is the form of ghosts, revenants, the undead – embodiments of the past that will not stay where they should be but insist on invading the "now"' (O'Toole, 2012).

'The time is out of joint'

O'Toole's comment leads us inevitably to a consideration of haunting and the spectral. This chapter proposes to read the Irish ghost estates in terms of Derrida's famous essay of 1993, *Spectres of Marx: The State of the Debt, the Work of Mourning and the New International* (translated 1994). It may seem a little surprising to use the lens of neo-Marxism to analyse this embodiment of the contemporary gothic home, but there are two valid reasons for using *Spectres of Marx* as a lens though which to view the ghost estates. One is Derrida's idea that time does not exist in a simple chronological fashion. Looking at images of the ghost estates one is reminded of Derrida's idea of the 'spectral moment, a moment that no longer belongs to time' (Derrida, 1994: xix). In a hauntological sense these ghost estates are adrift in a temporal rift, caught between construction and completion, vacancy and inhabitation (we are reminded here of Derrida's famous citation from *Hamlet*, 'The time is out of joint' (I.v.211)). This usage of non-linear time in relation to commodities such as ghost estates is also borne out by Melinda Cooper in her 2008 work, *Life as Surplus: Biotechnology and Capitalism in the Neoliberal Era*, where she argues that the present, when viewed in terms of speculative futures of capital accumulation, is an empty present, haunted by possible futures (Cooper, 2008). (Indeed, in a later work of 2011, she argues for a reconsideration of the financial network as a complex system 'characterised by non-linear dynamics and susceptible to suggest changes of phase state' as a truer reflection of its unpredictable state and of its uncertain future (Cooper, 2011)).

The second rationale for reading the ghost estates through Derrida is to explore the ghost estate as a commodity that has lost its value. Ghost estates are essentially spectral forms of fluctuating economic and cultural value. Their very being is problematised by their concurrent existence in several planes (what-they-might-have-been and what-they-are). They suffer from being both the thing-in-itself and its own simulacrum, one superimposed in front of the other. Valerie Anex's 2011 photographic project *Ghost Estates* helps to illustrate this point. In this work Anex presents the viewer with a flat documentary portrayal of suburbia as commodity, as a dream property marketed by colourful signs signifying 'Houses for Sale' and by a large, colourful canvas that shows an idyllic suburban landscape with expensive cars and well-dressed neighbours who stand in the driveways. However, on closer inspection of the photographs, the canvas poster is draped over a half-finished house, while the 'Houses for Sale' referred to in the advertisement lie soulless and empty behind the placard. The fracture of this vision is captured in the tension between sign and signifier, between the developers' dream and the homeowners' nightmare. Conor O'Clery puts it even more bluntly in his *Irish Times* article 'Ireland's bust leaves ghost houses and zombie hotels':

> From afar, many of these ghost estates look as if they are finished, but up close you find no cars in the driveways, no curtains in the windows and no sound but the wind stirring the weeds in the yards. In the cities the wind fairly howls through the open floors of unfinished apartment blocks, such as the skeleton of a 14-story building put up in Sandyford Dublin ... Incidentally, there is a fine-looking

10-story apartment block right beside the 14-story shell that seems like a nice place to live, with residents sunning themselves on the balconies. But on closer inspection you will find it is an illusion, a giant illustrated canvas draped over another empty concrete block like a shroud. (O'Clery, 2010)

In these estates, the hopes of the past, the crushing reality of the present and the uncertainty of the future all fill these empty houses. Their value has been lost, economically, physically, emotionally. Slavoj Žižek, in his 2003 book *The Puppet and the Dwarf: The Perverse Core of Christianity*, addresses this idea of advertising as 'fantasmic space':

As we know already from Marx, the commodity is a mysterious entity full of theological caprices, a particular object satisfying a particular need, but it is at the same time also the promise of 'something more', of an unfathomable enjoyment whose true location is fantasy ... The function of this 'more' is to fill in the lack of a 'less', to compensate for the fact that, by definition, a merchandise never delivers on its (fantasmatic) promise. (Žižek, 2003: 145)

The suburbs, always a gothic landscape in the truest sense – a space literally *in-between* city and country, spaces somewhere between rural and urban – has become darker, more problematic, a haunted landscape of ghost estates. The most logical point at which to enter this discussion of the ghost estates is the recent past: the Celtic Tiger era of 2000–08, which caused the production of the ghost estate phenomenon in Ireland.

Haunted by the (recent) past: before the fall

In 2007, a year before the Irish housing dream imploded, Irish artist Aideen Barry curated a series of shows by seven international artists collectively titled *Subversion and the Domestic*. The venue was an unusual one: her own suburban, semi-detached home in Claregalway, County Galway. One of the invited artists, Dominic Thorpe, decided to reveal the uncanny nature of the house in the form of large plastic letters across the façade that spelled the message 'It's Not My Place'. *It's Not My Place* (Thorpe, 2007) is a play on words, literally meaning both 'this is not my home' and 'I don't have a right to engage with this', but also expressing the trope of contemporary home as a site of anxiety. The semi-detached form of Barry's house adds to this feeling of disorientation by presenting the viewer with both a 'normal' house and its uncanny Doppelgänger side by side, a visual trick also used by artist Valerie Anex in her *Ghost Estates* series. The location of the project within the confines of suburban Galway was a deliberate curatorial choice by Barry, who makes work about the uncanniness of suburbia. Barry has described her personal experience of living in the heart of Celtic Tiger suburgatory, identifying it as a gothic site of anxiety:

> It's a very un-Irish landscape – and unlike in the past when you knew your neighbours and cared for each other – suddenly you didn't know who your neighbour was. The domesticity that I'm interested in came out of this space. I was living in one of these houses and all of the people in the estate were all obsessed with materiality and being perfect and clean. And this is where my anxiety manifested itself. (Gilsdorf, 2011: 1–2)

Critic Cliodhna Schaffrey, in her essay 'Unhomely homes', written as part of the House Projects, termed Thorpe's work as 'a subversive piece of contemporary art that throws up issues around ownership and belonging'. 'It becomes', she writes, 'a critical entry point in which to discuss our relationship to the places and homes in which we live today' (Schaffrey, 2009b: 10). This entry point allows us to begin analysing this unease surrounding the concept of home by reflecting on the problematic legacy of the Celtic Tiger, through the varied and powerful responses of fine art to these anxieties. During the boom days of the Celtic Tiger, the size of Irish suburbia changed dramatically. Funded by global neoliberal economic lending policies, it expanded, developed and extended far from its original boundaries. The definition of the Dublin commuting belt widened to include journeys of two, three, even four hours. Developers were eager to fulfil the growing hunger for housing by building estate after estate, and banks were equally eager to fund both these developments and the mortgages to buy within them. This startling rate of development was facilitated by a faulty national and regional planning process. In their excellent National Institute for Spatial Analysis (NIRSA) Working Paper of 2010, Rob Kitchin *et al.* analyse the effect of poor planning policy in Ireland and identify it as one of the main causes for the escalation of the 2008 crisis. In doing so they specifically cite both Derrida and Marx: 'A new spectre is haunting Ireland – the spectre of development run amok' (Kitchin *et al.*, 2010: 5).

Neoliberal market economics led to the wholesale selling of houses en masse, and the unstable planning process in the country together with reckless lending from the banking sector facilitated it. Coen and

Maguire summarise the morass of ill-thought-out planning and development policies succinctly –

> [W]hilst the Department of the Environment, Community and Local Government is responsible for planning legislation, much remains in the hands of 88 local planning authorities, 29 county councils, 5 county borough corporations, 5 borough corporations and 49 town councils. The system remains weak, ad hoc and often devoid of actual planning. (Coen and Maguire, 2012: 11)

The forces of neoliberal economic policy and corrupt planning practices therefore created a very gothic narrative of excess, reckless lending and reckless consumption, resulting in over 300,000 houses lying idle across the country. According to the NIRSA report of 2010, the definition of 'ghost estate' has been refined to the technical term used to describe an estate in which over 50 per cent of the properties lie unfinished or uninhabited (Kitchen *et al.*, 2010). There are over 650 ghost estates that fit this NIRSA definition across Ireland (O'Callaghan, 2011). These new ghost estates are uncanny, *unheimlich*, in the truest, most direct sense of the word – unhomely. They are non-homes, and in some cases never-homes. These empty houses are Doppelgängers of their inhabited counterparts, familiar yet unfamiliar. The ghost estate is a profoundly gothic entity, haunted and *in-between* in every sense of the phrase – in between country and city, rural and urban, built and finished, empty and occupied. The ghost estates are defined by alterity – by what they are not – 'normal' estates. The houses within them are non-houses; in ontological terms their very existence is problematised. They are the supreme gothic example of not only the ruined home, but the failed home. In their essay 'Death of a tiger: The collapse of Irish property dreams', Coen and Maguire explicitly reference Derrida (and Marx) in their reading of the Celtic Tiger as central to the realisation of these estates: 'The spectre of Ireland's Celtic Tiger stalks the landscape, and the social costs of the spectacular financial and property-market collapse continue to mount' (Coen and Maguire, 2012: 5). But the Irish home is also haunted by much older spectres: the traces of postcolonial angst, the fear of dispossession and the notion of the home as dangerous space.

Haunted by the (less recent) past

The haunting of these ghost estates is by spectres both old and new. Derrida would seem to agree: 'And this being-with-specters would also be, not only but also, a politics of memory, or inheritance, and of generations' (Derrida, 1994: xviii). In one sense, these ghost estates are simply another manifestation of the long tradition of ghost towns, left as a legacy of ruins from gold rushes in America and Australia. Ancient or mock-ancient ruins are one of the most gothic visual tropes of all. They are celebrated in classic gothic texts, faked by architects such as Wyatt and simulated by artists such as Salvator Rosa. Indeed, Rose Macaulay, in *Pleasure of Ruins* (1953), claims 'ruin pleasure must be, at one remove, softened by art' (454).

In his October 2011 show, *Settlement*, Anthony Haughey engages frankly with this notion of the aesthetic ruin and its place within the historical canon of visual art practice. His photographic landscapes of ghost estates use the idiom of classical painting to evoke a sense of timelessness; the buildings assume the gravitas of a Poussin temple; the photographs are irradiated with the serene, purifying light of a Claude Lorraine. The light also represents a gothic, liminal space – the threshold time between dusk and dawn. Haughey describes the thinking behind his process in a 2010 interview with Sarah Allen: 'By photographing between dawn and dusk in the penumbra or half-light, the combination of darkness, long exposures and artificial light draws attention to the destruction of the natural environment.' He has robustly defended charges of attempting to aestheticise a social crisis: 'Art can provoke, raise questions and generate a critical conversation around key societal issues whilst maintaining a tension between aesthetics and politics' (Allen, 2010). Although the unnervingly beautiful images and serene quality of light capture the attention, the images are also haunted by what is absent – the inhabitants of these settlements. As Cian O'Callaghan writes in the introductory essay to *Settlement*: 'The absence (or oblique traces) of human life in the photographs highlights the uncanny decoupling of these houses from their function as places of dwelling' (O'Callaghan, 2011: 33). The houses presented here have transcended their failed role to become something else.

Haughey's work combats the idea that art of protest and criticism cannot be aesthetic. However, it is not only the visual history of the ruin that concerns us. Haughey's underlying vision also refutes these ideas of the Irish ghost estates being a 'natural ruin'. The Irish ghost estates sit helplessly amid the traumatised landscape that has been torn up to accommodate them, many of them never used for their intended purpose. In the case of these Irish ghost estates, the echoes of the past resonate in the present. The empty houses of the estates are a physical reminder of the return of the repressed in Irish history. The Irish countryside is littered with historical ruins of home that carry with them the shadow of invasions and colonial anxieties – ruins of the Irish monasteries sacked, of great houses burned down, of Famine villages abandoned. It is worth noting the explicit links that economist David McWilliams has drawn between the ghost estates and their earlier precursors, the Famine villages. 'In the years ahead, these ghost estates, like our famine villages, may stand testament to a great tragedy which, although predicted by concerned observers, was never fully appreciated until the morning the crops failed' (McWilliams, 2006). The parallels with Famine Ireland of the 1840s are striking. Although the Great Famine offered the more ghastly statistics, with over 2 million Irish people dying or emigrating in the late 1840s, as with the current housing crisis, the gothic saga of the Famine was caused by British economic policy and the colonial system of landownership, which led to overreliance on a single crop. In both instances the crisis of home is linked with the forces of foreign capitalism, causing a repercussive effect of dispossession, eviction and abandonment of homes. After Ireland gained independence, there was a strong postcolonial desire to reverse these centuries of controlled ownership. In the early years of the twenty-first century, this sense of land hard won and the unregulated excesses of the private rental market (particularly in the capital city of Dublin) created a sense of mingled anxiety and desire in relation to homeownership – a kind of growing *land hunger* that could only be satisfied through the excesses of the Celtic Tiger build. The build being unsustainable and perpetuated only by the neoliberal economic policy of lending meant that, yet again, Ireland found itself was littered with abandoned homes. The ghost estates illustrate a horrid and inevitable return to this past, and the awful circularity of Irish history.

Haunted by the present

On the most westerly tip of Ireland, on the island of Achill, stands one of the strangest monuments of the twenty-first century. If you struggle up the rutted path on a mountain overlooking the village of Pollagh, you will find an extraordinary structure dubbed *Achill-henge* by the locals, a concrete edifice of 4-metre-high columns arranged in a circle some 100 metres in diameter. Achill-henge is a present-day recreation of Stonehenge constructed on the edge of the Atlantic (McNamara, 2011). Created from poured concrete in a hurried act of guerrilla construction in 2011, this structure rises out of the boggy ground to dominate the landscape. There are many fascinating aspects to *Achill-henge* but perhaps the most surprising is that it was not constructed by an artist, but by property developer Joe McNamara as one of a series of visual protests he has launched since falling €3.5m in debt to the Anglo-Irish Bank. McNamara, who was subsequently jailed for three days for unauthorised building, has hinted that *Achill-henge* is a 'tomb for the Celtic Tiger' (McGreal, 2012). There are connections from this monument to the Celtic Tiger development boom and the legacy of the surrounding landscape in Achill. Just a few fields away from the monument lies a deserted Famine village, another speaking memorial to the failed Irish home. The material used – poured concrete – is ugly and brutalist in its raw state, the resulting monument offering an easy parallel between itself and the poorly constructed, partially finished ghost estates, the legacy of the Celtic Tiger. *Achill-henge* ties together many salient features of the ghost estates – the debt, the developer, the bank and the art of protest. McNamara's use of the visual language of art to protest the ghost estates is significant. For in 2011, the year *Achill-henge* was erected, art was infused by a new spirit of resistance.

This artistic culture of opposition was inspired by global riots and protests against the impact of neoliberal economic policies in Europe, especially in Iceland and Greece. It was also infused by a native Irish spirit of rebellion stemming from centuries of occupation and control under the British Empire. In 2011, demonstrations and protest marches in Ireland reached their apogee with the Occupy movement, which commandeered sites of commerce in several Irish cities. A similar spirit of confrontation permeated Irish art. In January and February of 2011, a series of artist-led events were held in Dublin under the umbrella title of NAMARAMA. The object of these film-showings, walks and activities was to draw attention to the crisis of living in the shadow of the Celtic Tiger. Unsurprisingly, the ghost estates recurred as a motif throughout. In fact, the advertised line-up for the opening night reads like a *Who's Who* of the visual culture of the ghost estates:

[The] Opening night will reveal a host of video work from film-maker Eamonn Crudden with his work, *Wallets [Full] of Blood* featuring zombie bankers who stalk the dead republic, plus visual artist Elaine Reynolds with her illuminating work *On/Off States* that shows her unique resourcefulness of properties deemed 'not viable for completion' under NAMA categorisations. Other work includes photo stills from award-winning photojournalist Kim Haughton with her haunting betrayal of the barren landscape of Ireland's Midlands entitled, 'Shadowlands' and work from artist Chris Timms who pays satirical tribute to 90s sci-fi icons investigating Ireland's deserted landscape. (NAMARAMA, 2011)

NAMARAMA is indicative of a wave of socially engaged art that called for public participation and used techniques of assembling audience, encouraging debate, screening films and above all, audience participation and involvement. NAMARAMA not only included passive acts for the spectator, such as the viewing of film pieces, but also participative acts, such as a quiz with no winners hosted by artists, and a guided tour of Dublin's financial district with a free-to-download mobile phone app that allowed visitors to take their own tour of the scene of the birth and death of the Celtic Tiger economy in the Dublin Docklands.

Through these acts of resistance, the housing crisis itself is represented as a gothic event – a disturbing catastrophe of epic dimensions resulting in a generation of haunted houses and traumatised inhabitants. The sad tale of these ghost estates is a real-life gothic saga of greed and folly, punished by a terrible loss of wealth and stability and leading inevitably to ruin and desolation. Even the discourse around these estates is gothic: dry legal, economic and political parlance of the Irish housing crisis takes on a gothic inflection. McWilliams likens the housing crisis to a disease: 'Like every infectious virus, the housing boom got into our pores. You could feel it' (Henley, 2010). This conflation of the language of economics and of the gothic is illustrated in one simple event, the organisation of a protest walk on 30 October 2010 that staged demonstrations outside the homes of Dublin's richest citizens (the top 1 per cent) who had accumulated their wealth through association with neoliberal economic policy, Celtic Tiger enterprises or tax evasion. The event was designed as a Halloween treasure hunt, and the call for participants on the Workers Solidarity Movement website urged those taking part to make explicit in their costumes the link between neoliberal economic policy and the gothic: 'Participants are encouraged to wear fancy dress along the theme of Zombie developers, Vampire bankers, Ghost estates and Ravenous black holes' (Workers Solidarity Movement, 2010). In their 2000 article 'Millennial capitalism: First thoughts on a second coming', Jean and John Comaroff conduct a linguistic analysis of these gothic terms as they occur in economic parlance.

> A striking corollary of the dawning Age of Millennial Capitalism has been the global proliferation of 'occult economies'. These economies have two dimensions: a material aspect founded on the effort to conjure wealth – or to account for its accumulation – by appeal to techniques that defy explanation in the

conventional terms of practical reason; and an ethical aspect grounded in the moral discourses and (re)actions sparked by the (real or imagined) production of value through such 'magical' means. (Cited in Coen and Maguire, 2012: 16)

Other commentators refer to ghost estates, the dead boom, dead houses, zombie bankers, and even borrow the American legal term 'zombie houses' to describe houses where the title deeds are left incomplete (Conlin, 2013). This idea of the estates as zombie entities is explored by film-maker Eamonn Crudden. In his short film *Houses on the Moon* (2009a), the first of his trilogy of cinematic commentaries on Ireland's boom and bust, *Wallets Full of Blood*, he neatly couples the setting of a ghost estate with a metanarrative of zombies and consumerism. Crudden samples Dennis Hopper's voice from the audio track of Romero's *Land of the Dead* to use him as a central figure of corrupt and psychotic authority as he tries to maintain his ghost town against an invasion of zombie bankers, maddened with consumerist excess and run amok. The zombie analogy is particularly interesting; the flesh-tearing monsters spliced into the footage seem clichéd and cartoonish – the real undead menace emanates from the rows of zombie houses, animated by Crudden's lens, his technique of capturing reflections in the rainy windows creating an eerie effect of a simulated half-life taking place within. The real horror, the real monster in *Houses on the Moon*, is the ghost estate itself.

Ghosts of the estates

So far, this discussion has revolved around the estates and the art that charts and explores the economic and planning circumstances that led to their creation. What of the people within these estates? What of their real-life horror stories of debt, negative equity and loss of community? The ghost estates appear as scars on the landscape that symbolise the trauma and the unhealable wounds of the people trapped within. In Coen and Maguire's excellent 2012 sociological study of a suburban area in Dublin (under the fictive name of Olcote Village) they offer a description of how the inhabitants are haunted by the failure of the Celtic Tiger: '[T]heir dream-homes represent, to borrow from James Joyce, nightmares from which they cannot awaken' (Coen and Maguire, 2012: 7). National Institute for Spatial Analysis researcher Cian O'Callaghan's current project, 'Memories of the everyday present: Haunting, absence, and the spectral performance of everyday life in the Irish Ghost Estate', aims to carry out an analysis of both the media commentary surrounding the ghost estates and the people who live on them. O'Callaghan writes:

> This project deploys a research methodology based on discourse analysis of media and political debates to explore how ghost estates have been mobilised as a vehicle to represent the Celtic Tiger crash, and 'oral history' interviews with residents living on ghost estates to explore how they reconcile past and present realities ... Together with facing stark fiscal and social realities, people must now reconcile how their own personal biographies intersect with this collective catastrophe. (O'Callaghan, 2013).

When we examine how neoliberal economic policy construes home as commodity, it follows that when this commodity loses value, normative notions of comfort and security in relation to domesticity are consequently subverted.

The shifting relationship between house as commodity and occupier as consumer is explored by artist Aideen Barry in her stop-motion animation film of 2011, *Possession* (Barry, 2011). Set on a ghost estate in Galway, *Possession* centres on strong themes of desire, consumption, excess and confinement. In *Possession*, Barry plays with the different meanings of the word: her agitated protagonist slips between possession of the house and being possessed by it. In one sense, *Possession* plays with the gothic trope of the imprisoned woman to illustrate Barry's equation of the confined housewife with hysteria, slippage and eventual madness. In another sense, it is the ultimate horror story of the ghost estate, where the inhabitants become haunted, or even possessed, by its *unheimlich* nature. This traumatised protagonist strives to be the perfect housewife and consumer: inspired by glossy magazines she tans her arms in the oven, cuts the grass with her hair, sucks up dust like a hoover, and cooks excessively and eats compulsively. For all her efforts she is ultimately subsumed by the house, devoured whole by her own regurgitated baking. The traumatised occupant of the home is finally atomised; the house has moved from being a possession to possessing her wholly. In the story of the ghost estates, therefore, the consumer becomes the consumed.

Some sonclusions

These ghost estates hold a mirror up to the effects of global neoliberal economic policy in Ireland, when massive, international, unregulated lending met flawed national planning regulations. The image it reflects is stark. When the hyperinflated property bubble of the Celtic Tiger burst, it spilled out a landscape haunted by ghost estates, failed promises and unpaid mortgages. These ghost estates present us with a vision of the gothic home in contemporary culture that is aligned firmly to political, economic, geographical and social change in modern Ireland. As the end of Barry's *Possession* hinted, we cannot consider in full the impact of the ghost estates in Ireland without reference to their likely or imagined future. In this chapter we have looked at these estates as revenant spaces, as contemporary gothic homes that evoke spectral memories of past gothic homes that have appeared throughout Irish history. Uncanny, revenant, traumatised, these spaces present and re-present themselves in Irish contemporary fine-art practice as site, as protagonist and as metaphor. These estates and their constituent houses can be considered as buildings that have lost their value as commodities, as places filled with lost possibilities. They can also be examined as spaces adrift in time, caught in the circular but overlapping movement of time between past, present and future. Fine art plays a role in terms of signalling these different meanings, imaginatively responding to these sites in terms of history, recasting them as places of horror and sensation and articulating the fears of the people who live in them. The art of the ghost estate aims to provoke and disturb. It telegraphs the crisis, it signals the voids, and it reimagines these ghost estates as symbolic spaces, revenant places. It looks back to the past to contextualise these recent ruins, and in doing so, raises questions as to their future. But what of the future? What does the future hold for these estates? The short answer is that we cannot answer with any degree of certainty. The National Assets Management Agency are currently in the process of documenting all of the ghost estates and separating them into categories – capable of full development, capable of usage for social housing, or not viable for completion. In the next cycle, therefore, the current landscape of dead houses may look very different. However, several important questions remain. What happens if we fail to learn from the crisis of home in contemporary culture? In September 2014, the *Irish Independent* ran an article: 'House hunters queuing for five days before new homes go on sale' (Fegan and O'Regan, 2014). The article contains a quote from Ronan O'Driscoll, director of Sherry FitzGerald, who declared:

> There are about four parties there at the moment, but we'd expect it to grow over the next few days. They'll probably use tents. I've been involved in this business for 25 years, and I haven't seen anything like this since 2006. Even at the height of the boom, I never remember people queuing on a Tuesday, for a show house opening on a Saturday. That's unprecedented in my view. (Fegan and O'Regan, 2014)

This occurrence, this frantic queuing to buy, has been hailed as evidence of economic recovery for Ireland. The more sobering revelation is that as a nation, there has been little learning from the painful lessons of the ghost estates. 'Progress', as George Santayana commented, 'far from consisting in change, depends on retentiveness … when experience is not retained … infancy is perpetual. Those who cannot remember the past are condemned to repeat it' (Santayana, 1905: 45). It seems that although the ghost estates echo the history of the failed home, they may also point with some prescience towards the future. The circularity of the narrative of the ruin in contemporary Ireland reveals the frightening possibility that these ghost estates may not be the last in a long line of gothic failed homes in Irish culture.

References

Allen, Sarah. 2010. 'Anthony Haughey exclusive interview: *Settlement*'. *Prism Photography Magazine* 4. Available at https://sarahmarieallen.wordpress.com/2012/08/30/anthony-haughey-exclusive-interview-settlement/.

Coen, Catriona, and Mark Maguire. 2012. 'Death of a tiger: The collapse of Irish property dreams'. *Anthropological Notebooks* 18(1): 5–22.

Conlin, Michelle. 2013. 'Special report. The latest foreclosure horror: The zombie title'. Reuters.com, 10 January 2013. www.reuters.com/article/2013/01/10/us-usa-foreclosures-zombies-idUSBRE9090G920130110.

Cooper, Melinda. 2008. *Life as Surplus: Biotechnology and Capitalism in the Neoliberal Era*. Seattle: University of Washington Press.

Cooper, Melinda. 2011. 'Complexity theory after the financial crisis'. *Journal of Cultural Economy* 4(4): 371–85.

Cummins, Emma. 2011. 'Pathological geographics: The materiality of the global financial crisis'. Unpublished MA thesis, Goldsmiths, University of London, September 2011.

Derrida, Jacques. 1994. *Spectres of Marx: The State of the Debt, the Work of Mourning and the New International*. Trans. Peggy Kamuf. New York: Routledge.

Fegan, Joyce and O'Regan, Mark. 2014. 'House hunters queuing for five days before new homes go on sale'. *Irish Independent*, 3 September.

Gilsdorf, Bean. 2011. 'At home on the edge: Interview with Aideen Barry'. *Daily Serving: An International Publication for Contemporary Art*, August: 1–2.

Haughey, Anthony. 2014. 'Anthony Haughey: *Settlement*'. Paper delivered at Encircling Suburbia Conference, in VISUAL Carlow, 12 September.

Henley, Paul. 2010. 'Ghost estates testify to Irish boom and bust'. BBC News, 30 April. http://news.bbc.co.uk/2/hi/europe/8653949.stm.

Keohane, Kieran. 2009. 'Haunted houses and liminality: From the deserted homes of the "faithful departed" to the social desert of schismogenesis'. *International Political Anthropology* 2(1): 127–40.

Kitchin, Rob, Justin Gleeson, Karen Keaveney and Cian O'Callaghan. 2010. 'A haunted landscape: Housing and ghost estates in post-Celtic Tiger Ireland'. NIRSA Working Papers Series 59.

Macaulay, Rose. 1953. *Pleasure of Ruins*. London: Thames and Hudson.

McGreal, Edwin. 2012. 'Decision on Achill-henge expected this week'. *The Mayo News*, 17 July. www.mayonews.ie/news/15697-decision-on-achill-henge-expected-this-week.

McWilliams, David. 2006. 'A warning from deserted ghost estates'. 30 September. www.davidmcwilliams.ie/2006/10/01/a-warning-from-deserted-ghost-estates.

O'Callaghan, Cian. 2011. 'Haunted landscapes'. Introduction to Anthony Haughey, *Settlement, The Photography Review* 65: 33.

O'Callaghan, Cian. 2013. 'Memories of the everyday present: Haunting, absence, and the spectral performance of everyday life on the Irish "ghost estate"'. Irish Research Council, http://irishresearchcouncil.ie/intro_slide/memories-everyday-present-haunting-absence-and-spectral-performance-everyday-life-irish-.

O'Clery, Conor. 2010. 'Ireland's bust leaves ghost houses and zombie hotels'. *Irish Times*, March 28: 4.

O'Regan, Donal. 2014. 'Limerick man to live in house he "broke into"'. *Limerick Leader*, 5 January. www.limerickleader.ie/news/business/business-news/limerick-man-to-live-in-house-he-broke-into-1-5786643.

O'Toole, Fintan. 2009. *Ship of Fools: How Stupidity and Corruption Sank the Celtic Tiger*. London: Faber and Faber.

O'Toole, Fintan. 2012. 'Gothic realism in the here and now: Haunted houses of a dead boom'. *Irish Times*, 1 September.

Poe, Edgar Allan. 1839. *'The Fall of the House of Usher' and Other Writings*. London: Penguin.

Santayana, George. 1905. *The Life of Reason: The Phases of Human Progress*. Auckland: The Floating Press.

Schaffrey, Cliodhna. 2009a. *Pantoffeltier: Slipper Animal*, from catalogue to *Unit* exhibition, Portlaoise, curated by Cliodhna Schaffrey and Sarah Searson.

Schaffrey, Cliodhna. 2009b. 'Unhomely homes', from House Projects. Dublin: House Projects and Atelier Project: 14–163.

Siggins, Lorna. 2012. 'Galway ghost estate comes to life with sean-nós and dance for one night only'. *Irish Times*, 19 April. www.irishtimes.com/newspaper/ireland/2012/0419/1224314925677.html.

Wall, William. 2011. 'We imagine the police', in *Ghost Estate*. Knockeven: Salmon Poetry.

Workers Solidarity Movement. 2010. '1% network Halloween treasure hunt around Ballsbridge'. www.wsm.ie/c/halloween-treasure-hunt-shewsbury-road.

Žižek, Slavoj. 2003. *The Puppet and the Dwarf: The Perverse Core of Christianity*. Cambridge, MA: MIT Press.

Digital links to art works cited

Anex, Valerie. 2011. *Ghost Estates*. www.valerieanex.com/index.php/ghost-estates/.

Barry, Aideen. 2011. *Possession*. www.aideenbarry.com/Possession.html.

Baxter, Paddy. 2012. *Vacancy*. http://vimeo.com/46749319.

Crudden, Eamonn. 2009a. *Wallets Full of Blood: Houses on the Moon.* http://vimeo. com/3269259.

Crudden, Eamonn. 2009b. *Wallets Full of Blood: Roscommon Death Trip.* http://vimeo. com/13167154.

Crudden, Eamonn. 2009c. *Wallets Full of Blood: Zombie Banker Blues.* http://vimeo. com/4292136.

Cummings, Cindy and O'Neill, Rionach. 2012. *The Rambling House.* www.mapping-spectraltraces.org/mst5-the-rambling-house.html.

Haughey, Anthony. 2011. *Settlement.* http://anthonyhaughey.com/projects/settlement/ and http://settlementexhibitiondotcom.wordpress.com/.

Haughton, Kim. 2010. *Shadowlands.* http://kimhaughton.photoshelter.com/gallery/Shadowlands/G0000ChCUrmHIMoY/.

Klute, Vera. 2009. *Home Is where the Heart Is.* www.veraklute.net/pages/portfolio/home1.html.

McGarrigle, Conor. 2011. *NAMAland.* www.walkspace.org/namaland/; with tour and talks at www.walkspace.org/namaland/news.html.

McNamara, Joe. 2011. *Achill-henge.* www.bbc.co.uk/news/magazine-17034637.

NAMARAMA, Market Studios. 2011. http://themarketstudios.ie/wp-content/uploads/2013/05/Namarama.pdf.

Reynolds, Elaine. 2010. *On/Off States.* www.publicart.ie/main/directory/directory/view/onoff-states/6e2e879abc22c92697e1827d5bdca86e/.

Reynolds, Elaine. 2011. *On/Off States.* www.elainereynolds.info/ON-OFF-STATES.

Thorpe, Dominic. 2007. *It's Not My Place.* http://dominicthorpe.net/project/subversion-and-the-domestic-house-projects/.

Part IV

Crossing borders

9

Steffen Hantke

Gothic meltdown: German nuclear cinema in neoliberal times

Introduction: nuclear cinema between normality and catastrophe

Given the number of accidents that have taken place in nuclear power plants around the world since the commercial use of the technology became widespread in the 1950s, it is surprising how few films there are that depict such accidents. Compared to the number of films devoted to nuclear war – an event that, unlike catastrophic meltdowns in Sellafield (1957), Three Mile Island (1979), Chernobyl (1986) or Fukushima (2011), has never actually taken place – the catastrophic nuclear accident never acquired its own cinematic genre. If anything, it exists as a mere subgenre of the nuclear disaster film alongside such classics as Peter Watkins' *The War Game* (1965) or Nicholas Meyer's *The Day After* (1983). But then even these films are entries into the larger genre of the disaster film, a genre in which it matters little whether the disaster in question is nuclear, viral or natural in nature as long as it is spectacularly apocalyptic. Differences between nuclear devastation as a result of military or civilian technology vanish within this larger generic pool.

As a sub-genre of the disaster film, nuclear accident films may have produced the occasional box office success such as James Bridges' *The China Syndrome* (1979), but have failed, as of yet, to produce films with lasting appeal. Most likely, these films are too narrowly responsive to a specific historical moment to achieve cultural resonance beyond their topical moment. If *The China Syndrome* retains its claim to cultural relevance, it is perhaps less as a film about nuclear disasters and more as an entry in the cycle of post-Watergate conspiracy films, alongside Alan Pakula's *The Parallax View* (1974) and Sydney Pollack's *Three Days of the Condor* (1975). As a specific historical incident triggers a short-lived cycle of cinematic responses, each film is driven by a high degree of topical urgency that implies the topic's prospective erasure from the discursive sphere as soon as the sense of imminent danger has faded or been superseded as the media cycle turns. A coherent response from a global audience, attuned to the global consequences of a possible accident, is also hard to come by, since urgency and longevity of a social panic would differ substantially depending on the historical and geographic distance from the nearest actual event. Given the relative silence on the matter in between cycles, one might conclude that the public is not as worried about nuclear accidents as it is – or as it has been – about nuclear war. Those taking their paranoid cue from post-Watergate conspiracy films might also wonder whether the nuclear lobby has successfully exercised control over the public debate so as to manage or even suppress expressions of concern, especially of a more sensationalist, alarmist or even apocalyptic manner. Historical events have shown that information policy is as much in the hands of those who cause accidents as those trying to manage them; between the Soviet Union's handling of Chernobyl and the Tokyo Electric Power Company's handling, via the Japanese Government, of Fukushima, no agent of nuclear power would shy away from mobilising political and economic power to massage public opinion.[1] One thing is beyond debate, however. Given the industry's safety record, the surprising lack of cinematic representation is definitely not a sign that the civilian use of nuclear power is safe and thus does not provide reason for concern. Persistent popular resistance to the civilian use of nuclear technology around the globe testifies to the opposite.

Resistance to nuclear energy in its civilian applications also cuts to the core of the political significance of the technology and its economic exploitation. Protected by the State against espionage, terrorism and citizens' protest, nuclear power plants are nonetheless sites of corporate power. Private enterprise, often in the form of massive corporate entrepreneurial effort, and State power intersect within these sites. No other industry, with a comparably idiosyncratic architectural iconography, represents that amalgamation of State and corporate power better (the international arms trade might come close, but, to the extent that it is not nuclear arms being traded, lacks the same high degree of national and international regulation, just as it lacks a comparable architectural iconography). Depending on the historically specific shape assumed by this intersection, nuclear power is thus *the* most typical representation of neoliberalism, not in some idealised form of free-market capitalism, but in its most recent incarnation, which fuses the concerns of the modern security state, with its unique set of economic and social priorities, with the profit motive of corporate power. What is typical of this form of neoliberalism is not 1980s-style privatisation and deregulation, implemented by conservative governments in nations from the USA to Britain and Germany. Experiencing its heyday under centre-left administrations in all of these countries (Clinton, Blair, Schröder), this new type of neoliberalism has received its boost from the so-called global 'War on Terror', as a perpetual mode of political crisis, and the global banking crash that started in 2008, providing its economic equivalent. Neoliberalism after 2001, and then again after 2008, could count on revitalised anxieties about nuclear power plants, dormant for decades after Chernobyl, not as potential technological liabilities in themselves but as targets of potential terrorist attacks (see Wells, 2012). Similarly reconceptualised as semi- or quasi-terrorist activities, public protests against nuclear waste transport and storage, as seen within the framework of the security state, are now more than ever the object of renewed State scrutiny and suppression.

As during historical moments following an actual nuclear accident in the 1950s (Sellafield), 1970s (Three Mile Island) or 1980s (Chernobyl), the post-9/11 debate is perpetually refocused on the technology's dangers and risks, a psychological arena in which the nuclear industry is now as much a cause for concern as its detractors. To an audience of popular culture – in the USA and other member nations of the nuclear club, but perhaps all the more so in Germany, where commentators have diagnosed a 'German Angst', a 'unique tendency of the Germans toward hysteria' when it comes to matters of nuclear power – it hardly comes as a surprise, therefore, that representations of nuclear power often fall back on the vernacular of the gothic (Radkau, 2011). Unsettling scenarios are driven by fears of intimate bodily penetration, contamination and abjection, all dear to the horror film and certain forms of science fiction intimately connected to horror as an adjacent genre. They encompass those grand and horrific scenarios that fuel the imagination of the disaster and post-disaster survival narratives. Often it is nuclear technology itself – shielded as much behind barriers of concrete as behind barriers of secrecy erected and maintained by the modern security state – that functions as a complex gothic trope at the heart of popular narratives. Gothic iconography lends itself to a representational arsenal intent on expressing discomfort. What better to concentrate, embody and express feelings of unease than nuclear power plants, those forbidding fortresses of a familiar yet mysterious technology that have towered broodingly over natural and cultural landscapes like gothic castles?

The imagined disaster that comes with an accident in a nuclear power plant – what, again, in the German parlance is referred to as a GAU or Super-GAU, i.e. the 'größte anzunehmende Unfall', the gravest accident imaginable – intermingles the discourse of neoliberalism with that of the gothic. When David Harvey reminds us that the 'process of neoliberalization [has always] entailed much "creative destruction"' (Harvey, 2005: 3), his citing of Joseph Schumpeter's famous dictum is less a reference to capitalism's ability endlessly to renew itself from within, and more an anticipation of Naomi Klein's concept of 'disaster capitalism', i.e. the implementation of neoliberal reforms without the public's informed consent in the disorienting and delimiting aftermath of catastrophe, be it natural, terrorist or economic (Klein, 2007). Disaster films are well suited to the demands of chronicling, legitimising or critiquing such creative destruction in their depiction of how life goes on after disaster strikes. More specifically, disaster films about civilian nuclear accidents would seem perfectly poised to serve that function to nuclear power as a technology emblematic of recent neoliberal politics.

The films I would like to examine in order to explore this hypothesis about the confluence of gothic representations and neoliberal politics within the realm of nuclear power – Gregor Schnitzler's *Die Wolke* (*The Cloud*, 2006), Andreas Prochaska's *Der erste Tag* (*The First Day*, 2008), and Volker Sattel's *Unter Kontrolle* (*Under Control*, 2011) – all deal with nuclear power in the European context and from a uniquely German perspective. Schnitzler's film specifically targets a teenage audience, while Prochaska's film is a made-for-TV movie, and Sattel's film is a documentary. Despite these formal and generic differences, all three share that deep unease-bordering-on-hysteria Joachim Radkau has described as a 'unique "German Angst"' – a tone familiar to the gothic. More importantly, all three films' production dates fall into the time period when the Chernobyl disaster of 1986 had been long past, and before the occurrence of the Fukushima disaster in 2011. Lacking the direct historical and topical urgency that tends to impose restrictions on other films, and emerging from a national and geographic context that, unlike, for example, the USA, the UK or Japan, has not had any first-hand experience with nuclear disaster, the three films have more direct access to the neoliberal implications of nuclear power. That they still chose to do so by mobilising the possibilities of the gothic – either within the vernacular of the disaster genre, or with an eye for the unsettling effects of the technological uncanny – testifies to an unease with nuclear technology that extends far beyond the singular disaster.

Die Wolke: displacing political critique

In order to explore the gothic dimensions of nuclear discourse, I would like to begin with Gregor Schnitzler's 2006 film Die Wolke. Although this is, at first glance, the least gothic of the three films in its depiction of a nuclear accident, a reading of the film in the context of its literary source material, Gudrun Pausewang's novel of the same name for young adults, will shed light on what strikes me as a uniquely gothic historical dimension to nuclear disaster – one that emerges from the return of the (historical) repressed. While the production of film may have been spurred by the twentieth anniversary of the Chernobyl disaster as a commercial opportunity, Pausewang's novel, published in 1987, is a direct response to that same disaster. Pausewang mentions Chernobyl explicitly and repeatedly while the fictional meltdown of the nuclear reactor in Grafenrheinfeld propels the novel's protagonist, fourteen-year-old Janna-Berta Meinecke, on her odyssey across post-disaster West Germany. In fact, Pausewang opens with a long newspaper advertisement, published originally in Die Zeit on 23 May 1986, 'four weeks after the reactor accident in Chernobyl' (Pausewang, 1987: 11).[2] The advertisement, written by a 'group of friends, seven men and women', and signed, in their name, by Inge Aicher-Scholl, 'the sister of Hans and Sophie Scholl', announces a major theme in the novel – the failure of politics and of politicians to protect the population from nuclear accidents.[3] 'Our politicians have played dead' (7), the group claims, 'not a peep from those gentlemen who like to talk'. The State 'has gone underground' (8). Against a general background of uncertainty, anxiety and sickness, individual politicians avoid taking responsibility; only one, the group claims, spoke up: Herr [Friedrich] Zimmermann (German Minister of the Interior). He denounced the Russians for their inhuman information policy, irresponsible because it had no other goal than to 'keep calm, don't get excited, let some grass grow over it all, nuclear policy mustn't be jeopardised' (8). If Chernobyl were to repeat itself somewhere in the world, 'politicians would yet again prove themselves incapable of doing anything about it' (10).[4]

The novel itself bears out this critique. Keeping the actual nuclear accident itself off stage, Pausewang focuses on her female teenage protagonist, who starts out as one of the myriad refugees from the affected region. Janna-Berta then becomes herself contaminated during a downpour on her way to safety and spends some time in a refugee camp near Schweinfurth where she loses all her hair. After recovering from the more serious effects of contamination, she moves in with her Aunt Helga in Hamburg but returns to a friendlier part of her extended family closer to the evacuated zone down south. In the final scene of the novel, she returns to her home town, a small village named Schlitz. Along the way, Janna-Berta loses her immediate family to the catastrophe; witnesses the death of her little brother Uli in a car accident during the evacuation panic, a death she feels responsible for; and sees several friends die during her journey from the effects of fallout. Months after the incident, the final scene of the novel finds her in an encounter with her grandparents, who have spent the entire duration of the crisis in the privileged safety of a Spanish island, and who insist upon the resumption of a bourgeois normality predicated on the repression of any discussion of the incident and its casualties. The novel's final line – 'And then Janna-Berta pulled off her cap [hiding the sight of her bald head] and started to speak' (223) – defiantly opposes this regime of silence, postulating the crucial political significance of the historical witness as a precondition of collectively learning from disaster and changing nuclear policy.

Alongside this arc of a political *Bildungsroman* for teenagers, the critique of State authority announced in the prefatory newspaper advertisement is played out whenever authority figures make an appearance. In the first hours after the meltdown, official information over the radio oscillates uselessly between the authorities downplaying the incident in order to avoid a panic and insisting that they are doing everything they can in a grave crisis (30). When the radio fails to deliver vital information about wind direction, Janna-Berta suggests her friends pull over the car and test the wind for themselves (23). Police officers in charge of facilitating the evacuation are inefficient: 'The officers, who made their way among cars while cursing and yelling, appeared ridiculous' (45). Even worse, when the Minister of the Interior comes to visit the emergency medical facility near Schweinfurth where Janna-Berta is temporarily 'stored', the visit is clearly a political photo-op, the man himself willing to make improvements but woefully misinformed as to the seriousness of the situation. The fact that a small improvement does, in fact, occur after this official visit is counterbalanced with a deeply unsettling anxiety surrounding rumours, neither verified nor discounted, that the police, in order to keep those seriously contaminated near the site of the accident from spreading the contamination, have been shooting escaping civilians point blank. It is especially this desperate and callous brutality that makes the State appear weak and ineffectual, which then justifies Pausewang's demand for a more competent, prepared and efficient State apparatus.

In order to sustain this call for a strong State protecting its citizens, Pausewang avoids engaging fully with neoliberalism's demand for unfettered entrepreneurial opportunity in the realm of corporate endeavour. Just as the nuclear reactor and the technical failure itself remain consistently off stage, there is only one single mention of those who run that facility, the nuclear industry. It occurs during a televised debate in which politicians on one side claim that, in a democracy, 'we are all to blame for what happened', while, on the other side, a 'representative of the company running the power plant' refuses to accept the blame by complaining 'But we always pointed out that there was a residual risk ... Surely you won't deny that!' (163). Except for this single acknowledgement that the plant was run by a private company – and that, therefore, responsibility might ultimately lie with corporations rather than the State – the novel is not interested in exploring the link between this private industry and the political power structure in which it is embedded. The focus remains consistently on the State and its failure to control and contain the risky technology and the subsequent disaster.

The novel's disinterest in the convergence of State and corporate power stems from another item on the ideological agenda, which announces itself with the signing of Inge Aicher-Scholl's emblematic name to the newspaper advertisement that precedes the novel. The novel's suggestion of possible human rights abuses at the hands of the State resonates with the call for eyewitnesses and their stand against the repression of historical memory. As much as Pausewang is responding to Chernobyl, she is also an author, born in 1928 in Bohemia, who knows that the imaginary nuclear disaster in Grafenrheinfeld will inevitably evoke that original disaster – that essential foundational myth of West Germany after 1945 – which is Nazi Germany and that tyrannical regime's defeat in the Second World War. Not just to an author whose biography directly links her to the 1930s and 1940s, but to a public born and raised long after, historical awareness of the war is a matter deeply entrenched in German historical self-awareness. The fate of the novel's protagonist recapitulates German suffering in the course and the aftermath of the war. Like the civilian population during Allied bombing, survivors are cowering in cellars and basements to escape from the radioactive cloud. During the early stages of the evacuation, refugees are crowding the roads in overloaded vehicles, recreating German refugee treks escaping west from the advancing Red Army during the final year of the war. Later scenes in the novel recreate the harsh treatment of these refugees by those at a safer distance from the catastrophe, their ostracisation based on the outward signs of otherness: a complex textual move that also evokes the marginalisation and dehumanisation of Germany's Jewish population prior to and during the war. In this context, it is significant that the crucial location for Janna-Berta's flight is not the congested roads, but a railway station – a nightmarish setting of overcrowded trains that recalls the forced deportations of the Holocaust as much as it does the masses of displaced German civilians in headlong flight from the advancing Red Army.[5]

Pausewang's *overwriting* of the nuclear accident by way of mapping the Second World War and the collapse of the Third Reich onto the imagined disaster may accomplish the goal of critiquing the German inability to acknowledge the past in order to correct present mistakes. Not by coincidence does the novel end with a defiant stand of the younger generation against the complacency and amnesia advocated by their elders. But it also has the curious side effect of stripping the nuclear disaster of its unique features, almost as if Pausewang's imagination, failing when confronted with an 'unimaginable' event, domesticates the event by rewriting it in the familiar cultural and historical vernacular.[6] Coupled with its author's disinterest in corporate responsibility, the novel's insistent demand for a stronger State fails to address the problematic question, raised by the reference to Nazi Germany, of where exactly State strength turns into State tyranny.[7] Instead of reading the state's woeful lack of preparedness for nuclear disaster as an index of that state's priorities – an agenda in which industrial competitiveness obviously outranks concerns over civic safety – Pausewang is left with little else as foundation of a political critique.

Gregor Schnitzler's cinematic adaptation of Pausewang's novel – by now a staple in the German high school curriculum – presents a dramatic reworking of the source material. Given the generational shift between 1987 and 2006, which not only renders implausible characters who could speak about the Second World War from personal memory but also recognises its audience's collective lack of personal experience with the historical event, the film eliminates the Second World War sub-text that is essential to the novel.[8] The film also reimagines Janna-Berta (she is now called Hannah) and her solitary journey from one surrogate family to the next as a romantic love story with Elmar, a minor character who, cynical and too smart for his own good, exits the novel when he commits suicide in a fit of despair. No such existential darkness is allowed into Schnitzler's film; after being repeatedly separated, the two teenage lovers are reunited in the final scene, which has them drive off towards the horizon with Elmar at the wheel and with Hannah's hair – figuratively speaking, since she has still not recovered from hair loss – flying in the wind.

Refocusing the protagonist's solitary journey as a romantic narrative, the film tightens its focus dramatically, restricting the novel's expository excursions into historical context and political analysis. The disaster in the public realm is seen more strictly through the personal perspective of the teenage protagonist, who no longer serves as a conduit for contextual information but as the psychological, emotional and affective point of viewer identification. Recognising the star potential in the actress Paula Kalenberg playing Hannah, Schnitzler revels in close-ups of her expressive face at its most dramatically emotive. Dramatic impact comes less from rational political awareness and more from private trauma – the loss of her mother, the tragic death of her little brother entrusted into her care, the separation from Elmar – almost to the point where the film steers clear of any political dimension to the disaster. The nuclear accident matters only in so far as it provides emotional incentive for the private personal journey towards romantic reconciliation and personal fulfilment. With different reasons but the same degree of obliviousness, the cinematic adaptation of *Die Wolke* fails to confront the idiosyncratic nature of the nuclear disaster that ostensibly drives its plot – a depoliticisation I will return to in my concluding remarks.

Der erste Tag: neoliberal disaster

Andreas Prochaska's *Der erste Tag* tracks the events following a catastrophic accident at a nuclear power plant. Unlike *Die Wolke*, which covers a period of several months, *Der erste Tag* limits itself, as its title indicates, to barely the first twenty-four hours after the disaster. Much like *Die Wolke*, however, it never takes its audience inside or even close to the actual site of disaster, opening with a wide shot of the Tuchowany power plant at sunrise, while sirens start up signalling the invisible emergency inside. Prochaska revisits this shot twice as the day goes on, but otherwise shows no interest in returning to the territorial origin, the ground zero, of the crisis. This visual ellipsis is as programmatic as the film's title; its interest lies exclusively in tracing the collective and institutional responses to nuclear disaster during the day of its occurrence, mapping these administrative processes on to an ensemble of characters (two of whom, incidentally, correspond to the teenage lovers in whom Schnitzler's film is exclusively interested). In equal measures, the film divides its attention among various characters in the Austrian town of Horn, right on the border between Austria and the Czech Republic, and another set of characters in different official positions, both in the affected border region itself and in the capital, Vienna, all involved with generating and managing the official response to the disaster. In the interplay between these personal and official trajectories, as well as that of the various levels of geographical and personal proximity *to the accident* and degrees of institutional responsibility *for the accident*, the film lays out a broad panoramic view of a narrowly confined time period.

As a disaster film, it follows as many of the conventions of the genre as *Die Wolke*. The opening scene construes social and bodily vulnerability by showing a pregnant woman sending her five-year-old son back to bed early in the morning. The intimate domestic setting, as well as the emblematic display of the conventionally most vulnerable victims of disaster (i.e. women – and pregnant ones at that – and children), signal the seriousness of the disaster to come. Similarly conventional is the fact that the little boy, when going off to kindergarten, forgets his teddy bear, for which the mother needs to go back into the house. For similarly sentimental reasons, Uli, younger brother to the protagonist in *Die Wolke*, carries a teddy bear (unaccountably changed into a stuffed monkey in Schnitzler's adaptation) when he dies in a hit-and-run accident. That accident is replayed in the death of the single most important man in the small town of Horn, who is killed by a hit-and-run driver while warning his neighbours of the approaching danger; he dies needlessly as a result of the panic that spreads at the news of the disaster.

While the film is shot in a semi-documentary style (favouring hand-held cameras, rapid- or whip-pans substituting for cuts or dissolves, and frequent overcorrected zooms), its deployment of tropes from the disaster film is almost disappointingly conventional. Despite its explicitly open-ended concept – i.e. to cover the *first* day only – the film nonetheless strives towards narrative closure. Characters who are separated will be reunited (e.g. a father going in search of his son who, oblivious to the danger, is taking his girlfriend for a ride on his motorcycle), and all journeys undertaken lead away from the danger, either privately (a Government official's young pregnant wife taking their five-year old to her sister's) or institutionally (e.g. the young female photographer undergoing decontamination and ending up in a holding facility in what used to be a public pool). As much as the conventional nature of these elements might make the film disappointingly predictable, they nonetheless hold together events that, in their casual daily occurrence, produce beautifully poignant moments as well.

One of them is the unsettling scene at the end of the film in which the mayor of Horn is aimlessly staggering through the abandoned streets of his town; it points to yet another unresolved motif. Many of the central characters have been caught in the thunderstorm that rains radioactive fallout down on northeast Austria. The two teenagers playing truant, the girl's mother and father, the boy's father, and the female photographer – all of them are severely contaminated. Though never explicitly acknowledged, their deaths are evoked as a medical certainty, a representational ellipsis that relegates them to the outside of the representational space of the film itself. The first day, the film argues, is only the beginning of potentially far more gruesome things to come. There is a post-nuclear future here that, individually and collectively, is just as much going to be about nuclear energy as the past and the present used to be. What at first glance had appeared as conventional narrative closure is revealed as a device that points towards a space of unspeakability, a space where physical abjection and death await.

Among these larger administrative structures, the one that also falls into the realm of cognitive and political repression is the political and geographic organisation of Europe. Least of all, Prochaska's decision to have the accident occur at a power plant in the Czech Republic rather than in Austria itself (all of the characters in the film are Austrian, none are Czech) is motivated by a desire to address intra-European immigration issues. After all, the Austrian administration's first response is to police the border and to limit the flow of contaminated bodies and objects into its own territory. There is also a recognition that cheap labour traverses that border as a matter of regular economic exchange, marking the difference, within the European Union, between more and less developed economies. Objectively speaking, the film reflects the practice of locating power plants, if at all possible, along the territorial boundaries of the State. In case of an emergency, this practice ex-territorialises or at least trans-territorialises the spread of contamination, allowing states to draw on resources not their own in order to contain the damage – a strategy that might strike one as either pragmatic or cynical. Since radioactive contamination expands along natural vectors, aligning itself with wind direction and natural geographic features and ignoring political boundaries, the disaster not only stages an unsettling eruption of nature into the realm of the political but also demands an uncomfortable recognition of the inequalities within the European Union. Again, the film gestures towards the outside of the representational frame, to what remains unsaid and unacknowledged, to suggest the full extent of the disaster and its management.

While the film meticulously charts the administrative and institutional responses to the crisis, tracing the ways in which representational and bureaucratic structures adapt to, and thus process and manage, the unfolding catastrophe, it simultaneously insists that these responses will be inadequate to the rationally extrapolated dimensions of the disaster. Unlike Pausewang's critique of the State's inadequacy in controlling the technologies it unleashed, there is no institutional failure in Prochaska's film: everything goes according to plan, every agent in the process performs adequately, the machinery does exactly what it was designed to do. What emerges is a portrait of the legitimisation of State power through procedure, an emptying out of concrete political content in favour of an embracing of procedural accuracy, effectiveness and entrainment. This is a far cry from Pausewang's moralising critique of the weakness and inefficiency of the State abandoning its citizens, just as it falls short of the convergence of Pausewang's warning – that State power might turn fascist as the disaster challenges its legitimacy – with the tenets of what Naomi Klein has called 'disaster capitalism' administering or exploiting disaster in order to entrench itself more deeply.[9] Just as the administrative machinery in *Der erste Tag* lacks the menacing fascist overtones of *Die Wolke*, it does not require the disaster to be implemented – it is already there, fully formed, waiting to swing into action. If anything, *Der erste Tag* shows intra-European state power as already fully, and somewhat unspectacularly, engaged in the neoliberal project. The film articulates a clear awareness that the long-term effects of the disaster are going to be even worse than those visible within the narrative itself – just as the origins of the system producing and administrating the disaster precede the narrative. With origins and results of the crisis screened out, the institutional administrative response figures as a systemically integral aspect of the disaster itself, of the catastrophe for which it is responsible and of the larger administrative structures in which it occurs.

Unter Kontrolle: in the ruins of the nuclear industry

Volker Sattel's *Unter Kontrolle* (2011) hinges on exactly this idea articulated in *Der erste Tag* – that, when it comes to nuclear power administered neoliberally, procedural efficiency legitimises itself over concerns about the amelioration of human suffering, ecological devastation and social disruption. Yet *Unter Kontrolle* also stands out among the three films I am discussing because it is not a feature film but a documentary, and because it takes its audience exactly into the space that remains strictly off screen in *Die Wolke* and *Der erste Tag*. In fact, access to nuclear facilities that are otherwise subject to strict security measures – that is, the ability to take his camera inside and bring to the audience images hitherto unseen from behind the walls and the representational apparatus shielding nuclear reactors from public view – might be the film's major selling point. Subtitled 'An Archeology of Atomic Power' – a reference to Foucault's notion of tracing formations of knowledge and power – the film promises to have its audience peek behind this new iron curtain of the neoliberal age.

And yet in stark contrast to this thrilling promise, which is not only inherent in the film's approach but also part and parcel of its marketing strategy, Sattel presents this inside view in a style more pared down and austere than the one adopted by Prochaska in *Der erste Tag*, and diametrically opposed to Schnitzler's melodramatic style in *Die Wolke*. Stripped of all non-diegetic sound, *Unter Kontrolle* is shot almost consistently in agonisingly slow lateral pans or tracking shots; camera movement left-to-right and vice versa dominates, while vertical movement is reserved for a few significant moments (e.g. the transition to the film's segment about the underground storage of nuclear waste). Just as there is no non-diegetic soundtrack, there is no narrator, and only in a very few interview sequences does the audience get to hear the voice of the interrogator, presumably Sattel himself, from outside the frame. Otherwise, all interviewees speak unprompted; their names and functions, never provided through inserts, are revealed only in regard to the contents and contexts of their speech. The result is a slow and deliberate film, stylistically understated, and, for being so cool, all the more unnerving.

As much as the film seems to eschew, at first glance, gothic excess in camera movement and editing, the gothic's more melodramatic hyperbole also seems absent from the visuals of its subject matter. Among the film's stylistic features, it is colour selection that ties it back to Prochaska's emphasis on institutional legitimisation in *Der erste Tag*. Roaming through reactor cores, nuclear facilities, waste dumps, and bureaucratic and research facilities, Sattel's camera tends to emphasise the standard-issue, institutionally bland pastels of faded plastic and Bakelite. Harking back to an institutional washed-out 1970s retro look that complements the shrill palette of the period's consumer goods and popular fashions – a historical marker established in an early interview reminding us that most German reactors are twenty-five years old or older – these pastels evoke a sense of the mundane, the trivial, that stands in sharp contrast to the risks and dangers contained within the technology itself. Blandness also recurs in any of Sattel's compositions that feature empty rooms, straight lines and open angles. Human beings appear either in long shots, where their features are unrecognisable almost to the point of dehumanisation, or in medium close-ups. Just as the film avoids oblique angles, high- and low-angle shots, or dramatic shadows that might allow access to depth of field, there are no close-ups that might reveal human emotion. Extreme close-ups are strictly reserved for technology. The bureaucratic and technocratic jargon that runs through virtually all interviews completes a panorama of a technology and its human and institutional adjuncts in which bland surfaces conceal the dangers underneath.

While gothic excess and hyperbole are strikingly absent from the film, it is exactly this suppression of affect, replicated by way of Sattel's style, from which the gothic component of the film emerges. Nuclear power, wielded by a powerful industry and facilitated by a variety of regulatory bodies, might stage itself in concealed spaces, either entirely invisible, hidden underground or secured behind razor wire, or oddly self-contained within facilities inserted uneasily into natural and cultural landscapes. And yet, as the film slowly reveals, nuclear power has invaded all aspects of everyday life, a silently creeping force just below the threshold of conscious recognition. From street signs commemorating the scientific pioneers of nuclear technology to the detritus of nuclear technology circulating unrecognised through the economy and consumer culture, nuclear power is invisibly ubiquitous.[10] The awareness of this ubiquity is inherent in all images the film assembles, as it is spoken and testified to in every interview. And yet a mechanism is at work here that suppresses this awareness more effectively than the secretive nuclear industry or the security state ever could. *Unter Kontrolle*, in other words, evokes nuclear power and the state of affairs it helps to create as a deeply uncanny construct.

In revealing the ubiquity of nuclear technology, the film assumes a perspective that appears strikingly prescient considering its release date in advance of the Fukushima disaster and the subsequent German policy move towards a long-term abandonment of nuclear energy in favour of other, predominantly renewable energy sources. As the film slowly advances from the inside of nuclear reactors, through surrounding technological, bureaucratic and institutional layers, and towards the more mundane aspects of everyday life, it also traces a historical trajectory that reaches from the infancy of the technology in the 1950s, via its heyday between the 1960s and 1980s, to the present and – in that final segment – towards the immediate and none too distant future. The film ends with a meditation on the end of nuclear energy. Depending on one's perspective, this death of nuclear power has already occurred without anyone noticing, or is unlikely ever to occur; to put it in a gothic metaphor, nuclear power is weirdly undead.

Die Wolke and *Der erste Tag* project the abolition of nuclear power into an imaginary future, either as the democratically desired result of the lesson learned from history or as the inevitable outcome of economic and political strictures. But *Unter Kontrolle* states that such an abandonment of the technology has, in fact, already occurred (albeit only in the sense in which the two other films, not to mention the German Government, think of 'abolition'). According to Sattel, Germany is riddled with facilities, some of which were either decommissioned after an accident rendered them commercially non-viable, while others were abandoned during or immediately after construction as a result of financial or political changes. Add to this number the facilities decommissioned as a result of age and technological obsolescence alone, and the overall image that emerges is one of a postindustrial landscape dotted with the beautiful, virtually indestructible ruins of a technology both dead and alive.[11]

As one of Sattel's interviewees laments the scientific careers ruined by the public's gradual disenchantment with nuclear technology since its hopeful beginnings in the 1950s, the film urges its audience to revise its assessment of the technology it had put on display earlier. Instead of the technological sublime that resonates with many of the film's images, the new context, retrospectively evoked, now places emphasis on the fact that the immense size, the grand and awesome scale of the facilities, speaks of the technology's historical obsolescence. In an age in which biotech and digitech provide the parameters for techno-logical relevance and innovation – defined largely by miraculous feats of miniaturisation and flexibility – large-scale industrial instal-lations such as nuclear power plants are always already ruins, their abandonment and demise written into their outsized dimensions. From the endless miles of pipes and cables revealed in slow tracking shots, to the long shots of massive turbines and heat exchanger coils, nuclear power, the film insinuates, is basically nothing more than a nineteenth-century steam engine coupled to a twentieth-century heat source. In a twenty-first century setting, it is an oddly anachronistic technology, a folly, a relic.

Nonetheless, in suitably gothic fashion, it is this undead technology that still rules the land. The nuclear industry, Sattel's film concludes, is in the process of performing a gradual shift from an industrial mode of production to a postindustrial mode of processing its own historical obsolescence, and discursively framing, bureaucratically administering, and institutionally managing the waste it has produced and the damage it has caused. Sattel's view matches David Harvey's thumbnail defini-tion of neoliberalisation as 'the financialization of everything', which erases the commonsense distinction between technological relevance and obsolescence as well as economic success and failure (Harvey, 2005: 33). Instead of producing electricity, nuclear technology is now predominantly geared towards reprocessing its increasingly rare and thus prohibitively expensive raw materials, packaging and storing its detritus, managing and policing its storage facilities, and recycling pieces of its technology broken down into components so small that their tainted origins are effectively concealed and their inconspicuous circulation through the global economy is ensured. The fact that the industry's functioning remains an important item on the agenda of the post-9/11 security state places it firmly in the realm of neoliberal poli-tics. What Sattel's film makes explicit is firmly suppressed in *Die Wolke* and begins to emerge in *Der erste Tag*: that even in cases of catastrophic meltdown and historical obsolescence, nuclear technology within the neoliberal regime is always 'under control'.

Conclusion: monetising failure

Read as a continuous narrative, all three films taken in sequence tell the story of the gradual neoliberalisation of West/Germany, each with a different deployment of gothic tropes in service of various thematic concerns. As several East Asian economies, Britain and the USA were pursuing a dramatic turn towards neoliberal policies during the 1970s and 1980s, it was West Germany that, thanks to its relatively strong unions and its 'social democratic traditions' held out and only made that same turn when the economic stresses caused by the divided nation's 'hasty reunification' began to make itself felt (Harvey, 2005: 90). Pausewang's failure in *Die Wolke* to read the Chernobyl disaster as an economic fable, and her focus instead on its (perceived) analogies to the collapse of the Third Reich – a failure replicated in 2006 by her novel's cinematic adaptation – testifies an absence of economic anxiety, a reliance on social stability and a confidence in State authority as the final instance of nuclear control typical of the period. Although the novel stages the disruptive return of the repressed, reading the ghosts of West Germany's fascist past into its catastrophic future, it is not yet historically positioned to link neoliberal politics and gothic tropes as its successors.

While Pausewang can hardly be blamed for not being more sensitive to economic developments that were barely emerging in Germany during the 1980s, Schnitzler's film version must stand up to the criticism of having failed to rectify these oversights by updating the source material to fit a fully neoliberalised (and now reunited) Germany after the drastic policies of the social democratic administration under Gerhard Schröder during the 1990s – an administration comparable to the second wave of radical neoliberalisation, after Reagan and Thatcher in the 1980s, of Blair in Britain and Clinton in the USA. The Schröder administration's so-called 'Agenda 2010', delivered in March 2003, fits Naomi Klein's thumbnail definition of neoliberalism by aiming at 'the elimination of the public sphere, total liberation for corporations and skeletal social spending' (Klein, 2007: 15). What is worse, while Pausewang still explicitly references the anti-nuclear protests during the 1960s and 1970s, Schnitzler's film denies this oppositional history by not reaching back to this history, presumably because it must appear remote and irrelevant to a teenage audience in 2006. If anything, the depoliticisation of the nuclear disaster in his film reconstructs the historical moment – twenty years after Chernobyl, but only five years before Fukushima – as one in which all political opposition has ceased and civil society has made its peace with nuclear energy. The quiet before the fictional storm in the film comes across as a perfectly hermetic private world of middle-class affluence, destabilised temporarily in order to allow its return on equally private terms. Perhaps it is in this high degree of depoliticisation that neoliberalism can be read as having accomplished its goal of becoming 'incorporated into the common-sense way many of us interpret, live in, and understand the world' (Harvey, 2005: 3).

All of these economic, political and ideological anxieties, uncertainties and blind spots, bracketed by both versions of *Die Wolke*, surface with a vengeance in *Der erste Tag*. The administration of disaster management by way of mass evacuation, border policing and forced decontamination of a deterritorialised population reflects beautifully the impotent outrage on display at protests against neoliberal policy whenever privileged Europeans happen to be among those policies' losers. No matter whether these protests target Castor transports of nuclear waste across European borders, or whether they are directed against a company such as Nokia abandoning its production site in Bochum in 2008 in search of cheaper labour markets in Eastern Europe, the trope of the disaster always makes an appearance when those used to receiving the economic profits from neoliberal policies are suddenly reduced to producing these profits for someone else's benefit. What Prochaska's film pulls into the discursive sphere around the concept of the nuclear disaster are also anxieties about the interplay between national boundaries and transnational European sovereignty (e.g. immigration, uneven development), as well as the long-term expenses of nuclear energy, dismissed or altogether denied in the two versions of *Die Wolke*.

It is exactly with this long view of nuclear energy, and with a vision of the fully accomplished neoliberalisation of German society, that Volker Sattel enters the discussion with *Unter Kontrolle*. Historically speaking, Sattel still operates without awareness of the impending disaster at Fukushima. But unlike Schnitzler's and Prochaska's films, *Unter Kontrolle* stands out against the background of the global economic crisis starting in the autumn of 2008, a crisis often seen as both an indictment of neoliberal policy and, in its unfolding and gradual management, as evidence that neoliberalism will allow no alternatives to itself even in its moments of abject failure. What emerges is a strangely compelling (not to mention horrifying) vision of neoliberalism as sublime: a system with spatial ambitions of transnational and even global scope, which also claims unlimited historical dimensions as it claims universal applicability and projects itself forwards into the future – an inescapable, overwhelming and awesome construct. Nuclear technologies embody all these ambitions. Starting with the images of concrete nuclear sites and facilities as versions of the technological sublime, Sattel goes on to emphasise the vast historical space into which this technology is practically projecting itself, producing elements that are going to last millennia. Analogous to these historical spaces is the economic sphere through which, according to Sattel's film, minute particles of nuclear technology – stripped, recycled and repurposed – are going to circulate as a result of the industry's shift from production to postindustrial management. This is an economy in which breakdown, financial loss and abject failure can still be monetised so that traditional boundaries or points of orientation (loss/ gain, winner/loser etc.) are dissolved.

Since the disaster at Fukushima in 2011 – which is far from contained and still ongoing at the time of writing in early 2014, as if to confirm Sattel's analysis – the German Government under the leadership of Angela Merkel, newly confirmed to a third legislative term in 2013, has announced the abandonment of nuclear energy in favour of renewable energy. This turn in policy – referred to as the 'Energiewende', the turn or turnaround in energy policy, analogous to the nomenclature applied to Germany's so-called reunification ('die Wende') – came as a surprise to most, since, immediately preceding the announcement, that same Government had just opted to renew operating licences for some of Germany's oldest nuclear power plants. Whether the recent policy shift in response to Fukushima is being implemented in good faith or not is a matter to decide for those paying close attention to the interactions between the State and the handful of monopolistic corporations controlling the German energy market. But then the question about the viability of renewable energy is moot; the nuclear industry, regardless of whether reports about its demise may have been premature or not, has entrenched itself so deeply as a postindustrial mode within the larger national and even European economy that it will continue to exercise its undead grip on all of our lives in these national and trans- or even post-national spaces. And as the gothic would have it, we may not know if it is with us or not, but we are sure to feel that twinge of unease every time we make a purchase, flip a switch or hear a siren going off.

Notes

1 Recent examples of such media-consciousness might include online blogs such as 'Nuclear Street', which advertises itself as 'Pro-nuclear power blogs: Blogs written by individuals, companies, and government agencies about nuclear power'.

2 All translations from the original German are, unless otherwise noted, the author's own.

3 Hans and Sophie Scholl were members of the 'White Rose', a notable anti-fascist resistance group during the Third Reich. Captured by the Nazis, they were executed in 1943 when both were in their early twenties.

4 Pausewang also employs a similarly documentary strategy by citing, 'in slightly altered form', passages 'from official drafts of disaster emergency plans' whenever we hear official announcements over the radio, as a footnote to the novel informs the reader (Pausewang, 1987: 28).

5 Though the emergency medical facility itself does not have explicit features of a concentration camp, one might also see a Holocaust reference in the physical description of Janna-Berta as she sees herself in the mirror, a victim of radioactive fallout: 'Sunken eyes, pointed chin, pale skin, lifeless, shaggy hair. In the much-too-big night shirt they had put on her, she looked like a ghost' (Pausewang, 1987: 82).

6 I am borrowing here from the discourse not of nuclear accidents but of nuclear war as conceptualised by attempts at formulating Nuclear Criticism (Rosenberg, 2013), in which the concept of nuclear disaster appears as a version of 'the unthink-able', occurring in a space of fiction (46), 'resist[s] specificity by spilling over geo-graphic, temporal, or other "imagined" border' (48), and generally falls into the realm of 'radical negativity' (51) that defies the imagination while simultaneously occupying and imposing upon it.

7 Had the novel been written a few years later, Pausewang would have had the oppor-tunity to observe West German State power being mobilised massively against anti-nuclear protests at sites of nuclear power plants, and at storage and reprocessing facilities, largely triggered by the experience of Chernobyl.

8 Pausewang might have seen this complete elimination as an ironic confirmation of her critique of German historical amnesia and its dangers. The fact that the film represses the name of the actual nuclear power plant as it is used in the novel (Grafenrheinfeld) by replacing it with the fictional 'Markt Ebersfeld' further con-firms this ironic point.

9 Klein does depart from the term 'neoliberal', however, as she emphasises the return of a state power to the scene that, under neoliberal guidance, would have been rel-egated to a supportive mechanism for corporate power; her preferred term would be 'corporatist' (Klein, 2007: 14–15).

10 It is important to point out that the film presents the manner in which nucluear detritus is rendered unrecognisable not in conspiratorial terms but in economic ones. Sattel meticulously outlines how scrapped components of nuclear technol-ogy are thoroughly disassembled, reconfigured and repurposed before they are reintroduced into the circulation of commodities through the larger economy: that they are stripped of any trace of their former existence. This is not an act of decep-tion perpetrated on the consumer, but an inevitable side effect of the technological

malleability of the artefacts themselves and a corresponding flexibility of a market ready to accommodate any commodity regardless of its origins.

11 Most striking among the images produced in evidence of this diagnosis are those of a nuclear reactor and its surrounding compound used for a town fair: a children's merry-go-round is placed in front of the egg-shaped reactor; a carousel rises up inside one of the vast cooling towers, spinning its riders towards the edge of the tower and the circle of blue sky above. Tracking vertically down along the same cooling tower, Sattel's camera reveals that the imposing tower has been painted and that, at its base, it has been surrounded with a large circular awning, all elements beautifully defamiliarising the emblematic shape and colour of the facility.

References

Harvey, David. 2005. *A Brief History of Neoliberalism*. Oxford: Oxford University Press.

Klein, Naomi. 2007. *The Shock Doctrine: The Rise of Disaster Capitalism*. New York: Henry Holt.

Pausewang, Gudrun. 1987. *Die Wolke*. Munich: Ravensburger Buchverlag.

Radkau, Joachim. 2011. 'Das Gute an der "German Angst"'. Geo.de. 11 August. www. geo.de/GEO/natur/oekologie/kernkraft-das-gute-an-der-german-angst-69334. html.

Rosenberg, Aaron. 2013. 'Specters of totality: The afterlife of the nuclear age'. In Michael Bouin, Morgan Shipley and Jack Taylor, eds, *The Silence of Fallout: Nuclear Criticism in a Post-Cold War World*. Cambridge: Cambridge Scholars, 45–58.

Walker, Mike. 2013. ' "Big, ugly, and scary"; or, How Hollywood has misinformed the public about nuclear power'. 6 August 2013. https://nuclearstreet.com/pro_ nuclear_power_blogs/b/science-history-nuclear/archive/2013/08/06/quot-big-ugly-and-scary-quot-or-how-hollywood-has-misinformed-the-public-about-nuclear-power.aspx.

Wells, Jane. 2012. 'Are nuclear plants safe from attack? Millions spent since September 11 to beef up security', NBC News.com. 11 December. www.nbcnews. com/id/3072967/ns/business-check_point/t/are-nuclear-plants-safe-attack/ #.VHGGYE0cTcs.

Filmography

Der erste Tag. 2008. Dir. Andreas Prochaska. ARTE.
Unter Kontrolle. 2011. Dir. Volker Sattel. WDR/ARTE.
Die Wolke. 2006. Dir. Gregor Schnitzler. Concorde Filmverleih.

10

Agnieszka Soltysik Monnet

Border gothic: Gregory Nava's *Bordertown* and the dark side of NAFTA

In the past twenty years, hundreds of women have been murdered in the border town of Juárez, Mexico, and thousands more have gone missing.[1] Many of them worked in the mainly foreign-owned factories known as *maquiladoras* that once promised to make Ciudad Juárez a showcase for the North American Free Trade Agreement (NAFTA) and for neoliberalism on the North American continent more generally.[2] Few of these murders have been solved, and most have never been properly investigated. Scholars and activists have shown that Juárez became a killing ground for rapists and murderers preying on women – spawning a new term, 'femicide' – as the result of a complex convergence of factors, including sexism, racism, State indifference, police corruption and corporate negligence that made female workers particularly vulnerable to after-hours violence.[3] Neoliberalism and its profit-seeking ethos of placing corporate interests before workers' rights have underwritten and magnified all these factors. According to the cruel logic of the bottom line, it has simply been cheaper to replace women than to protect them. As a result, the murders have continued with impunity as State authorities and corporate interests colluded to keep the murders quiet, fearing that media attention would expose the exploitative working conditions in the hundreds of factories in Juárez (and over 5,000 in Mexico as a whole (Borderplex Alliance, 2012)).

Gregory Nava's 2006 film *Bordertown*, a gothic thriller starring Jennifer Lopez and Antonio Banderas, and based on the real circumstances of the murders and their failed investigations, is a relatively high-profile attempt to expose this situation. The film draws heavily on gothic imagery and conventions, such as live burial, forgotten crimes, aristocratic villains and dismembered bodies, and especially the female gothic, with its emphasis on the imprisonment and instrumentalisation of women, in order to suggest that border towns such as Ciudad Juárez are contemporary forms of hell created by neoliberal practices that prey especially on young female workers. The film echoes a long-standing literary tradition of depicting unsafe working conditions in gothic-inflected terms, such as Herman Melville's 'Tartarus of maids' (1855) and Upton Sinclair's *The Jungle* (1906), but updates this critique by a pointed engagement with issues raised, for example, by Gloria Anzaldúa's *Borderlands/La frontera* (1987), Achille Mbembe's 'Necropolitics' (2003) and Henry A. Giroux's notion of the 'biopolitics of disposability' (2006). Thus, the film exposes how the combined forces of neoliberalism, patriarchy and continuing postcolonial disenfranchisement of native populations produce the Mexican–American border as a gothic space – a permanent state of exception, in Giorgio Agamben's terms – where women workers' bodies are subject to control, exploitation and violence (Agamben, 1998; Fragoso, 2002: 6). Agamben has famously revived the classical Roman notion of a *homo sacer*, a person who stands outside both human and divine law, and who is defined by their capacity to be killed. More importantly, as Zygmunt Bauman specifies, the *homo sacer* is someone who can be 'killed without fear of punishment' (Agamben, 1998: 85; Bauman, 2003: 133). This accurately describes the necropolitical situation of indigenous and working women in the area of Juárez since the dawn of the NAFTA era.

The prehistory of the *maquiladoras* begins with the violent and fraught relationship between the United States and Mexico dating back to the nineteenth century. Mexico gained its independence from Spain in 1821, but by the 1850s had lost half its territory to the United States through the Texas Revolution (1836), the US–Mexico War (1846–48) and the Gadsden Purchase (1854). In the late nineteenth century, according to Monica Muñoz Martinez, 'shifting racial hierarchies, the massive transfer of property from Mexico to Anglo hands, and the industrialization of agriculture – which assigned Mexicans in the American southwest to manual agricultural wage labor – led to a particularly violent period in the US–Mexico border region' lasting through the early twentieth century (Muñoz Martinez, 2014: 665). During this period, thousands of Mexicans were killed with relative impunity by Texas Rangers and other vigilantes in order to enforce white privilege and propertied interests (662). In the twentieth century, the Bracero Program of 1942 allowed US agricultural companies legally to acquire male labourers from Mexico during the Second World War and the decades after. When it was terminated in 1964, 200,000 workers were left jobless and the Mexican Government initiated the Border Industrialization Program (BIP) the following year.

This was the beginning of the export processing plants known as *maquiladoras*, which aimed to attract foreign investors by offering cheap labour with relaxed safety and health conditions. Advantages included 100 per cent expatriation of revenues, weak toxic dumping regulations, and workers who could be made to work longer hours and much cheaper wages than in the home countries of the firms that set up factories there. This programme clearly anticipated the trends linked to contemporary neoliberal policies and had the added side effects of uprooting people from their traditional land and homes and increasing the overpopulation in Mexico's northern states (Gutiérrez, 2004: 65). In fact, as David Harvey has observed, falling prices of agricultural goods due to State-sponsored agribusiness in the USA, coupled with predatory tax policies in primarily indigenous states such as Oaxaca and Chiapas, have forced large sections of native peoples off their land and funnelled them to the *maquiladora* factories as migrant wage labourers – forming a new class of 'landless proletariat' (Harvey, 2003: 145).[4] The factories in turn preferred to hire women and girls because they were perceived as more docile, compliant, and willing to accept longer hours and lower wages, in addition to having smaller and more nimble hands (though they are not paid more for their allegedly greater dexterity). By 1994, when NAFTA was signed, women outnumbered men in the approximately 300 factories in Juárez. After NAFTA, the number of *maquiladoras* grew rapidly, with women continuing to be hired preferentially, working day and night shifts at the factories, which functioned twenty-four hours per day. According to Edward A. Avila, 'various forms of social inequity and violent labor practices emerged from a complex social arrangement conditioned largely by the mutually determining forces of global capital and local racialized and gendered relations of power' (Avila, 2012: 7). These conditions set the scene for the twenty-year murder spree that *Bordertown* addresses.[5] The murder of women in Juárez officially dates back to 1993, when the first victims were found, and involves over 400 bodies and nearly 5,000 women still missing (Sadowski-Smith, 2009: 75–94, 90n1).

Amnesty International and other organisations have demonstrated that the murders were largely ignored by local police and the corporations involved, as well as the governments of both Mexico and the United States (in keeping with the trend under neoliberalism of state governments toeing the corporate line instead of protecting workers). In fact, since drawing attention to the murders created negative publicity for the *maquiladoras* and threatened to expose the sub-standard working conditions, local and national authorities colluded actively to silence efforts to expose the murders. Since most of the women working in the factories come from other parts of Mexico, and many hope to cross the border into the United States eventually, they are regarded as temporary labour by the factory managers, justifying lower wages and a high turnover rate. According to Julia Monárrez Fragoso, 'the practices of the maquiladora industry towards the workers reveal a consume and dispose cycle' (Fragoso, 2002: n.p.). In other words, the women workers of the free trade zone are considered 'disposable', in a logic that Henry A. Giroux has termed a 'biopolitics of disposability', a 'new and dangerous form of biopolitics' in which entire populations are relegated to 'invisibility and disposability' (Giroux, 2006: 181–2). Under these conditions, certain racial and sexual populations – here we speak of indigenous women – are effectively abandoned by the State and find themselves living in a permanent state of exception, as mentioned before, subject to violence and unable to claim State protection or services – de facto denationalised.

Gothic spaces, gothic border

This is the complex nexus of factors that Gregory Nava's film sets out to present. Framed as a gothic thriller, the film is not exactly a murder *mystery* – since the perpetrators of the specific crime depicted in the film are known to the spectator from the start – but a horror-tinged investigation of the social, economic and political system that allows the killers to strike repeatedly and with total impunity. Through its narrative, dialogues and settings, *Bordertown* indicts the factory owners and managers and the governments of Mexico and the US, and specifically names NAFTA as creating the conditions that allow these murders to happen. The plot focuses on two women: a 15-year-old *maquiladora* worker who is raped and strangled and left for dead in a shallow grave, Eva (Maya Zapata), and an American journalist, Lauren Adrian (Jennifer Lopez), investigating the murders for a

Chicago newspaper. The film is as much about Lauren as it is about Eva, and involves a gothic sub-plot using dreams and flashbacks in which she slowly recovers her own past of violence and dispossession as a Mexican child adopted by an American family. After Lauren goes into the factory undercover as a worker in order to lure the killers into attacking her, one man is arrested but a sinister second killer remains at large. Eva recognises this second man at an exclusive reception for local and national elites where she has accompanied Lauren, allowing Lauren to discover his identity. However, the story she writes about Eva and the *maquiladora* industry ends up being censored by her own corporate-owned newspaper, while Eva panics and tries to cross the border into the United States illegally. Nearly dying from suffocation and heat when the smugglers abandon the car with her locked in the trunk (a form of live burial that represents another gothic aspect of the US–Mexican border today), she is found by border police and deported back to Juárez. The two women and the killer converge on Eva's shanty-town home where Eva arrives just in time to save Lauren from being killed herself.[6]

As can be seen from this description, the film is, on the face of it, a social problem drama. It integrates several large social issues into a narrative focusing on two women, and can be seen as heir to the tradition of literary naturalism. Recalling that naturalism originally emerged to narrate tensions of social class and capitalism at the turn of the century, one can see that *Bordertown* shares many of its thematic preoccupations and political tendencies. It is also a gothic thriller, with a sadistic aristocratic villain; a young female victim-heroine; claustrophobic and confining spaces; a character haunted by a violent and repressed past; a stifling climate of constant fear; and a visual repertoire of graves, body parts and charred corpses. Scholars have recently begun to explore the many hybrid texts that combine these two modes (Elbert and Ryden, 2016). Charles Crow has suggested that 'Gothicism and naturalism are both devoted to shaking bourgeois complacency, revealing unsettling truths that society tries to conceal from itself' and confronting us with 'a universe of vast forces that can overwhelm and terrify the individual' (Crow, 2009: 103). In addition, he says, a key image common to both modes is 'the cage in which … we are trapped' (103). However, while naturalism was effective in exposing the machinery of exploitation under industrial capitalism, the gothic genre has emerged as better suited to addressing the unique monstrosity of neoliberalism and its spectral financial transactions, irrational market worship and predatory spirit. As Henry A. Giroux terms it, the age of neoliberalism is an age of 'dark times' and 'zombie politics' (Giroux, 2011: back cover).

An early example of gothic naturalism, and one that establishes many of its key tropes – a cage-like work space, the factory as a kind of hell, reified workers resembling dead things – was Melville's 'The paradise of bachelors and the Tartarus of maids' (1855), which also happens to be one of the first literary critiques of globalisation and the disparities that it creates. The piece is more of a sketch than a story, contrasting a cosy London club for bachelor lawyers, featuring sumptuous dinners and much drinking, with a freezing-cold paper mill in a remote mountain location in New England, where pale girls perform rote assembly-line tasks to produce paper. The narrator dwells on the deathly pallor of the girls – showing how they come to resemble the dead paper that they produce – and depicts the factory, though chilly and well lit, as a kind of modern hell, a 'Tartarus'. What link the two worlds are the invisible networks of a modern communication society, which in the nineteenth century depended on paper, produced by working women and used in all manner of legal and other documents by men such as the lawyers. Though separated by continents, gender and class, the bachelors and the maids are inextricably linked by the same global economy, though the relationship is starkly uneven. While the men drink and eat in their warm club dining room, the girls work and waste away at their machines in the snow-bound mill. Like a concentration camp, the remoteness and design of the site are intended to enhance absolute control over the bodies of the workers. Anticipating a trope that would become a regular feature of critiques of alienated industrialised labour, Melville's narrator observes that the girls seem to the 'machinery as mere cogs to the wheels' (Melville, 1997 [1855]: 328). The entire mill is a terrifying place, linked to death, not only in the pun of the 'unbudging fatality' that governs the machines, but also by the deadly dust particles and mind-numbing repetitiveness that it involves. Finally, the narrator imagines he sees the 'pallid faces of all the pallid girls' themselves 'passing in slow procession along the wheeling cylinders' to some inexorable fate (333–4).

Bordertown also depicts the modern *maquiladora* as a kind of cage-like hell. This is shown when Lauren Adrian goes undercover and spends a day drilling screws into electronic components and we see how claustrophobic her work space is. In addition to the loud din of the factory there is a voice over the loudspeaker constantly exhorting the women to work faster and scolding the workers in specific lines for falling under the quota, creating an impression of relentless surveillance and discipline, keeping the women working at a dizzying pace throughout their shift. According to Arturo Aldama, women at these factories often work 'fourteen hour days, with two strictly enforced bathroom breaks of ten minutes each' (Aldama, 2003: 26). When Lauren's shift is over, a loud buzzer sounds and the women are told to leave quickly because the next shift begins in ten minutes. At several points throughout the sequence the camera pans up and above the factory floor to reveal an enormous mechanised space of hundreds of work stations – uncanny and infernal in its density and repetitiveness. From the camera's elevated perspective, workers no longer resemble cogs in a machine so much as ghosts in an infinite circuit-board. Nearly invisible in their electronic cages, the women seem to disappear into their work stations at the factory – before disappearing for good on their way home. If one of the causes of the uncanny is a blurring of boundaries between the quick and the dead, one can see a form of the uncanny at the *maquiladora* – giving way to the abject when the women workers are found dismembered in the desert nearby.

If the *maquiladora* is a kind of contemporary 'Tartarus of maids', the city just outside it is no less a gothic space for women. Instead of bright white light, the city glows with the red neon lights of strip joints, bars and brothels, where women's bodies are bought and sold and controlled in other ways. Instead of tight schedules and assembly-line discipline, women wear tight-fitting clothes and johns follow girls into semi-private back rooms where they couple standing up. If one space looks highly controlled and the other chaotic and lawless, the logic of instrumentalisation, the consuming and disposing of women, is the same on the streets as in the factories. Here too women are mere objects, mere bodies, used and discarded. The film follows Lauren into this cacophonous space when Eva runs away from her hotel room. Nava films the scene with rapid cuts, garish light and loud background noise to emphasise the violence and dehumanisation of the border sex trade, which reduces Mexican women's bodies to commodities in an infernal marketplace – a space of constant traffic and despair.

A third gothic space in the film is the shanty-town outside Juárez where migrant indigenous people like Eva and her mother live. Unable to afford housing in the city, internal economic refugees such as the indigenous populations of Oaxaca are forced to construct homes from debris and to steal electricity, at a high risk of electrocution, from the power lines that pass through their make-shift camp. This shanty-town serves as a visual shorthand in the film for the marginalised position of indigenous people within Mexico itself, an internal colony of sorts, dispossessed of its traditional lands, forced to migrate towards the factory areas along the border, ignored by police, unprotected by normal legal institutions, considered primitive and superstitious even by the most well-meaning Mexicans. The Mexican indigenous population often lives in a permanent state of exception, a life marked by precariousness and uncertainty, and the film's treatment of the shanty-town scenes underscores this. For instance, when an accidental fire starts, the flimsy structures quickly go up in flames and serve as a hellish backdrop to the film's climactic scene, when Lauren is herself nearly killed. Red lights, shaky camera, flashbacks to their earlier attack, rapid editing and the roar of the fire all contribute to make the squatter's camp a kind of inferno as the villain strangles her.

In addition to these three specific gothic locations, the border itself is explored as a gothic space in this film, as it has been in critical literature in recent years. In *An Intellectual History of Terror*, Mikkel Thorup identifies the 'frontierland' as a space of terror as well as a 'specter which haunts statist order' and therefore a place of permanent violence and exception to the rule of law (Thorup, 2010: 64). This definition is partly true for the Mexican–American border, in so far as it is a place where normal laws – including labour and safety laws – often do not apply or are not enforced, but it fails to recognise the regimes of discipline that are also present in order to ensure the proper functioning of the factories that constitute the main legal revenue along the border (drug trafficking being the principal illegal economy in this area). A more complex term that scholars have applied to the specific nexus of violence and control that characterises the free trade zones of the Mexican–American border is 'necropolitics'. According to Achille Mbembe, necropolitics involves 'contemporary forms of subjugation of life to the power of death' (Mbembe, 2003: 39). In other words, contemporary biopolitics in a postcolonial or neocolonial context assume an aspect characterised by a state of exception (in Agamben's sense) where power is exercised mainly outside the law and racialised subjects are defined as 'disposable' (Mbembe, 2003: 23, 27).[7] In the film we see this dynamic at work in the way State sovereignty has ceded its power to corporations, and subordinated its institutions – including law-enforcement – to the imperative of corporate profit. As a consequence, workers' deaths are silenced rather than investigated, women are tightly disciplined on the factory floor but left unprotected once they finish their shift, and indigenous migrants are left to live or die in their squatters' camps along the border after being dispossessed of their land and forced into wage labour.

However, the most important and influential theorist of the border is Gloria Anzaldúa, whose 1987 book *Borderland/La frontera* changed the way scholars and activists thought about this concept, and inaugurated 'border theory' as a mode of critical enquiry. In a book that was as unconventional and border-crossing formally as its author was politically and personally, Anzaldúa mapped out the Mexican–American border as an endemically violent space, '*una hiera abierta* where the Third World grates against the first and bleeds' (Anzaldúa, 1987: 39). An 'open wound', the border is a site of particular danger for women and especially Indian women, who are preyed upon by both 'Anglo' and Mexican men.[8] It is a space of uncertainty and ambiguity, ambivalence and paradox. As such, it is also, for Anzaldúa, a productive space where a new kind of consciousness – one that is more open to ambivalence and ambiguity, less committed to maintaining traditional categories and binaries – can emerge. Anzaldúa writes of a new 'mestiza consciousness' that can be produced by the encounter of two 'incompatible frames of reference', or world views, and we see that happening in the film through the character of Lauren, who undergoes important changes, and most notably a political awakening, through her experiences on the border (78).

Gothic heroines, gothic villains

Lauren's narrative arc is in fact a classic gothic one of growth through an encounter with a hidden world and a personal descent into darkness. For two centuries, gothic narratives have offered stories of terror as female *Bildungsroman*, and *Bordertown* is clearly heir to this tradition. The first interesting thing about the two female characters is that they are initially presented as opposites: the privileged American woman, blonde, educated, with a career, and the young Indian girl, working in a factory at fifteen, vulnerable and powerless to defend herself. Yet, as the film progresses, the gothic trope of the double is increasingly present, as Eva's story stirs Lauren's repressed memories of her own childhood in Mexico. Her parents, it slowly emerges, were also migrant workers, and both were killed, her father before her eyes. These memories are initially stimulated by Lauren's encounters with Eva, but later in the film Lauren begins to have flashbacks in which her memories are intermingled with Eva's. When she dyes her hair back to its naturally dark colour and dresses in Eva's factory clothes, the two women look like twins. Finally, when Lauren is alone on the bus with the bus driver she is trying to catch, she finds herself living out Eva's story exactly as it was told to her, in every detail. In this way, the film uses the double motif to show that two people who seem to come from very different worlds and have incommensurable identities can find themselves reduced to the same vulnerability as women, especially women of colour.

On a more empowering level, Eva and Lauren are two variants of the classic gothic heroine: the socially disenfranchised victim who survives and tells her story, and the middle-class sleuth who enters the gothic space in order to solve a mystery and finds herself. Eva is initially the paradigmatic gothic victim, the socially marginal person whose testimony about her injury carries no social capital and is dismissed as untrue or delusional. Because she is indigenous, everyone, including the concerned newspaperman and the wealthy patroness Teresa (Sonia Braga), who takes her into her home, believe that she cannot distinguish fact from imagination. Thus, when she insists there was a second man attacking her, no one believes her. The fact that she refers to this second attacker as the devil, 'el Diablo', only makes her story seem more fantastic, the product of her 'primitive' culture and Indian superstitions. Lauren is the Ann Radcliffean heroine, the middle-class woman of privilege who enters into a dark and labyrinthine world on an investigative quest only to discover that this world is far darker than she suspected and that she herself is implicated in it. Lauren's character thus experiences an important evolution in the film, as she discovers her own connections to the border culture she comes to investigate, and recovers her repressed childhood memories of trauma and dispossession. She learns that she is not so different from Eva at all, and that she could easily be one of the women in a grave outside Juárez. The film ends with a device from the horror film, that of the 'final girl', as Eva fights the mysterious killer in the last scene, knocking him out and into the fire.

This killer is also a classic gothic villain in the sense that he is a wealthy man from an old and well-connected family. An heir to the aristocratic tyrants of the classic gothic novel, the man is virtually untouchable despite the fact that he is a serial rapist and murderer. When Eva survives his attack and comes forward with her story, it becomes apparent that the police are working in collusion with him to find and silence her. Although he appears on many occasions throughout the film, he never utters a word, which renders him distinctly uncanny and almost supernatural. As a sadist and psychopath – he strikes Eva even after she is unconscious and bites her viciously on the breast – he is literally a monster. Moreover, these bites not only identify him as a serial killer responsible for the many other women's bodies found with identical bite marks, but also evoke comparisons to the gothic figure of the vampire. Like the classic gothic monster, Eva's rapist strikes female victims under the cover of both night and his aristocratic privilege, destroying them as he takes his pleasure, and seems able to materialise and disappear with supernatural stealth as he stalks her throughout the film. By representing the wealthy villain as a vampiric figure, the film also makes him into a personification of the predatory effects of the neoliberal political economy that keeps women like Eva living in precarity: unsafe at work, unsafe on the streets and unsafe in her shanty-town home.

Thus, the real villain in the film is NAFTA itself, and the neoliberal policies that shaped it, especially as these exploit and exacerbate the existing power structures along racial and gender lines. The results of the NAFTA agreement, which came into effect in 1994 – linking Mexico, Canada and the United States in a 'free trade' arrangement – have been typical of neoliberal policies elsewhere in the world. Trade has indeed increased but the beneficiaries have mainly been corporations and wealthy elites. In Mexico, many new billionaires were produced in the first decade of NAFTA while workers on either side of the border saw no benefits at all. In fact, many US jobs migrated south of the border while Mexican workers' wages have remained pitifully low – around $6 or $7 a day – since 1994. These results are not surprising, given that low wages and maximum corporate profit are the whole point of the *maquila* industry, not job security or a living wage. The agreement also tied the US and Mexican economies more closely, so that when the USA suffered its recession in 2008, many people in Mexico lost their jobs as well. The result has been a large influx of immigrants crossing illegally into the United States in order to survive, much larger than the pre-NAFTA annual numbers.

In short, one of the main results of NAFTA has been a wholesale disruption of populations – a variation of what David Harvey calls a key dynamic of neoliberalism, 'accumulation by dispossession' (Harvey, 2003: 137–82). The tendencies of neoliberalism to push populations away from their traditional homes to areas of industrialised zones such as the free-trade parks intersects with pre-existing Mexican policies in recent decades that have worked to dispossess indigenous populations, long protected under collective ownership by the Institutionalized Revolutionary Party, of their lands. In 1992 the Salinas Government began to prepare for NAFTA by privatising land, a trend that continued after 1994, when NAFTA came into effect at the same time as the peso was undergoing serious devaluation. Salinas' successor, Ernesto Zedillo (1994–2000), was a pro-NAFTA economist who continued the privatising policies already under way, including selling the state railway company.

The film presents these policies through Eva's back story, which involves being forced off her family land in Oaxaca because of an inability to pay land taxes. Eva's family is told to go to the *maquiladoras* to work to have money for the taxes, but she tells Lauren that she simply does not earn enough – that it is impossible to earn a living wage, much less to save money for a larger payment like a property tax. Her father has left to work in the United States several years previously, and they have not seen him since. *Bordertown* shows that the real consequences of NAFTA on ordinary people include the break-up of families; the dispossession of people from their homes and land; precarious working and living conditions in the towns along the border; and a culture of death, crime and predation on the most vulnerable. As indigenous women, Eva and her mother have become what Zygmunt Bauman calls 'human waste': internal refugees, suffering the plight of 'redundant' populations across the globe (Bauman, 2007: 28–45). They have been forced off their native lands, but are refused entry into any other; Bauman argues that such refugees do not change their dwelling place so much as '*lose* their place on earth', and are 'catapulted into a nowhere' (45). Achille Mbembe uses the even more gothic term 'necropolitics' to refer to the state of 'permanent class and racial exception' that confers on certain populations the status and living conditions of the 'living dead' (2003: 40). Although Mbembe writes about South Africa under apartheid and about Palestinians, his remarks apply in full measure to the situation of indigenous people, especially women, working and living around the free-trade zones in Mexico, and have been used as a framework to theorise their conditions by several scholars (Avila, 2012; Aldama, 2003; Fragoso, 2002).

By telling Eva's story in a gothic frame, *Bordertown* is able to critique contemporary neoliberal policies along the US–Mexican border in an accessible and popular form, and thereby situate itself in a long tradition of gothic literary activism dating back to the eighteenth century. As one recent study of gothic activism puts it, the gothic mode is 'particularly suited' to the task of 'influencing social change' (Ledoux, 2013: 7). Heir to this tradition, *Bordertown* borrows from the female gothic to create sympathy for vulnerable but intrepid heroines, and from naturalist gothic to expose the social and economic forces that condemn women workers to precarious lives. Recycling conventions such as the powerful aristocratic villain – a kind of vampire –who manipulates social institutions to his own selfish ends and preys on disempowered female victims abandoned by these institutions, the film shows the results of NAFTA on the US–Mexican border: consolidation of moneyed elites and predatory corporate practices on the one hand, and wholesale displacement and dispossession of the most vulnerable on the other. The gothic lends itself particularly well to the representation of such effects, not only because of its extensive toolbox of rhetorical devices to represent violence and dehumanisation, but also because of its skill at giving a visible form and face to what normally remains invisible – whether it is the predatory logic of neoliberalism or its many forgotten victims.

Notes

1 The first wave of murders began the 1990s but a second even larger wave has been unfolding in the last five years, according to the *New York Times* (Cave, 2012).

2 Signed by Mexico, Canada and the United States, and entering into effect on 1 January 1994, NAFTA created a trilateral 'free trade block' in which tariffs and barriers were to be reduced or eliminated entirely.

3 See Wright (2011) and Pantaleo (2006).

4 See also Schenwar (2008).

5 The murders in Juárez have not stopped; in fact, they have multiplied, from between 200 and 300 a year (both men and women) to nearly 300 a month in 2009, but the causes since the late 2000s include the violent drug war that has caused murders all over the country, making it even harder to identify and solve murders targeting specifically female victims. Figures cited in Bowden (2010), 246.

6 Although the film is fictional in its specific details, it is closely based on the actual circumstances of several Juárez murders. For example, although several serial killers have operated in the area, and some women were probably killed by boyfriends or husbands, at least some of the murders are thought to be the work of members of wealthy families, who prey on poor women for sport. Also, in 1999, a 14-year-old *maquiladora* worker was raped and left for dead by a bus driver in a scenario resembling that of the film, where the driver tells the girl, who is the last passenger on the bus, that he needs to go to a service station, before driving her to a remote location and strangling her (anon, 1999).

7 Susan George makes a similar point in a talk entitled 'A short history of neoliberalism', where she argues that 'the great new central question of politics is … "Who has a right to live and who does not"' (George, 1999).

8 When paraphrasing Anzaldúa I retain her own terms, i.e. Indian, Anglo, Mexican and Chicano (used for Mexican Americans).

References

Agamben, Giorgio. 1998. *Homo sacer: Sovereign Power and Bare Life*. Trans. Daniel Heller-Roazen. Stanford: Stanford University Press.

Aldama, Arturo J. 1998. 'Millennial anxieties: Borders, violence and the struggle for Chicana/o subjectivity'. *Arizona Journal of Hispanic Cultural Studies* 2: 41–62.

Aldama, Arturo J.. 2003. 'Borders, violence and the struggle for Chicana and Chicano subjectivity'. In Arturo J. Aldama, ed., *Violence and the Body: Race, Gender and the State*. Bloomington: Indiana University Press, 19–38.

Anon. 1999. 'Teen-ager survives vicious attack on bus'. *Amarillo Globe News*, 20 March. http://amarillo.com/stories/1999/03/20/tex_155-3670.002.shtml.

Anzaldúa, Gloria. 1987. *Borderlands/La Frontera: The New Mestiza*. San Francisco: Spinsters/Aunt Lute.

Avila, Edward A. 2012. 'Conditions of (im)possibility: Necropolitics, neoliberalism, and the cultural politics of death in contemporary Chicana/o film and literature'. Unpublished Ph.D. thesis, University of California, San Diego. Available at https://escholarship.org/uc/item/7sh1f55b.

Bauman, Zygmunt.2003. *Liquid Love*. London: Polity Press.

Bauman, Zygmunt. 2007. *Liquid Times: Living in an Age of Uncertainty*. Cambridge: Polity.

Borderplex Alliance. 2012. 'Maquiladora FAQ'. www.borderplexalliance.org/regional-data/ciudad-juarez/twin-plant/maquiladora-faq.

Bowden, Charles. 2010. *Murder City: Ciudad Juárez and the Global Economy's New Killing Fields*. New York: Nation Books.

Cave, Damien. 2012. 'Wave of violence swallows more women in Juárez'. *New York Times*, 23 June. www.nytimes.com/2012/06/24/world/americas/wave-of-violence-swallows-more-women-in-juarez-mexico.html.

Crow, Charles. 2009. *American Gothic*. Cardiff: University of Wales Press.

Elbert, Monica and Wendy Ryden. 2016. *Haunting Realities: Naturalist Gothic and American Realism*. Tuscaloosa: University of Alabama Press.

Fragoso, Julia Monárrez. 2002. 'Serial sexual femicide in Ciudad Juárez'. *Debate feminista*, 13th edn, Vol. 25, April. www.womenontheborder.org/sex_serial_english.pdf.

George, Susan. 1999. 'A short history of neo-liberalism'. Talk presented at Conference on Economic Sovereignty in a Globalising World, Bangkok, 24–6 March 1999. Available at www.globalexchange.org/resources/econ101/neoliberalismhist.

Giroux, Henry A. 2006. 'Reading Hurricane Katrina: Race, class, and the biopolitics of disposability'. *College Literature* 33(3): 171–96.

Giroux, Henry A. 2011. *Zombie Politics and Culture in the Age of Casino Capitalism*. New York: Peter Lang.

Gutiérrez, David Gregory. 2004. *The Columbia History of Latinos in the United States since 1960*. New York: Columbia University Press.

Harvey, David. 2003. *The New Imperialism*. Oxford: Oxford University Press.

Ledoux, Ellen Malenas. 2013. *Social Reform in Gothic Writing: Fantastic Forms of Change, 1764–1834*. Basingstoke: Palgrave.

Mbembe, Achille. 2003. 'Necropolitics'. Trans. Libby Meintjes. *Public Culture* 15(1): 11–40.

Melville, Herman. 1997 [1855]. 'The paradise of bachelors and the Tartarus of maids'. In Herman Melville, *The Piazza Tales and Other Prose Pieces 1839–1860*. Evanston and Chicago: Northwestern University Press and The Newberry Library, 316–35.

Muñoz Martinez, Monica. 2014. 'Recuperating histories of violence in the Americas: Vernacular history-making on the US–Mexico border'. *American Quarterly* 66(3): 61–689.

Pantaleo, Katie. 2006. 'Gendered violence: Murder in the maquiladoras'. *Sociological Viewpoints* (Fall): 13–23.

Sadowski-Smith, Claudia. 2009. 'Imagining transnational Chicano/a activism against gender-based violence at the US–Mexican border'. In Kevin Concannon, Francisco A. Lomelí and Marc Priewe, eds, *Imagined Transnationalism: US Latino/a Literature, Culture, and Identity*. New York: Palgrave, 75–94.

Schenwar, Maya. 2008. 'Oaxaca's government land grab'. *Truthout Archives*. www.truthout.org/archive/item/79013-oaxacas-government-land-grab.

Thorup, Mikkel. 2010. *An Intellectual History of Terror: War, Violence and the State*. London and New York: Routledge.

Wright, Melissa W. 2011. 'Necropolitics, narcopolitics, and femicide: Gendered violence on the Mexico–US border'. *Signs* 36(3): 707–31.

Index